Growing with
Your Child

Growing with Your Child:
Pre-Birth to Age 5

EDITOR: CHRISTINE LANGLOIS

CANADIAN LIVING'S HEALTH AND FAMILY EDITOR

In collaboration with the Canadian Paediatric Society and

The College of Family Physicians of Canada

A **Canadian Living** Family Book

🆎

Ballantine Books

A Division of Random House of Canada Limited

ACKNOWLEDGMENTS
pages 283–291 adapted from *Well Beings*, 2nd ed., 1996, Canadian Paediatric Society

PROJECT TEAM
Project Editor: Jean Stinson
Preliminary Research: Susan Pedwell, Danyael Halprin
Fact-checking: Laurel Aziz
Index: Christopher Blackburn
Cover and book design: Hambly & Woolley Inc.
Cover photograph: Barbara Cole
Props courtesy of UpCountry
Brush drawings: Bob Hambly
Watercolours: Lisa Smith
Photo credits: page 17, Ed Gajdel; and generous parents

Publisher: Caren King
Editorial Director: Bonnie Baker Cowan

CANADIAN CATALOGUING IN PUBLICATION DATA
Langlois, Christine (Christine Anne)
    Growing with your child : pre-birth to age 5
"A Canadian Living family book."
ISBN 0-345-39858-0
1. Child rearing.   2. Parent and child.   3. Child development.   I. Title
HQ769.I.243   1998   649'.122   C97-931630-8

Ballantine Books
A Division of
Random House of Canada Limited
1265 Aerowood Drive
Mississauga, ON L4W 1B9
Canada

Canadian Living
Telemedia Communications Inc.
25 Sheppard Avenue West
Suite 100
North York, ON M2N 6S7
Canada

1998 99 2000 01 02 FP 5 4 3 2 1
Printed and bound in Canada by Friesen Printers

Contributors and Advisors

Canadian Living Contributors

Lynne Ainsworth
Cindy Barrett
Okey Chigbo
Marcia Kaye
John Keating
Sharon McKay
Julie Ovenell-Carter
Susan Pedwell
Laura Pratt
Mark Witten
Kim Zarzour

Expert Advisors

CANADIAN PAEDIATRIC SOCIETY
Emmett Francoeur MDCM, FRCPC
Associate Professor, Paediatrics, McGill University
Frank Friesen MD, FRCPC
Manitoba Clinic, Winnipeg
Danielle Grenier MD, FRCPC
Associate Executive Vice President, Canadian Paediatric Society
    Liaison: Elizabeth Moreau

THE COLLEGE OF FAMILY PHYSICIANS OF CANADA
Janet Dollin MD, CCFP
Assistant Professor, Family Medicine, University of Ottawa
Carol P. Herbert MD, CCFP, FCFP
Head, Family Practice, University of British Columbia
Walter W. Rosser MD, CCFP, FCFP
Chair, Family and Community Medicine, University of Toronto
    Liaison: Leslie Challis

Valerie Lee, *President, Infant & Toddler Safety Association*
Rena Mendelson, M.S., D.SC., *Professor of Nutrition, Ryerson Polytechnic University*

Contents

Foreword

Children are Canada's most important resource. In recognition of this fact, **Canadian Living** has developed a useful and timely guide for Canadian parents who are engaged in the critical activity of parenting infants and preschoolers. *Growing with Your Child* collects the wisdom of both professionals and parents to offer the most current thinking on child development and care in a Canadian context.

This guide for parents complements materials that have been produced for health-care professionals who are directing their efforts toward making Canada child-friendly. The College of Family Physicians of Canada commissioned a task force on child health which reported in May 1997 on the health status of Canadian children and suggested ways in which family physicians and other health-care professionals could improve practice and enhance child health. The Report, entitled "Our Strength for Tomorrow: Valuing our Children," highlights the fact that, in a country of affluence, too many of our children grow up in less than optimal circumstances. Too many children face the challenges of poor nutrition, inadequate parenting and abuse, and have consequent increased vulnerability to emotional and physical illnesses and injuries. While all illnesses and injuries cannot be prevented, there is increasing recognition that providing the optimal start for children will prevent many problems and minimize the disabling effect of other problems. It is essential that we all do our part toward achieving this goal—parents, health-care professionals, politicians, and Canada's many different communities.

Among the recommendations of the Task Force are specific suggestions for ensuring that family physicians make their offices child-friendly; help women deliver the healthiest babies possible; promote, support, and protect breast-feeding; prepare for pediatric emergencies; identify child maltreatment; work to improve the emotional and mental health of children; and provide appropriate medical care for the disabled child. These "10 Step" guides for family doctors bear striking resemblance to some of the suggestions for parents that appear in *Growing with Your Child.* The synergy between parents and family physicians, working toward the common goal of providing the best possible environment for children, has the potential to change the outcomes for individual children and for Canadian society.

This common purpose is exemplified in the CFPC's "10 Steps for Improving the Emotional and Mental Health of Children." The Task Force recommends that family physicians:

1. support prospective parents.
2. promote establishment of secure attachment to a nurturing caregiver.
3. advise parents of their children's need for positive stimulation.
4. be a good role model for parents.
5. help parents define appropriate roles for themselves.
6. help parents to express their love for their children appropriately.
7. encourage parents to spend time with their children.
8. assist parents in gaining effective parenting skills.
9. help parents have reasonable expectations for their children.
10. encourage parents to appreciate people who are different and to value the strengths of others.

These recommendations parallel the advice for parents in *Growing with Your Child* which includes specific suggestions for understanding and guiding children as they move through the formative developmental stages.

As the most important supporting characters in the drama of early childhood development, parents need and deserve the best advice possible from those whom they trust. Their partners in child care include their own extended families, nurses, physicians, midwives, pharmacists, early childhood educators, physiotherapists, occupational therapists—to name only some. *Growing with Your Child* adds to the information resources that help parents develop as child-care experts themselves. It provides guidance for their collection and critical assessment of information and advice, and promotes the notion that parents have the capacity to decide what is best for their young children.

But *Growing with Your Child* is not only a resource for Canadian parents, it is also worthwhile reading for health-care professionals. Materials such as Canada's Food Guide are more clearly presented here in a user-friendly way than in any medical textbook that I have seen. The health professionals who use *Growing with Your Child* as their own guide for advising prospective and new parents will find suggestions for enacting the recommendations of The College of Family Physicians of Canada and improving the health of Canada's children.

Carol P. Herbert MD, CCFP, FCFP
Chair, National Committee on Child and Adolescent Health
The College of Family Physicians of Canada

Introduction

One of the contributors to *Growing with Your Child* teases me often about suffering from "baby lust" since we started working on this book. And she's right. As I sat at my computer editing the chapter on the newborn, I ached instead to be holding a tiny baby and smelling that wonderful new baby smell. With the next chapter, I wanted to be bouncing a six-month-old on my knee and making silly faces to hear her laugh out loud. And so it went. Each new section brought back memories of when my own two teenagers were small and reminded me of wonderful moments with other children in my life—my nieces and nephews and the children of friends.

So if you're a reader who is just beginning your journey as a parent, I'm a little envious of all those funny, happy, exciting moments that await you with your tiny charge. The time with your children when they're small is truly a special time. But I don't want to suggest that your role is easy. For most of us there is no life change as all-encompassing as becoming a parent; the responsibilities, especially early on, can be overwhelming. When your baby is crying and you don't know why, when your toddler starts screaming and kicking because it's time to leave grandma's, when you're exhausted at the end of the day and can't face reading one more bedtime story, you can easily feel inadequate in your role. But remember that you have so much experience and knowledge to draw on from other parents and from experts, who can help you through your confusion and give you the support you need to regain confidence in your instincts.

That's really what this book is all about—synthesizing all the very best information about how your child will develop and grow, and how, as a parent, you can best foster his development. This information has been gleaned by a talented team of **Canadian Living** contributors from dozens of experts across the country who generously gave their time to be sure we included everything you need to know about breast-feeding, nutrition, baby's sleep habits, toilet teaching, and how your child learns to walk and talk. We wanted to assemble information and advice that reflects the fact that you're raising your child in Canada. In *Growing with Your Child*, you'll find out what to expect when you give birth in a Canadian hospital, you'll learn about your baby's nutritional needs based on the latest information from Health Canada, and you'll be able to check an immunization schedule that matches the one your doctor uses. You'll also find lists of all-Canadian resources to help you with any special needs.

As a new parent, your relationship with your child's doctor will be very important. So I'm proud of the fact that *Growing with Your Child* has been edited in collaboration with both the Canadian Paediatric Society and The College of Family Physicians of Canada. Their input was invaluable in making sure the information reflects the most current and accurate information on your child's health, safety, and development.

> If you're like most parents, you'll find that you get support and encouragement from talking with other parents who are living through the same age and stage with their child as you are with yours. So throughout the book, you'll find advice and observations from other parents across the country. Some might make you laugh, some might make you cry, but all will make you think.

Parents love to give each other advice and, as someone who has been parenting for almost eighteen years, I've both received and offered my share. But the best advice has been offered from one parent to another through the ages: Be aware of how fleeting your baby's first months and early years will be, and take pleasure in and attend to all your child's changes and accomplishments from that first tiny smile to the first solo bike ride. Have a wonderful time together because, before you know it, your tiny baby will be a teenager, and you'll be amazed and thrilled at what a wonderful young person she has so quickly grown to be.

Christine Langlois
Toronto, October 1997

Before Baby Arrives

You've never been so interested in the world of babies as you have been since you became pregnant. Whether you're an expectant mother or father, as you wait for your child to arrive, you watch other parents for clues as to what's ahead for you. You listen to all the funny stories, all the horror stories, and try to imagine how you will react when it's your turn to care for a newborn. You've heard about babies with colic whose waking hours are one extended wail, about hollow-eyed fathers who are getting little sleep, about mothers who fill the time between feeding and changing diapers with feeding and changing diapers. And you've observed melt-your-heart moments between infants and adults that leave you aching to hold the tiny new person who will soon come into your life.

Preparing Emotionally for a First Baby

Sometimes the conflicting emotions of anticipation and anxiety can be overwhelming. But these emotions may play a part in preparing you to become a parent. Since a baby brings major changes to your life, a little upheaval during pregnancy helps a couple adapt to the turmoil that's typical of life with a new baby. If, however, you find your emotions are too close to the surface, look at your schedule. A daily walk is one way to ease stress. When you're overtired, you react more strongly to negative feelings, so grab a nap during the afternoon whenever you can. Develop a routine that helps you wind down and relax at the end of the day.

Activities like preparing space in your home for a nursery, washing baby clothes, and collecting the necessary equipment will make the baby's impending arrival more real for you. Pick up on opportunities to talk with other expectant parents—their comments and suggestions will get your mind in gear. Register for prenatal classes early in your pregnancy through your hospital or public health unit, or check the Yellow Pages under Prenatal Classes.

Besides learning about the mechanics of birth and the techniques that will help you with labour and delivery, you will have a chance to talk with others about the whole experience. Sometimes in the context of a free-wheeling classroom discussion, one partner will mention a concern that you both can discuss and resolve together after class. Be sure to ask your doctor if you can arrange a tour of the hospital services.

Your own parents are bound to be excited by the prospect of grandchildren. Ask them about their memories of when they were expecting you. From the time we were children ourselves, we never tire of hearing stories about our past. Listen to their recollections and continue the story-telling tradition with your own children.

Some Typical Pre-Birth Worries

I'm not sure I'll be a good parent.

The fact that you're reading this book means that you want to learn about how your child will grow and develop and what he will need from you. That willingness to learn is key to becoming a responsive and understanding parent. Find out as much as you can, not only

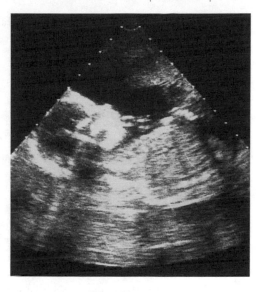

A routine ultrasound offers a first glimpse of the baby.

from books but also from spending time with the children of your friends or relatives. Offer to babysit, to hold a baby for a few minutes, to change a diaper. If you would like the opportunity to pose your questions to experts, contact your local public health unit or family services association about parenting classes in your area.

You may also be worried about your ability to be a good parent because you, as a child, did not receive good parenting. This is a good time to reflect on your positive and negative childhood experiences and to get professional help if childhood memories of abuse surface.

Sometimes I'm afraid our baby might not be born healthy.

Worry about the baby's health is probably the most common anxiety of expectant parents. And knowing that the likelihood of a problem is very slight doesn't necessarily calm your fears about your baby. For the record, Canada's infant mortality rate for children under one year of age is 6.3 per 1,000 live births, one of the lowest in the world. But if worry about your fetus consumes your days and nights, try talking out your fears with your partner who may be experiencing the same emotions. Sometimes just talking out your fears will help both of you. Your doctor or your midwife can help you find answers to specific concerns. Above all, continue to provide the best possible environment for your developing fetus.

I worry that the baby will put a lot of stress on our relationship.

Your relationship with your partner will certainly change when a baby joins the party. You might be noticing changes already. The focus of the relationship shifts to the baby and away from the other partner. But you're still the same team and this is an adventure that, if embarked on as a team, will enhance your relationship. If romantic moments occur less frequently, don't allow them to disappear. Take the time daily to hold hands, to hug, to share some intimate thoughts even if you are unable to do anything else

I'm not sure we can afford a baby.
The good news about babies is that they don't care about fancy gear and designer clothes. Put the word out to other parents that you're accepting hand-me-downs, check garage sales for equipment (but be aware of safety requirements), and join a toy-lending library—these methods will stretch your budget over several more months, even years. A debatable benefit is that your household expenses may be lower because you won't have as much SEE PAGE 273 time for socializing and entertaining.

I watch the news at night, and I wonder if it's right to bring a new life into a world that is rife with danger.
It's easy for a parent-to-be to feel overcome by all the worst-case scenarios. Try to focus on the positive. Remember, you live in a democratic country that is not at war, that is not subject to drought and famine, and that has a decent health-care system. And you are providing your baby with an immediate environment that is safe and loving. Perhaps this tiny soul you're bringing into the world will make news herself by growing up to develop a cure for AIDS or to lead an environmental crusade that will result in cleaner air.

Right from birth, a baby can grasp a finger.

Who to Invite to the Birth

Fathers need no invitation. It's normal practice for dads to coach their partners through labour as well as through prenatal classes and to be an active participant in the delivery. But if your partner is not available, invite someone else to fill that supporting role. A woman in labour needs an emotional bolster. As hospitals cut back on staff, you may find it helpful to bring your own support staff—which should ensure that you'll get ice chips or a back rub when you need it.

A private, intimate delivery is the alternative chosen by many couples. However, some like to have a second support person even when the father can be present. How do you choose that special person who will help you and your partner bring your baby into the world? You might ask a friend or a relative—maybe your own mother or sister. It's one of those jobs that can aptly be described as woman's work. Apart from their male partner, women tend to favour having other women around them as their active support during labour. But both partners must feel comfortable with the support person, since you will all be spending hours together in very close quarters. Your second support person should be someone who:

➤   is available day or night and able to take time off work, if required.
➤   will prepare for the role by reading about the process of labour and delivery, by meeting with your doctor or midwife, and by attending one or more prenatal classes with you.
➤   supports your expectations for labour and delivery, including your preferences on medication and medical intervention.
➤   will remain calm and communicative.
➤   will support the baby's father if he becomes anxious.

In hospitals, deliveries can be done by obstetricians, family physicians, or midwives. Several regions in Canada have or are developing midwifery legislation to regulate training and certification. If a couple chooses to use a midwife for delivery, she will also provide care during pregnancy and physical and emotional support throughout labour. Unless there is a medical emergency, she will deliver the baby.

Overall, amost all Canadian babies are born in hospitals. However, about one-third of babies delivered by midwives are born at home. If you're planning to have your baby at home, you might have a primary team of your partner, a midwife, and a doctor. The Canadian Paediatric Society does not recommend home births because, while most births are uneventful, unexpected emergencies do occur. In these emergencies, the survival of the mother and her infant may depend upon the expertise and equipment available only in a hospital.

A doula is another possible addition to your team, although doulas are not yet covered by provincial medicare. The original Greek word *doula* meant *female slave*, but today's practitioners of the profession define their role as *one who mothers the mother* since doulas provide emotional and physical support during labour. Unlike midwives, doulas have no medical role and do not perform medical procedures of any kind. They make several home visits during the pregnancy and after the birth for help with breast-feeding or other baby concerns. Expect to pay between $300 and $600 for their services, although volunteers are often available for high-need mothers. Doulas are found across the country, and they are increasing in numbers. Call Doulas of North America (DONA) (206-324-5440) or the Labour Support Association & Registry (LSAR) at (905) 842-3385 or (905) 844-0503 for information about doulas in your area.

Planning for Postpartum Help

For first-time mothers, it's really important to plan for help in the first few weeks at home, because many Canadian hospitals discharge mothers and their babies twenty-four hours after the birth. Especially if you're planning to nurse, you'll need the help of a knowledgeable mom with experience, since your major focus will be on learning how to breast-feed. Your helper could be your own mother, your mother-in-law, your sister, or a friend. Even if no one is able to stay with you, or if you and your partner prefer not to have company, identify other mothers who will visit you or answer your questions on the phone.

Find out from your hospital what postnatal services it provides, and ask for the phone numbers of professional help on which to call if you run into any feeding problems. Check with your local public health unit to see if a public health nurse (PHN) could provide postnatal visits. The Victorian Order of Nurses (VON) will also make both pre- and post-natal visits to your home to help you resolve baby-care concerns and arrange for light house-keeping and laundry services through a home support program. Midwives and doulas also include home visits in their services.

You and your partner will both feel somewhat confused after the excite-ment and hard work of birthing. You will need time to focus on the baby, not on laundry and vacuuming. If you deliver by cesarean section, you shouldn't do any lifting for some time, so it's likely you'll need help. If you can afford home help, have them come during the first weeks to do the housework, leaving you free to tend your baby.

Family members may offer to help, but consider the quality of your relationship with them before you accept. Some couples welcome a mother or mother-in-law, or both sets of parents, moving in for a week or more. Grandparents can provide a wealth of wisdom and support for a new family, but this is a highly emotional and sensitive time for you and your partner so you need to choose your helpers wisely. If you're secure enough with your folks and able to assert your feelings calmly, then this time together can be very special for all of you. It could also be the begin-ning of a close relationship between your baby and her new grandparents.

When people ask what you need, don't be too shy to tell them. Gifts of oven-ready casseroles or a dinner ready for the table are timesavers; so is an offer to take an older sibling out for the afternoon. Most guests are thoughtful and sensitive to the parents' needs, but don't bother to stifle your yawns if your visitors forget that their presence might tire you or make more work for you when what you really need is a nap.

Discussion Points for Parents-to-be

When the first contraction signals that your baby is on the way, the decisions you will have to make come thick and fast in the following hours and days. Prior to that busy time and while it's still just the two of you, talk through some of the issues you know will arise. Remind each other that your decisions don't have to be carved in stone, that you'll most likely review them after you've had some input from the addition to your family.

Birth Plan and Newborn Care Plan

A birth plan, written by you and your partner, describes how you want your labour and delivery to proceed—insofar as you have control over these events. Your family physician, obstetrician, midwife, or doula can explain which options are open to you and could even help you prepare your plan. This is a good topic for your prenatal class, where other expectant parents

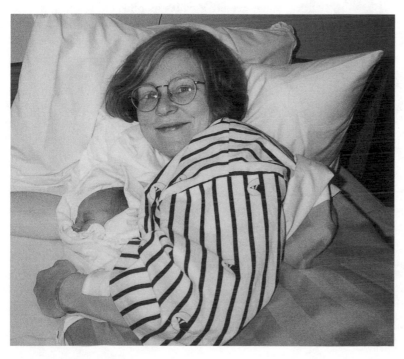

Mother and baby
doing well in hospital.

Before Baby Arrives

as well as the instructor should have lots of ideas. The plan can be as simple or as detailed as you like. It should cover the medications you want or don't want, your preferences about moving around during labour, the roles your partner and support person will play, and what medical interventions you would prefer.

A newborn care plan should cover your wishes for how your infant will be treated while in the hospital, whether he will stay with you immediately after the birth, and whether he'll be allowed sugar water while in the hospital nursery. Discuss your plans with your family physician or midwife and take into consideration your hospital's restrictions for birthing rooms. Even though you should be prepared to accept changes as you move through the experience, the process of working through these plans ahead of time makes it much more likely they'll occur as planned.

What Newborns Look Like

It's not uncommon for parents to think their newborn baby looks perfect in every respect. Yet most newborns show obvious signs of the laborious journey through the birth canal. Typically, a baby born vaginally will have a large pointed head, puffy eyes, and flattened nose. She may have a full head of hair or she may look bald. She may be covered in a white, creamy protective coating, called vernix, and in fine body hair, called lanugo. Newborns often have swollen genitals and breasts. Their nipples may secrete a white or pink fluid, and girls may have some vaginal secretions. Babies born by cesarean section will look less the worse for wear.

You may wonder why every other baby in the hospital nursery is so odd-looking compared to your little beauty. But chances are, a few years down the road when you're looking at her birth photos, you'll be surprised to see how obvious are the marks of birthing to which you had previously been blind.

Banking the Umbilical Cord Blood

Because the umbilical cord blood contains a very high concentration of stem cells (the basic units in the bone marrow responsible for producing all red cells, white cells, and platelets), it provides a perfect match for a bone marrow transplant should the baby need it in the future. It is also more likely to provide a good match for siblings with a blood-related illness such as childhood leukemia (one child in 1,000), or parents with another life-threatening disease. Also, because the stem cells have not yet built up antibodies, they are more compatible with a greater number of unrelated people in need of cell transplant.

You might consider either donating your newborn's umbilical cord blood to a cord blood bank or storing it for your child's or a family member's future use. The process of collecting the blood involves no risk or pain to mother or baby, since it's collected within twenty-four hours of the birth from the clamped umbilical cord that remains with the placenta. However, expectant parents who are interested in the possibilities should obtain information and counselling early enough in the pregnancy to make arrangements for testing and for the collection and storage of the blood.

The procedure has been adopted in several Canadian and U.S. centres. The Alberta Cord Blood Bank, associated with the University of Alberta in Edmonton, is a public resource that accepts cord-blood donations from hospitals across the country and makes it available to the general public. It charges no fees for collection or storage. The Bank's phone number is (403) 492-2673.

Other private programs for collecting and storing this blood have begun in Vancouver and Toronto, offering parents a once-in-a-lifetime opportunity to store the blood collected from their newborns for future use. The Toronto Cord Blood program at The Toronto Hospital (416) 340-3323 accepts referrals from Ontario residents only. It operates on a cost-recovery basis, charging fees to collect the cord blood ($600) and subsequent annual fees ($100) to store it. Your own hospital should be able to provide you with information about these programs or others that might become available in your area.

Circumcision

Should you or shouldn't you? Some choose to circumcise for religious reasons; others so that the boy's genitals will be the same as his father's. But the Canadian Paediatric Society states that there is no medical reason to circumcise a baby, and several provinces no longer cover circumcision under their medical insurance plans.

Circumcisions are generally performed without anesthetic because there is no general or local anesthetic safe enough to give to newborns and because, up until recently, the medical profession believed that newborns didn't feel much pain or that they wouldn't remember pain. Using the data from three separate studies, researchers from The Hospital for Sick Children in Toronto analyzed records on vaccinations given to eighty-seven infants between the ages of four and six months. The results of the study, published in February 1997, found that male babies who had been SEE PAGE 20 circumcised reacted to the pain of the vaccination to a greater degree than did the female babies or the male babies who had not been circumcised. Another related study concluded with a recommendation that, during the circumcision procedure, a topical anesthetic be used to provide adequate pain control. Circumcision does pose some risks: Infection, hemorrhaging, and improper healing affect from two to ten per cent of circumcised newborns.

Breast-Feeding

Most Canadian newborns begin life as breast-fed babies for the clear reason that breast-feeding is best for both them and their mothers. Breast-feeding is a learned art that comes easily and naturally to many new mothers but, for others, the learning curve can be steep in the first few weeks. There are some women and men who, for various reasons, are not comfortable with the idea of breast-feeding. Now is the time to talk about your feelings, to read as much as you can about the subject, and to make your choice.

SEE PAGE 31

Sleeping Arrangements

There are differing viewpoints on the topic of sharing your room and your bed with your baby, and you may revisit this particular issue several times during your offspring's childhood. Prior to the birth, you and your partner should discuss your feelings about safety, convenience, comfort, and privacy, but leave the topic open for reconsideration.

SEE PAGE 52

"I can remember, with our first child, my husband lying in a sleeping bag on the floor with his hand on the baby's back trying to get him to sleep in his crib. We smartened up with the others and just let them in our bed if they wanted. We got really smart and put a double bed in one of the kids' rooms and some nights that's where we ended up!"

JEANNE, MOTHER OF FOUR, BISHOP'S MILLS, ONT.

Diapers: Disposable or Cloth?

Fortunately, this is a decision that can be changed as easily as…a diaper. Cost, convenience, and the environment are the factors you should take into consideration. Your baby may show a preference, but he will make his point later.

Disposables are certainly convenient. They're fast and easy to change, they're very absorbent, and they're easily disposed of—initially. Although it's illegal to dispose of human feces in landfills, many people still roll up dirty diapers and toss them into the garbage. About 240,000 metric tons of disposable diapers hit landfill sites in Canada each year—the single largest non-recyclable component of household garbage. But human waste dumped in landfill sites instead of sewers or septic systems contaminates our soil and groundwater, so discard any solid waste in the toilet before throwing the diaper out.

Disposable diapers can easily cost more than double the amount of cloth ones, even with the cost of laundering included. Though it's true that disposable diapers require less frequent changing because of their higher absorbency, sometimes parents change them less often than they should, which can cause the baby to develop diaper rash.

Because of environmental concerns, cloth diapers are regaining some of their popularity. You can now buy fitted cloth diapers, with Velcro fasteners or belts and in different sizes, which offer great improvements in changing efficiency and in protection over the old-fashioned kind of cloth diaper. Plastic pants, the old ill-fitting, moisture-retaining bottom burners, are being replaced by diaper covers made of breathable fabrics that manage both to protect your lap and to be kind to sensitive baby bottoms. You can wash them yourself or, if your community has a diaper service, hire it to pick up, launder, and deliver on a weekly basis.

Be aware that some babies have sensitive skin that reacts to the chemicals used in the manufacture of disposables; others react to wet cloth. Your baby will let you know if he has a preference. And there's no reason why you can't use both: cloth diapers at home; disposables away from home.

Choosing Your Health-Care Team

The arrival of a new baby usually means that parents develop a much closer relationship with their family physician and perhaps add a pediatrician to their health-care team. In large cities in central Canada, there are more pediatricians to choose among, and parents don't usually require a referral from their family physician. But smaller towns and rural areas often don't sustain a pediatric practice, although specialists may make weekly or monthly visits to the local hospital or clinic.

As your child's primary health caregiver, your family physician usually brings her knowledge of the whole family and its medical history to bear in her treatment. She can handle day-to-day medical problems and make the appropriate referrals to specialists like a pediatrician, if necessary. For most Canadian parents, a pediatrician requires a referral from a family physician before examining a child.

If you wish to add the services of a pediatrician, it's important to choose one before your baby is born. Begin your search by discussing the question with your family physician or with other parents who share your childcare views. Set up an appointment with one or two to find one with whom you're comfortable and whose attitudes toward treatment match your own.

Although your child probably won't need to visit a dentist before the age of three, make inquiries about dentists who treat lots of children. Their experience with kids, their knowledge of children's growth and development and how to keep them comfortable may make dental check-ups fun instead of an ordeal.

Choose your complementary health-care professionals with the same thoroughness with which you choose your doctors and dentists. Chiropractors and naturopaths are licensed practitioners with their own colleges and professional associations. Your pharmacist is also an important source of information, someone who can answer your questions about prescription drugs and help you choose appropriate over-the-counter medications.

Maternity Leave and Parental Leave

You will want to learn as much as you can about the options both parents have in taking leave from work to care for your newborn. To find out which standards apply to you, you might check first with your employer's human resources department, then with the Ministry of Labour or its equivalent in your province or territory. Minimum provincial employment standards regarding leaves of absence and job protection vary from province to territory.

At the federal level, the government pays mothers on *maternity leave* through Employment Insurance. If a pregnant woman has been employed for at least 700 hours in the last 52 weeks before she gives birth, then she is entitled to 17 weeks of maternity leave (which includes a 2-week unpaid waiting period). The benefits equal 55 per cent of the individual's earnings over a certain number of weeks up to a maximum of $413 per week in 1997.

Employment Insurance also entitles either parent (adoptive parents are included) to 10 weeks of paid *parental leave*. The parental leave benefits can be claimed by one parent or divided between them. Whether you are a birth or an adoptive parent, the parental leave must be taken within one year of the child's birth. Information about these benefits is available at any Human Resources Development Canada (HRDC) office or Canada Employment Centre (CEC). Check the Blue Pages of your phone book.

Some family-friendly corporations or employers may offer benefits beyond the money and job protection offered by federal and provincial governments. You might be able to negotiate an extended leave with your employer, whether paid or unpaid, to stretch your time at home with baby. One partner might be able to secure a leave of absence or a sabbatical to start when the other's parental leave ends. Some couples save up vacation time and tack it on to their leave.

Childcare Options

You might think it's a little early to be discussing childcare when your baby isn't even born. But good childcare, particularly if you want a daycare setting, can be difficult to come by in many Canadian communities. Some daycare centres have waiting lists for infant care that are 18 months long.

Ask your friends what worked best for their children, visit a few neighbourhood daycare centres and childcare providers to get a feel for what's available, and find out if a relative in the family could step in to take care of baby should you need her. Put your name on the waiting lists now. If it turns out you don't need or want the space, you've lost nothing or perhaps only a deposit.

If you decide to return to work after your maternity leave (and 80 per cent of mothers do return), your major concern will be securing good care for your baby while you're out of your home. You'll be glad you got a SEE PAGE 88 head start on the search.

Recording Your Child's Development

Some of us know the delight of rediscovering our baby selves through the baby books and mementos carefully kept by our parents. Consider that you've become the keeper of your family history, and discuss together how you'd like to record the story of your child and your life together. There will be so many remarkable, funny, magical moments, but you'll be so busy and weary that your brain won't be able to retain them all. A memoir will be an invaluable keepsake. Baby books are a delightful gift to receive, but a scrapbook or notebook in which you can record special moments will be just as precious. Write in it often, even if it's only a few lines; add photos and special mementos. (You might drop an inexpensive camera into the baby's diaper bag for spur-of-the-moment shots.) If that's not your style, select a large box with a tight lid as your baby's memento box and keep whatever holds meaning for you.

You may receive a Health Record booklet in the hospital or from your doctor. It contains specific sections in which to keep track of your baby's immunizations, illnesses, and injuries. It could prove an important source of information in the future, so you might also record in it any problems you experienced during pregnancy and a description of your delivery. Keep it up-to-date with charts of weight and height, results of dental and eye examinations, details of food sensitivities or allergies, and related notes on the family's health history.

Is There Sex after Baby?

If there weren't, there sure would be a lot of only children. But in the weeks or even months after a new baby arrives, you may wonder if passion will ever again come into the chaos called home life. Heed your doctor's warning to avoid intercourse for six weeks following a vaginal birth or four weeks after a cesarean. A new mother's body needs time to heal.

Both partners might worry that intercourse will hurt the woman, and sometimes it does—nursing mothers have little natural vaginal lubrication. Most new mothers, whether adoptive or birth mothers, usually feel little desire for sexual intercourse. When she's short of sleep and has a baby glued to her body half the day and night, a woman may not feel like sharing more of her physical self. But both of you need to share your emotional selves. Talking to your partner about how you each feel may be the sexiest thing you can do right now. Don't deny each other the intimacy of touching and cuddling, even if that's all you're up to.

When you are ready for sex, take it slowly. Have a lubricant at hand, if necessary, and don't forget contraception. You may ovulate even while you're nursing, and even if your menstrual period hasn't started again. Don't limit lovemaking to the evening when you both may be tired. Try to time romance for when your baby is asleep, but don't get too discouraged when she interrupts you. Babies seem to know when you would most wish not to be disturbed. Persevere. It will get better.

Home Essentials

These are the basics you'll want to have in the nursery space when you bring your baby home. It's wise to buy baby's clothing according to weight—a baby weighing more than 3.6 kg (8 lb.) at birth probably won't fit into the newborn size. Or buy the size three times the baby's age: for example, size 6 months for a two-month-old; size 12 months for a four-month-old.

Equipment

- → crib or bassinet
- → change table (any safe surface will do as long as it's the right height to prevent back pain)
- → bottles, nipples, formula, cleaning brushes and sterilizing equipment (if bottle-feeding)

Clothing

- → several undershirts
- → several stretchy sleepers for a winter baby
- → several short-sleeved cotton rompers for a summer baby
- → socks or bootie slippers
- → 6 to 10 receiving blankets
- → 3 dozen cloth diapers or disposable diapers
- → safety pins, 6 diaper covers or rubber pants (if using cloth)
- → diaper pail for cloth diapers
- → sunhat or warm cap and outerwear appropriate to the weather

Supplies

- → cotton swabs
- → diaper cream
- → thermometer
- → soap appropriate for baby skin
- → baby washcloths and hooded towel

Hospital Bag Essentials

It's best to pack it a couple of weeks before your due date, but include a list of last-minute items to add. Visit the hospital ahead of time, and take your documents with you so you can pre-register at Admitting.

The Paperwork

- health card
- proof of hospital insurance
- birth plan
- newborn care plan
- photocopy of pre-registration

What Mom Needs

- something comfortable to wear during labour (The Midwifery Collective of Ottawa suggests a man's large flannel shirt— very Canadian!)
- warm socks (not too tight) and slippers
- clothing for after the birth
- underwear (several pairs)
- nursing bra and breast pads
- personal toilet items
- sanitary pads (plus size)
- snacks, favourite juice (you may find apple, pineapple and orange juices too acidic at this time; try cranberry, grape or grapefruit)
- extra pillows
- massage oil
- lip balm
- music tapes and tape player
- big bath towels (the hospital can put them in the warmer for you)
- focal point (if you are using one during contractions)
- clothes to go home in
- facial tissues
- tennis balls (for back massage)
- magazines or light reading

What Dad and Support Person Need

- snacks, juice
- personal toilet items
- comfortable clothes
- notepaper and pen
- telephone numbers
- change for phone, or calling card
- reading material
- camera
- money for parking and incidentals, but avoid bringing a wallet.

What Baby Needs

- diapers
- clothing: undershirt, stretchy sleeper, cardigan, hat, booties,
- two baby blankets
- CMVSS[1]-approved infant car seat for the trip home

[1] Canadian Motor Vehicle Saftey Standards set by Transport Canada

The
Newborn

2

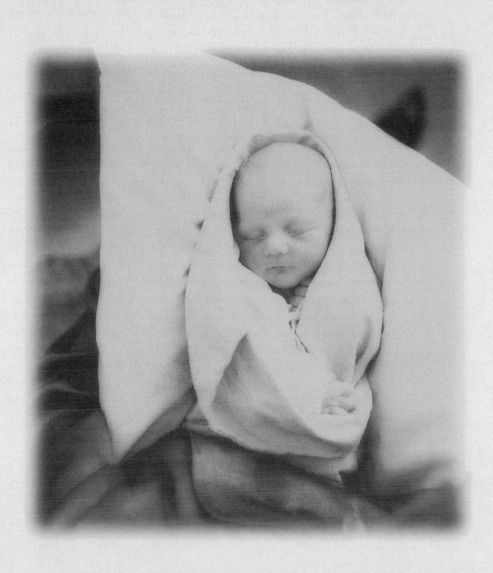

Your baby arrives with highly tuned senses but no understanding of the world he is entering. Once emerged from the confined, dim, and muffled world of the womb, a newborn must feel bombarded with stimuli, particularly light. He begins to collect information about the larger world outside the womb and, as he develops his senses of sight and sound, taste, smell, and touch, he learns more and more. Try to put yourself in your baby's tiny booties—by looking at the world from a baby's point of view, you'll learn how to respond to his needs.

The World through a Newborn's Senses

Sight

Unlike some animal babies, a human baby has sight at birth. But the lens of a newborn's eyes cannot yet adjust its focus to different distances—each child is unique but will be able to focus at a point within the range of 15 to 45 cm (6 to 18 in.). She can usually see a breast when it's offered, and she can see your face when you hold her up close.

At first, a baby moves her eyes in a jerky fashion, but fluidity of eye movement, distance vision, and binocular eyesight will improve over the first few months. Infants appear to prefer bright shades over dull ones, and to recognize high-contrast patterns. Checkerboard patterns appeal to newborns who appear to concentrate on the dividing line between colours.

Newborns watch moving objects more intently than stationary ones, and they favour curved shapes over straight ones. They like big objects that are brightly lit. And newborns love to look at faces, particularly their mother's. Some studies have shown that, as soon as a baby has recovered from the trauma of delivery, he will stare at his mother's face for up to an hour. Until about two months, most babies tend to scan the edges of a face more than the internal features.

Sound

Newborns can hear—indeed fetuses can hear as early as three months before they're born—but they don't always respond to sounds. Babies are born with the ability to inhibit noises selectively. Sometimes they respond, even in their sleep, to whisper-soft noises; sometimes an alarm can go off beside them and they won't even flinch.

Their preference is for human sounds over man-made ones, and for soft sounds—probably because they've grown accustomed to the muted noises of the womb. Studies of newborns have revealed that they react more strongly to female voices, suggesting the baby becomes attuned to her mother's voice through the wall of her womb. Babies can distinguish pitch and volume, and they can detect echoes that adults cannot, although they can't separate a sound from its echo. But a newborn cannot turn her head toward a sound until about three months, although she might turn her eyes in the direction of the sound.

Taste and Smell

The sense of smell is the quickest to mature and it persists the longest—into old age. As well, babies are born with more taste buds which, unfortunately, decrease as we grow into adulthood. A baby's senses of taste and smell are linked to people, particularly the centre of his world—his mother. One study found that very young babies prefer the smell of milk to that of sugar water. And babies suck differently on a bottle of human milk than on one containing formula. Although toothless, babies are born with a sweet tooth and demonstrate a preference for sweet breastmilk.

Touch

Babies can distinguish some textures from birth. Research studies reveal that babies react differently when they're given rough nipples to suck than when the nipples are smooth. Newborns are especially sensitive to the touch of others, which is why they enjoy baby massage so much. Newborns SEE PAGE 61 appear to prefer firm pressure to gentle stroking. The neural systems of infants are sufficiently developed to deliver a message of pain to the brain, although they can be distracted from mild pain by sucking.

Newborn Quirks

Why is my newborn's breathing so erratic?

Because a newborn's lungs are small, like everything else about him, his breathing may seem very shallow. That's normal. And it's also normal for his breaths to be of varying lengths, including an occasional worrisome 10-second pause during which he doesn't breathe at all. Called *periodic breathing*, this pattern is entirely natural for the first few weeks. Newborns also make snuffling noises because they breathe through their noses.

Why does my newborn sometimes cough and choke?

The fluid that filled her lungs in the womb was mostly squeezed out during birth, but excess mucus post-delivery is normal. And babies have tiny nasal passages, which often require a cough or a sneeze to clear.

Why does my baby's chin quiver?

A newborn's nervous system is not yet fully mature. Shaking arms and legs and a deceptive, jerky smile are also normal movements, especially when the baby's drifting to sleep. They'll subside by three months.

Do Newborns Feel Pain?

Some parents worry that babies might suffer the same discomforts that mothers endure during final labour and delivery. But a mother's body hurts precisely because it is being stretched to accommodate the baby's birth. Whereas, pain sensors on an emerging infant have demonstrated that the pressures of the birthing process are no more severe than the pressures on an adult's body just lying in bed.

This is not to suggest that infants don't feel pain. At The Hospital for Sick Children in Toronto, the analysis of videotapes and other records indicated that female infants and uncircumcised male infants showed a higher tolerance for pain during vaccinations than their circumcised counterparts. As lead researcher on one study, Dr. Koren said, "This demonstrates two important findings: It shows us that infants do, in fact, feel pain and that the pain is not short-lived as previously thought."

What are the little white pimples on my baby's face?
These tiny whiteheads—*milia*—are caused by clogging of the newborn's immature oil glands. They'll disappear within weeks without treatment.
Are birthmarks permanent?
There are different types of birthmark. Some birthmarks will grow in the first six months, then recede. The best approach for a parent, dismayed to discover her baby doesn't have the unblemished skin she pictured, is to leave the birthmark alone. It will either fade at its own pace or hold fast, in which case little can be done anyway. If concerned, discuss it with your doctor.
How well can babies hold their temperatures?
Not well at all. Newborns don't arrive with much insulating body fat, especially if they're preterm. Their sweat glands are poorly developed, so they can't rely on this cooling mechanism. And they can't shiver efficiently either, in an effort to warm up. What's more, a baby's skin is paper-thin, which makes it highly sensitive to sources of heat and cold. It is a parent's job, then, to protect her child from overheating and overcooling.
My newborn often lapses into bouts of hiccuping. Should I be concerned?
Not a bit. Hiccups in newborns are caused by a sudden irregular contraction of the diaphragm, and there's nothing you can—or should—do about it. The incidence of hiccups generally decreases significantly by five or six weeks of age.
Why does the doctor feel my baby's tummy?
In addition to a discussion about the infant's feeding, behaviour, development, and temperament, a well-baby visit with the doctor includes a complete physical examination. When a doctor feels the abdomen, she's look-

ing for any enlargement of the liver, spleen, or kidneys that might lead her to be suspicious about an abnormality that would require further testing.

How nervous should I be about the fontanelles?

The fontanelles, the soft spots where the sutures join the four bones of the infant's head, allow the head to adopt a passage-friendly shape for its journey through the birth shaft, and they accommodate the tremendous growth of the brain during the first year. When a baby is born, he generally has two soft spots. Although parents are sometimes alarmed to discover the seemingly insufficient protection between the cruel world and these vulnerable spots on their baby's head, they needn't be. The membranous tissue that covers the soft spots is extremely tough. Although the soft-to-hard transition varies from infant to infant, the posterior fontanelle generally closes up by about three months; the anterior one disappears between twelve and twenty-four months. When you hold your baby upright, the anterior fontanelle may appear a little sunken. If the baby is well, that depression is normal. In babies who have been ill, it may indicate some dehydration. When babies cry excessively, the fontanelles sometimes bulge. When you touch or wash the fontanelle, you needn't give it any more special treatment than you would your baby's tummy or feet.

What reflexes does my newborn have?

Moro or startle: This is a neurological reaction which causes the arms to move outward and then come together in front of the body, a reflex brought about by sudden movements or noises or the withdrawal of head support. You can calm your newborn somewhat by swaddling her.

Rooting: The baby turns her head towards the stimulus, most often her mother's breast. Touching her cheek or mouth will elicit this reflex.

Walking: If you hold your baby in a standing position with your hands under her armpits to support her weight and her feet on a flat surface, she will make stepping movements.

Sucking: When you touch her lips or the upper part of her mouth, your baby will begin to suck.

Grasping: When you touch the palms of your newborn's hands, the stimulation makes her grasp your finger; if you touch the soles of her feet, she will curl her toes.

Babinski: When you stroke your finger up the side of her foot, your newborn's large toe curls up.

Swallowing: Babies are born knowing how to swallow.

Gagging: To protect a baby from choking while she's learning to feed, the gag reflex automatically expels an object from her throat.

Hand to mouth: If you stroke your baby's cheek, she will turn her head in the direction of the touch, bring her hand to her mouth, and suck.

Tonic neck (fencer's reflex): If you turn your newborn's head to one side while she's on her back, you'll notice she thrusts her arm and leg of that side outward, while the opposite arm and leg flex.

Blinking: Your baby will instinctively close her eyes at a loud, nearby sound.

Withdrawal: In response to a painful stimulus on any body part, your newborn will withdraw.

A newborn will lift her head if placed on her stomach, close her eyes in response to a bright light, and turn her head away and flail her arms if you cover her mouth.

Hospital to Home

If there are no complications, new mothers are discharged with their babies just twenty-four hours after bringing them into the world. Some women enjoy getting back home to familiar surroundings as quickly as possible, others feel overwhelmed by their new responsibilities. Being home alone without supervised medical care may be frightening. If you have never breast-fed or experienced your milk coming in, so much is new. For both parents who have never bathed a baby or changed a meconium-filled diaper, the first few days home from the hospital can be very stressful.

New parents most often report that the sudden burden of caring for a new life is what worries them most. Accept that you won't leave the hospital knowing everything about raising an infant, but trust your abilities. Parenting is a learning process and, as long as you're equipped with the basics, you're as well prepared as you can be. Often, all that parents need is reassurance that they're doing a good job. If the baby is content, feeding well, sleeping, and doing all the things babies should do, new parents shouldn't worry.

If this is your first baby, you will both have questions about whether his behaviour is normal, whether he is feeding properly, whether he's healthy. The best way to satisfy yourself that all is well is to arrange for your baby to be seen by an experienced professional as soon as you need. The Canadian Paediatric Society recommends that you and your baby be seen within the first week of your baby's life.

But your need for transitional help may go beyond a 20-minute doctor's visit. The support that women used to get during a longer hospital stay can be replaced in part by at-home care. If you're at all worried about your baby's health or your own, get help. Ask your hospital for a list of resources and references for extra support near you. Be specific about your needs.

Many hospitals host regular educational sessions on a variety of topics for new parents. Also contact your local public health unit (check the Blue Pages in your telephone book) to arrange for visits by a public health nurse or a lactation consultant. Community assistance is probably available through other organizations, public and private, in your area.

"I finally had my son, after thirty hours of labour, on a Saturday. I left the hospital on Monday. I couldn't get any rest in the hospital, just an hour of sleep here and there. I was pretty depressed, and I found the whole thing pretty stressful. I'd baby-sat kids before, so I knew how to put on a diaper and that kind of stuff, but nobody told me just how exhausting having a baby would be."

SUSAN, MOTHER OF ONE, TORONTO, ONT.

When You Leave and Your Baby Doesn't

If your baby is preterm or has medical complications, you might have to leave him behind when you're discharged. If he's staying on for just four or five days, many hospitals have a parent's room where a mother can stay close and breast-feed. If he will be in hospital longer than a few days, you will probably be able to visit at any time and may stay, if you want.

Once your baby is strong enough to be independent of technological help, you can take him into a parent's room to get acquainted. Until then, enjoy your baby with your eyes, and talk to him in his incubator. As hospitals have adopted more family-friendly measures and medical staff acknowledge the value of human contact for premature babies, you will be given many opportunities for parent-baby interaction with your newborn. Some recommend "kangaroo care," in which the diapered baby lies on her parent's naked chest and benefits from the skin-to-skin contact. And as soon as the baby is medically stable, he is allowed to leave the incubator, especially once he is breast-feeding.

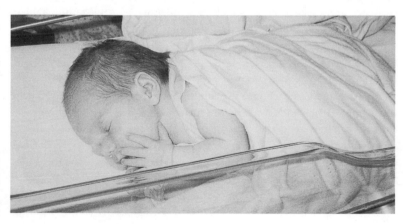

Even in the hospital nursery, a baby needs a parent's touch.

The Newborn

Preterm Babies

According to the World Health Organization (WHO), preterm babies are defined as those born two weeks early who weigh less than 2500 g (5 lb.). But obstetrical technology has improved over the past fifty years to the point where there isn't cause for concern unless the premature infant is under 1500 g (3 lb.). A doctor's decision to admit a newborn to the neonatal intensive care unit (NICU) depends on the degree and the cause of prematurity and any associated medical problem—or a very low birth weight. Typically, preterm babies weigh between 1600 g and 1900 g (about 3.2 lb. to 3.8 lb.) The smallest preemies can fit into an adult's outstretched hand.

Babies are born prior to their due dates for a variety of reasons, some of them baby-centred, most of them mother-centred. The baby may have abnormal chromosomes or an infection, and it's not unusual for twins or other multiple gestations to lead to preterm delivery. There may be problems with the mother's placenta, abnormalities in her uterus, or a history of illnesses such as congenital heart disease or kidney disease throughout the pregnancy.

Maternal substance abuse (cigarettes, alcohol, and illegal drugs) may also lead to preterm delivery. The most common abuse is maternal smoking, which inhibits the ability of the placenta to deliver enough blood to the fetus. As well, drug use, particularly of cocaine, leads to preterm, low-weight babies.

Appearance and behaviour

Some people say that preemies look like little birds. They have no fat, and their veins and arteries are visible through their translucent skin. Their sex organs are immature, and there may be no areola around the nipples. Their ears are sometimes flat or folded, and their skin colour responds to feeding and physical touch.

The smaller the baby, the less control she has over her body. If you lay a tiny preterm baby on her back, very often her hands, arms, and legs will splay out and shake a bit, or go all limp. In contrast, a full-term baby has the ability to recover from this prone posture into the flexed position that keeps him calm. A preterm baby doesn't yet have that control.

In the past, preemies were cared for flat on their backs under bright lights in a hospital's NICU. Now, care providers are encouraged to tuck the baby's arms and legs back into the comfortable, flexed position and to help them bring their hands near their mouths. Babies are positioned on their sides or tummies, and they rest on beds of sheepskin or lambskin under dimmed lights.

Preterm babies used to be characterized by long, thin faces, but now that they're placed on soft bedding, their faces appear rounder. Preterm babies cry less often than their full-term counterparts, because they just don't have the energy. Indeed, these babies often deal with stress by simply shutting down and doing nothing. Preemies face greater risk of long-term behavioural characteristics like learning disabilities, attention deficit disorder, trouble with visual-spatial concepts, difficulties hearing, and eye problems.

Caring for a Preemie

Basic care for a preterm baby differs somewhat from your care for a full-term baby.

➤ Be sure she's kept warm. Her lack of fat means she can't maintain her body temperature.

➤ She may require dietary supplements because her intestines do not yet have complete ability to absorb certain nutrients.

➤ She may require smaller, more frequent feedings.

➤ She probably sleeps more than a full-term baby, and may take longer than usual to settle into any pattern.

➤ Research has revealed that premature babies who receive lots of maternal contact, especially in conditions that simulate the movement they would have enjoyed within the womb, grow faster than babies in isolated, static care.

➤ You may explore the possibility of seeing a special developmental pediatrician, to stay on top of your baby's development.

➤ There are guidelines for transporting preemies in vehicles, and specially developed car beds are being evaluated.

Concerns and special care

Babies born between 34 and 37 weeks might experience some breathing difficulty, and they might not have the stamina to feed sufficiently, but generally they develop well. For preemies born at 24 weeks, there is considerably more cause for concern. Although they have all their parts, their bodies are entirely immature. Of greatest significance are the immature central nervous systems and lungs. These babies suffer the risk of severe lung complications, infection, feeding problems, and heart difficulties. They're prone to interventricular hemorrhages (bleeding in the brain) from the stress of delivery. Some of them suffer other problems of differing severity.

Another critical issue with small babies is a dangerous lack of glucose. If a baby doesn't have enough fat, she doesn't have the ability to generate sufficient glucose—the fuel for production of energy for survival. She can become hypoglycemic and suffer seizures or brain damage. Hospital staff watch the glucose levels of low-birth-weight babies very closely and, if there's any sign of hypoglycemia, they provide glucose intravenously.

Hospital stay

No matter how severe a premature baby's condition is to begin with, it's a hospital's goal to get her home with her parents, under the security of her own roof, as soon as she is medically able to be there. If a baby is born at 24 weeks, she'll usually stay in hospital for three or four months, or until she reaches 37 or 38 weeks of gestational age. For the babies who are born closer to term and whose conditions aren't complicated, hospitals send them home by 35 or 36 weeks, or as soon as they are gaining weight well.

Going home

Mothers of preterm infants are generally discharged after 24 or 48 hours, and, if the babies can be discharged within a few days of that, the hospital will often put the parents up in a parent's room so they can stay close and the mother can breast-feed. If the baby has to stay longer, parents are encouraged to visit at any time and parent's rooms are generally available for overnight stays.

Some babies go home with a rather complicated set-up, including oxygen and several medications. If the baby has had difficulty breathing and has damage to her lungs, she may require oxygen for a few months. These babies tend to be more irritable, and they don't sleep well, but most of a parent's attention must focus on the feeding of a home-bound preemie, because it's critical that the baby add weight as quickly as possible. But it's not unusual for parents to feel nervous when, after weeks of hospital care, this little creature becomes their primary responsibility. Parents in this situation do have one advantage: Most parents of preterm infants have become extremely knowledgeable about their babies and their required care by the time they take them home.

Development

A preterm baby has two ages: her actual age and her corrected age. She could be an actual age of six months (that is, she was born six months ago), but when you subtract the lost gestational time, she is really only three months old— her corrected age. This is a significant point. Parents of a premature baby have to measure her development by her corrected age, not her actual age, so they can set accurate milestones for her. Just because she may have been born eight months ago, you can't expect her to do what a regular eight-month-old does. After about two years, the child's age is measured by her birth date.

Slow development in a preterm baby is to be expected. There is some evidence to suggest that emotional warmth and stroking can help premature babies develop better. But if she isn't making any progress at all over a period of time, or if she seems unresponsive, talk about it with her doctor.

Feeding

If the premature baby is very small, feeding is a major concern. Preterm infants have to be fed every three hours to ensure weight gain. A daily weigh-in should yield a gain of about 1 to 2 per cent of her body weight daily. By the time she reaches the date she was originally expected, she should be approaching the weight of a full-term baby. Later on, premature babies may experience difficulties absorbing nutrients because of problems with their bowels. Premature babies all need to receive extra iron and vitamin supplements.

The Vulnerable Child Syndrome

Once a premature baby has recovered and has achieved a normal height, a normal weight, and a normal disposition, that child should be freed of the preemie label. The term "vulnerable child syndrome" is applied to the child whose parents are unable to make that adjustment. They forever regard their child as vulnerable because she was fragile at birth. This parental attitude sometimes makes it difficult for the child to develop like other children. There are some children who do not fully recover from the complications of their prematurity, and their special needs have to be tackled. But most preemies can have a normal childhood.

Attachment

Attachment is the dance of understanding between a baby and her parents. It is the parents' role to learn to respond to the baby's cues, to let her take the lead. And the baby's role is to signal a change in the steps, to let her parents know what she needs. Attachment is the act of sharing information and learning from each other. It begins at first meeting and deepens and grows over a child's whole life with her parents.

On a very basic level, attachment is critical to a child's development. Both mother and father have to feel invested in what happens to their baby. A mother, in particular, has to develop an interest in her baby. If she doesn't, she won't protect him. As for the child, among the first lessons he'll learn is the lesson of trust. If his needs aren't met, if his parents don't try to figure out who he is and what he needs, he won't learn trust. Luckily, for the majority of babies and their parents, a solid attachment emerges over time so that baby and parents feel that wonderful bond that will connect them throughout their lives.

Fathers provide a variety of touch and sound, thus helping their babies respond to change.

For some parents and their baby, the dance of attachment feels awkward at first, with lots of missed cues and false steps on both sides. Different babies present parents with different challenges, and some babies are very hard to read. Some mothers expect to feel an instant and overwhelming sense of love toward their baby and, when that doesn't happen right away, they feel inadequate, guilty, confused, and fearful. These feelings, combined with sleep deprivation and huge hormonal changes, can make the first postpartum weeks more hell than heaven for the mother. Try not to place too much significance on your confused feelings those first few weeks. Take comfort in the knowledge that you're not the first parent to feel this way, and trust that your relationship with your baby will develop with time.

You can make the acquaintance of your baby and stimulate a deep mutual connection in many simple ways. Give yourself time to just watch your baby and be amazed by her. Memorize what she looks like, carefully examine all her body parts. And let her, in turn, stare at your face and drink you in.

Fathers are very much a part of the attachment process that occurs in those early weeks. As you touch and hold your infant, you encourage her to use different muscle groups and parts of her brain that her mother may not reach. Fathers provide variety of touch and sound, thus helping their babies respond to change. Research indicates that fathers who are highly involved with their newborns have a positive effect on their child's development. In one study, fathers regularly talked and played with, soothed, fed, and changed their babies during the first month of life. At age one, their children scored significantly higher on developmental tests of motor skills, pattern identification, word recognition, and problem solving than those children who hadn't enjoyed the same paternal attention.

Attachment or Bonding—or Both?

In their 1983 book, *Bonding: The Beginnings of Parent-Infant Attachment*, two American pediatricians, Drs. Marshall H. Klauss and John H. Kennell, noted that it was beneficial for a mother to have the opportunity to "bond" with her infant immediately after delivery by holding her baby and having skin-to-skin contact. If that early contact happened, the mother's behaviour was more natural and more committed. But the message of that observation got a little twisted. Many people worried that, if the contact didn't happen, the relationship between mother and child would be permanently damaged. The bonding expectation caused a lot of grief for adoptive mothers and the many biological mothers who weren't able to hold their babies immediately.

Recognizing the concerns aroused by the original observation, Klauss and Kennell undertook a more focused follow-up study which demonstrated that the primary beneficiary of immediate skin-to-skin contact is the mother, not the baby. While it's beneficial for parents to spend time with their baby in that first twenty-four hours, it isn't damaging to the baby or to their relationship if that doesn't happen. Now experts extend the concept of *bonding* with the word *attachment* to describe the process that goes on over the child's whole life. For expectant parents, the important result of these studies is the improved experience of birthing in hospitals.

Sibling Attachment

New siblings almost always attach, on some level, to one another. Watching the relationship unfold is a wonderful experience for parents as it adds a whole new dynamic to the interactions of the family unit. The connection may take some time, though, and it may not always happen as you anticipated. Everyone comes into this world with a certain personality and a unique way of associating with other personalities.

Remember that siblings relate to one another differently from how they relate to their parents. Here are some tips for fostering the sibling connection:

➤   Don't force it. If it's going to happen, it will. Parental pressure and interference will only add stress.

➤   Use the baby's name from the start, so his older sibling can understand he's a person, and not a thing.

The Newborn

> Urge the older sibling to learn about the baby. The more you learn about someone, the more connected you feel to him.

> Listen to one sibling's complaint about another without judging. It's natural to get frustrated with another person who is always "in your face." To calm the waters, discuss these natural feelings with your children.

> Recognize that sibling rivalry is a fact of life, and don't overreact to the occasional flare-up.

> Just as important as a sibling's attachment to a new family member is her need to re-attach to her parents. Don't be surprised if your older child reverts to some babyish behaviour in the transition phase. It will pass.

"We were lucky. Our oldest child accepted each newborn very readily. I do have to be careful, however, if I do something special with one of the younger children, that I make plans with the oldest child to do something special with him. He needs to be reassured that I still love him and that I want to spend time with him."

COLIN, FATHER OF THREE, SCARBOROUGH, ONT.

Let the new sibling relationship grow naturally.

Breast-Feeding

The decision to breast-feed is a personal one and, increasingly, a common one. Canadian health organizations unanimously support breast-feeding, and they're spreading the message that breastmilk offers perfect nutrition and significant immunological and psychological benefits for the health of the babies. Certainly breast-feeding can't be beat for its practicality. Whenever the baby is hungry, mother offers a ready-to-serve, not to mention free, milk supply.

Ten Reasons to Breast-Feed

1. Breast-fed infants have increased protection against major illnesses like meningitis and diabetes.
2. Breastmilk also helps protect against minor illnesses including ear and gastrointestinal infections, diarrhea, and colds, and may help protect against Sudden Infant Death Syndrome (SIDS).
3. When breast-fed babies do get sick, they require hospitalization less frequently than bottle-fed babies.
4. Breastmilk offers superior nutrition.
5. The components of breastmilk change to meet the infant's changing nutritional needs as he grows.
6. Breast-feeding may protect against food allergies, if mother's diet contains only low allergenic foods.
7. Breast-feeding is convenient. There are no bottles to sterilize, no formula to mix.
8. Breast-feeding may save a family about $100 a month in formula and bottle supplies.
9. Breast-feeding is enjoyed by both mother and baby, and promotes attachment.
10. Women who breast-feed experience less ovarian and breast cancer.

Choosing to Breast-Feed

It's a decision each mother makes after considering all the available information and a constellation of family and community factors: How does she feel about breast-feeding? What does her partner think? Did her own mother breast-feed? Her sister? Her friends and neighbours? Will she feel comfortable breast-feeding in public? In the end, the decision lies with the soon-to-be mother, who may not always choose breast-feeding but who will choose what she feels is best for herself and her family.

About 80 per cent of Canadian mothers start breast-feeding in hospital;

by the baby's sixth month, 75 per cent are using formula alone or in combination with breast-feeding.

Beginning to Breast-Feed

With the birth of your baby and the expulsion of the placenta, the level of prolactin in your body rises, which stimulates the secretion of milk. Within the hour after birth, a baby's sucking instinct is at its strongest, and the baby will instinctively seek his mother's breast. When he wants to nurse depends on his quickly emerging personality. Some babies are slow to develop an effective feeding pattern; they seem to prefer to open their eyes wide and look around or to nod off to sleep. Other babies suckle vigorously and often. Let your baby breast-feed whenever he indicates an interest, and aim for a minimum of 8 feedings in 24 hours. Some babies may breast-feed as often as 10 to 12 times in 24 hours. Look for hunger cues such as changing facial expressions, sucking, rooting, and bringing his hands up to his face.

"When my wife breast-fed, I would participate by just being close. I would sit with my wife and son, hold his hand and caress it. Or he would use his hand to explore my face. Sometimes we'd make eye contact and just look at each other. There were special moments like this every day while we became a family."

ALLAN, FATHER OF ONE, OTTAWA, ONT.

From colostrum to mature milk

During the first days of nursing, your first milk (called *colostrum*) is thick, sweet, and yellowish. New mothers have between 2 and 20 mL each day for two or three days. Not only does it give complete nourishment, it also supplies antibodies that protect the baby from disease. It has a laxative effect that helps clear out the *meconium*, the dark greenish material (a baby's first feces) that is passed by the third or fourth day. If the baby is nursed soon after birth and frequently thereafter, transition milk (a mixture of colostrum and mature milk) will be flowing within three or four days (with a first child) and will last until about the tenth day when a mother's mature milk begins to flow.

Breast engorgement

On Day Three after the birth, when your milk production increases, you may look like a fertility symbol, but your painful breasts will make you feel like anything but a goddess. Day Three engorgement is almost inevitable. The best way to treat this and other engorgement (which may occur later if you miss a feeding or two) is to nurse the baby frequently. You may be able to avoid further engorgement altogether by giving your baby frequent, unrestricted opportunities to breast-feed.

Engorgement makes your breasts hard and nursing difficult. You might

"My daughter was what you would call a quirky feeder. She was born on a Monday, we came home from the hospital on Wednesday, and by Saturday she still wasn't nursing well. She would suckle for a few minutes and then stop. As a mother, I was getting so frustrated, and the baby was getting so frustrated. It was a real lose-lose situation. She wasn't a happy baby. She and I would walk the floor at two, three, six in the morning. I was at the breaking point. By then my milk had come in, and I was doing the warm-washcloths-and-shower thing. The engorgement made it hard for both of us; it was hard for her to latch on and painful for me. I was about to go to the drugstore and buy fourteen bottles and lots of formula. Then she decided to nurse really well. My daughter is very determined in the way she approaches her life. It's her way—or the highway."

SHARON, MOTHER OF TWO, WINNIPEG, MAN.

express some milk with a breast pump until your areola softens, which will allow your baby to latch on to your breast more effectively. To relieve soreness before nursing, have a hot shower, or apply heat to your breasts with warm compresses or hot wash cloths. Gently massage the breast to help the milk flow.

If your breasts are very painful, take a pain reliever twenty minutes before nursing. Acetaminophen will not affect your baby. After feeding, apply ice packs for fifteen to twenty minutes to help decrease swelling. With regular nursing, engorgement does eventually go away. **For more information on breast-feeding problems, see page 81.**

Normal jaundice and breastmilk jaundice syndrome

If your baby's skin is developing a distinctive yellow tint, he may have normal jaundice, which affects approximately 50 per cent of all babies in the second to fourth day after birth. Most babies do not require treatment for jaundice but, if a blood test shows that the level of serum bilirubin (bile in the blood) is excessively high, your doctor may suggest phototherapy (light therapy) to help speed up the elimination of the bile which causes the yellowish tint. All infants with jaundice need to be monitored by a physician because of the association of high bilirubin with brain damage.

However, breastmilk jaundice syndrome is a rare condition affecting 2 to 4 per cent of breast-fed newborns. It usually appears toward the end of the first week, peaks at ten to fifteen days, and may last three weeks or longer. Breast-feeding should not be interrupted because of either the normal jaundice or breastmilk jaundice syndrome. In fact, frequent unrestricted breast-feeding can be helpful to both the mother and the baby.

Who to turn to for help

The first three to five days after birth are crucial for successful breast-feeding. With the recent policy of discharging a new mother and child from hospital twenty-four hours after birth, the onus lies firmly on the shoulders of the new parents to find help with breast-feeding. You may think that breast-feeding will come naturally but, like most aspects of parenting, breast-feeding is a learned art. If you haven't set up breast-feeding support before your baby's birth, don't leave the hospital without a phone number to call with questions. You may also need someone who will meet with you, if needed, to coach and encourage you through any problems you may encounter.

Finding answers to a breast-feeding problem may be as simple as a phone call to your sister. Or maybe you have a friend who has nursed before, and you feel comfortable whipping off your top in front of her. She, too, has fallen in love with your baby and is more than willing to work with both of you on the mechanics of nursing. Or perhaps it's midnight, your breasts are rock-hard with engorgement, your baby's screeching, and you feel you have no one to turn to. You're wrong.

With the decrease in the length of the hospital stay has come an increase in support to breast-feeding mothers. A good place to start is the hospital where you gave birth. A nurse will be able to give you some over-the-phone help and, if your hospital has a breast-feeding clinic, you'll be invited to join. Some hospitals also have a "warm line" which new mothers can phone for advice and support. You could check with your family physician who is trained to help you or who may refer you to a nurse, a midwife, or a lactation consultant—a person who is fully informed about all aspects of breast-feeding. Another good source is your public health unit. Check the local or municipal Blue Pages in your telephone book. Public health nurses can offer everything from home visits to 24-hour phone-in lines to well-baby clinics to drop-ins.

La Leche League Canada may be a helpful source for you. *La leche* is Spanish for *the milk* and La Leche League is the largest women's health organization in the world, with more than three thousand breast-feeding support groups in forty-eight countries. Chances are that there's a group near you that can offer mother-to-mother support, monthly meetings, and telephone help. To locate your closest group, check for La Leche League in the business section of your phone book or call their Breastfeeding Referral Service at 1-800-665-4324.

You may also want to read *The Womanly Art of Breastfeeding* (6th edition, 40th anniversary, 1997), La Leche League International's runaway bestseller, considered by many as an essential resource for the breast-feeding family. Or watch one of their videos. The 60-minute video "The Art of Breastfeeding" was made, in part, by La Leche League Canada.

How to Breast-Feed

Breast-feeding is wondrous, but it's also sound science. It helps to understand the science to know why proper technique is necessary. After delivery, as estrogen and progesterone levels drop, the level of the milk-making hormone prolactin rises, and your baby's suckling stimulates nerve impulses that set off a biochemical response which keeps it high. Prolactin not only aids milk secretion, but also has a calming effect on the mother.

Milk is produced in your breasts but isn't available to your baby until it is "let down" into the milk ducts. When your baby suckles, she triggers your letdown reflex which releases milk into the ducts. When this happens, you may feel a tingling sensation, which some women describe as pins and needles. Each breast nipple contains 15 to 20 milk duct openings. When the baby continues to suckle on the areola (the pigmented area surrounding the nipple), the breast releases milk into his mouth. During pregnancy, the breast's areola enlarges and turns from pink to reddish brown. Although the milk is released from the nipple, the baby nurses from the areola.

You know that your milk has let down when your baby's suckling slows and his swallowing increases. At this point, your other breast may start leaking, and if you've given birth in the last few weeks, you may feel your uterus con-

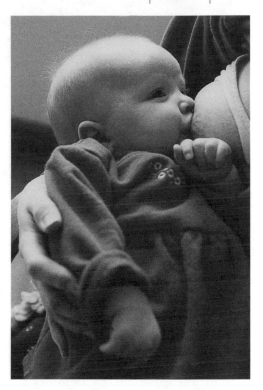

tract. Breastmilk is actually composed of two milks: foremilk and hindmilk. You produce the bluish-white foremilk between feedings. The foremilk, which your baby receives first, quenches her thirst. The higher-fat hindmilk is produced during the feeding. The hindmilk satisfies your baby's hunger—it's important to allow your baby to stay on each breast until she is satisfied.

When baby has latched on properly, she can suck contentedly, and you won't have sore nipples.

In the first few weeks, your breasts will feel hard as they adjust to producing milk. Later, as they become more efficient, they'll soften. Don't worry that, since your breasts are soft, you're no longer producing enough milk. Nursing promotes milk production. The more your baby nurses, the more abundant your milk will be.

Latching on and off

Proper positioning of the baby's mouth on the breast, known as *latching on*, ensures that your baby receives adequate nutrition and that you won't get sore, cracked nipples. To stimulate the baby's natural urge to suck, lightly stroke his cheek. He'll turn his head in the direction of the cheek you stroked. Or tickle his lower lip with your nipple.

Help your baby latch on by compressing your breast between your thumb and fingers, keeping your fingers away from the areola. By cupping the breast, you shape the areola to match the oval shape of the infant's mouth. Brush the nipple to the baby's mouth. When he opens his mouth wide, draw your baby to your breast so that his mouth covers most of your areola. The baby sucks on your areola, not on your nipple. If your baby is latched on correctly, nursing shouldn't hurt. If it does hurt and you see that your baby is sucking on the nipple rather than the areola, help him latch off and try again.

To stop your baby from nursing, gently put your finger in the corner of his mouth to break the suction. If you simply pull your baby away, you'll hit the ceiling with pain.

Breast-feeding positions

Breast-feeding is a time to relax with your baby. Get comfortable and use pillows to help support your arm and the baby. Vary positions to avoid sore nipples and to ensure draining from all the milk ducts. The following instructions are for feeding on the right breast. Reverse for the left breast.

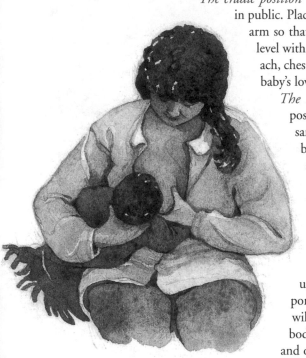

The cradle position This position allows you to nurse discreetly in public. Place your baby's head in the crook of your right arm so that baby is lying horizontally, with her mouth level with your areola. Turn the baby so that her stomach, chest, and knees are against your body. Place your baby's lower arm around your waist.

The side-lying position When you master this position, you'll be able to sleep and nurse at the same time. Lie on your right side, and place the baby so that his mouth is level with the areola on your bottom (right) breast. Use your bottom (right) arm to hold your baby in position. Take care not to lie on your baby's arm.

The football hold This position is especially useful for smaller babies or for a mother with large breasts. Hold your baby under your right arm, with your hand supporting the baby's head and neck. Your baby will be facing you and should be close to your body. Cup your right breast with your left hand and offer it to your baby.

Football hold

Feeding schedule—What schedule?

Feeding a newborn usually takes five to twenty minutes per breast, but thirty minutes per breast is not unusual. Don't look at your watch to see if your baby has finished feeding. Let her feed for as long as she likes or until she falls asleep.

Give your newborn frequent, unrestricted opportunities to breast-feed— a minimum of eight feedings in twenty-four hours. Since human milk can be digested within two hours, night feedings are essential. To stimulate and maintain your milk production, let your baby suckle at both breasts in turn at each feeding. For the subsequent feeding, let him start with the breast offered last. Can't remember which side to start on? Some women put a safety-pin on the bra strap of the breast with which the baby should start.

Feeding during growth spurts
When your baby suddenly nurses more frequently, she is probably going through a growth spurt. Typically, these growth spurts occur around two weeks, four to six weeks, three months, and six months. Help your milk production increase to satisfy your baby's hunger by resting, eating well, and nursing more often.

Burping
Some breast-fed babies never need burping. But if your baby tends to gulp back your milk, he may need to burp after each breast. Place him over your shoulder or legs and gently rub his back until he burps. Do not hit his back. And don't be surprised if the shoulder you're burping him on suddenly feels wet. Regurgitation is common with burping. You'll get in the habit of placing a towel or receiving blanket over your shoulder or leg before you burp the baby.

"When my son was born, I thought breast-feeding would be a piece of cake. I thought that I would just know what to do. The first six weeks were awful. He wouldn't open his mouth enough, so he'd just be nipple feeding. My nipples were so cracked and sore that when I nursed I'd be curling my toes because it hurt so much.

LESLIE, MOTHER OF TWO, CALGARY, ALTA.

Expressing milk
You may want to express your milk if you're suffering from engorgement, or if you have to miss a feeding and want to keep up your milk supply. To express your milk manually, use a large, clean bowl to collect the milk. Wash your hands, then place your thumb and forefinger on opposite sides of your breast where the areola meets the paler flesh. First push the areola back toward your chest wall with thumb and forefinger, then pull it forward while gently squeezing. Repeat, moving your hand around the areola.

If you would rather use a breast pump, manual ones are available at your pharmacy. Bulb (bicycle horn) pumps are not recommended because they can cause nipple trauma and are difficult to clean. If your baby is premature and requires long-term milk expression or you are returning to work in the first few months, battery-operated or electric pumps are recommended. Look for a full-strength pump that has a Y-connector for both breasts and a regular rhythmic pumping action. You can rent one from lactation consultants, public-health departments, or medical supply stores.

The Newborn

After you have collected your breastmilk, pour it into a bottle or plastic disposable bottle liner and store it in the refrigerator for up to two days. If you plan to freeze your breastmilk, use a glass or rigid plastic container, or a plastic storage bag, specially designed for freezing human milk and available from your pharmacy. Freezing milk in a bottle liner is risky because the seams may burst during freezing or leak during thawing. You can store breastmilk in the freezer compartment of your refrigerator for up to two weeks, for two months in a refrigerator with a separate freezer compartment, and in a deep freezer for up to six months.

Serve refrigerated breastmilk as you would formula. Defrost frozen breastmilk in the refrigerator, then shake well before warming. Never use a SEE PAGE 49 microwave to warm breastmilk.

Is Your Baby Nursing Well ?

The Canadian Paediatric Society offers these checkpoints for knowing that your baby **is** feeding well.

➤ You hear short swallowing sounds (making a caw sound) which gradually lengthen and deepen as your milk is released.

➤ Your areola, and your baby's jaw muscles move evenly as your baby sucks. You'll be able to see the movement of your baby's jaw right up to the ears.

➤ Your baby is content or asleep after feeding.

➤ The nursing process doesn't hurt you.

Your baby **is not** feeding well when:

➤ You hear a lot of lip smacking.

➤ You notice there's very little swallowing.

➤ Your baby isn't content after eating.

➤ The nursing process is painful for you.

Supplemental bottles

Nursing mothers should not provide supplemental bottles until the breast-feeding relationship is well-established, unless there is some initial concern about depriving the newborn of essential nutrition. Giving your baby supplemental bottles too early will only contribute to your breast engorgement, sore nipples, and poor milk production. Since sucking on the nipple of a bottle requires a different technique, using both at the beginning may confuse your baby. If she's only breast-feeding, your baby will perfect her sucking techniques. But once breast-feeding is established, you will be able to return to work, if you wish, while maintaining breast-feeding and supplementing occasionally with bottles.

Pacifiers/Soothers

The World Health Organization suggests that breast-fed babies not be given a pacifier or soother during the first few weeks because it may distract them from breast-feeding. As with supplemental bottles, your baby develops a sucking technique with a soother that's different from the one needed to breast-feed. Many babies who nurse satisfy their sucking needs at the breast; however, a soother may let you get rest between feedings.

SEE PAGE 108

Is Your Baby Drinking Enough?

Without a way to measure how much a breast-feeding baby is drinking, many parents feel anxious that he might not be getting enough. You can be assured that your baby is receiving adequate nutrition if, after the first week, when milk production has increased:

➤ You see your baby swallowing during a feeding, and he seems content and satisfied after feeding.

➤ Your baby nurses well at least eight times a day during the first few months.

➤ His bowel movements are soft or liquid and occur once or more daily for the first month. They are probably yellow or a green shade.

➤ His urine is pale yellow. He has six to eight wet diapers daily. (It's hard to determine if a diaper is wet when you use disposable diapers.)

➤ Your doctor feels your baby's weight gain is adequate.

Vitamin and Mineral Supplements

According to Health Canada, a nursing mother shouldn't have to supplement her diet with vitamins as long as she eats a well-balanced diet, which includes 1L (35 oz.) of milk or its equivalent daily. However, some physicians recommend that women continue to take their prenatal supplements while they are nursing.

As for your baby, you're feeding him the way nature intended, so squirting a vitamin supplement into his mouth may seem unnatural. But the major health organizations recommend it.

Vitamin D Both the Canadian Paediatric Society and Health Canada recommend that 400 IU of vitamin D be given to breast-fed babies daily to prevent rickets and promote natural growth. For the body to synthesize vitamin D, the skin must be exposed to sunlight. And Canada isn't famous for its sunshine. The Canadian Paediatric Society recommends that the dosage be increased to 800 IU daily during the winter for babies living in the Far North, where sunshine is extremely limited.

The Newborn

People with dark skin have a harder time synthesizing vitamin D. One study showed that, to produce a similar amount of vitamin D, people with dark skin may need up to six times as much sunlight as people with light skin. Rickets, caused by vitamin D deficiency has been reported among Native children in Manitoba and northern Ontario.

Iron Sufficient iron is provided in breastmilk for the first six months of age. After six months, your baby will maintain adequate stores if she eats iron-enriched cereal. Premature babies may need an iron supplement, but ask the advice of your doctor.

Vitamin B₁₂ If you follow a vegan diet, your baby needs a vitamin B_{12} supplement.

Concerns of New Breast-Feeding Mothers

Fatigue

You may find that fatigue interferes with your let-down and contributes to an inadequate milk supply. Check your expectations. When you're nursing a baby around the clock, don't expect to be able to do everything you did before the baby arrived. There is no pat solution to new-mother fatigue, especially if you don't have family help close by. But if a friend offers to take your older kids to the zoo for the day, say yes. If there's a choice between vacuuming and taking a nap, crawl between the sheets.

> If there's a choice between dusting and napping, take a nap.

What to eat

Fatigue can take away your appetite. Or you may be hungrier than ever before. To feed the nursing mother is to feed the baby. Small amounts of everything you eat end up in your milk. As you nosh your way through the lasagna your neighbour made, and the strawberry cheesecake your mom baked, your milk picks up the odours and flavours of the foods. This ever-changing taste spectrum of breastmilk will help your baby accept new foods when he's older.

There are no foods that you must eat while you're nursing, nor is it necessary to eat more while you're nursing. But it's important to eat well and nutritiously. To be sure you meet your nutritional requirements, follow Canada's Food Guide to Healthy Eating. Every day, have 5 to 12 servings of grain products; 5 to 10 servings of vegetables and fruit; 3 to 4 servings of milk products; and 2 to 3 servings of meat or alternatives such as legumes. It is not necessary to avoid specific foods or spices while breast-feeding, unless your baby shows evidence of food sensitivities or allergies.

SEE PAGE 183

SEE PAGE 44

What to drink
You may also be thirstier than ever before. A nursing mother produces up to 1L (35 oz.) of breastmilk a day. To combat thirst, some nursing women follow the rule: Whenever you pass a tap, take a drink. Other mothers sip a tall glass of water every time they nurse. If your urine is dark or cloudy, it probably means you are not drinking enough. It means it's time for a glass of water, milk, juice, a hot bowl of soup, or a pot of a weak herbal tea (avoid teas with high-alkaloid herbs). Limit coffee, tea, and colas. Not only can they dehydrate you, the caffeine in them may make your baby irritable.

Alcohol can pass into breastmilk. Although the occasional drink is considered compatible with breast-feeding, heavy consumption of alcohol interferes with your milk supply and is harmful to your baby. To minimize the amount of alcohol your baby receives, avoid alcohol for two hours before breast-feeding.

If you have a cold
Absolutely continue to breast-feed. Although you are exposing your baby to your germs, you're also protecting him with your antibodies.

Breast-feeding and your waistline
Breast-feeding naturally mobilizes fat stores, making it easier to shed the pounds you gained during pregnancy. But don't diet when you're nursing. Since we all store PCBs in our fat and crash diets mobilize the PCBs, a nursing mother may pass PCB toxins to her baby through her breastmilk. However, tiny amounts of pesticides and pollutants are found in all foods, including formula, so breastmilk is still considered the safest food for babies. Be aware that a diet with fewer than 1,500 calories a day will reduce your milk supply and contribute to your fatigue.

Contraception
Breast-feeding may offer some protection against pregnancy if the mother is exclusively breast-feeding the baby day and night. However, it is not reliable as a method of birth control. New mothers start ovulating as early as eight weeks after the baby's birth, so if they don't wish to conceive, they should use a contraceptive method. An IUD, diaphragm, or condom with spermicidal foam are the preferred choices. The progesterone mini-pill, implants, and injections increase milk secretions. For some mothers, the estrogen-progesterone pill occasionally reduces their milk production.

Smoking
If you smoke, you may feel more motivated to cut down, if not quit, since nicotine passes into breastmilk. Smoking more than ten cigarettes a day has been associated with decreased milk production and decreased ejection as well as with infant irritability and poor weight gain. Heavy smoking may give your baby nausea or diarrhea or it may cause her to vomit. Breastmilk

is still the best choice for your baby, so try to reduce the harmful effects on your baby by smoking only after breast-feeding, not before. To reduce the risks of second-hand smoke, don't smoke or allow others to smoke near your baby, since it increases the risk of SIDS.

Should breast-feeding feel this good?

Here's the best-kept secret about breast-feeding. Women's hormones for lactation and the sexual cycle are similar. Nursing can be sensually stimulating, if not sexually arousing. Health Canada has given its blessing on these feelings by stating that they are "normal."

Vegetarians and Vitamin Supplements

If you are a lacto-ovo vegetarian who enjoys both dairy and egg foods, breast-feeding will not pose dietary concerns beyond those of all nursing mothers. If you are a vegan who eats no animal products, then vitamin B_{12} supplements for both you and your baby are crucial. Health Canada recommends that nursing women who are vegans take a 1.5 mcg vitamin B_{12} supplement daily. Some babies of vegan mothers who haven't taken a vitamin B_{12} supplement during pregnancy or while nursing, and who haven't given their baby a B_{12} supplement, have suffered major neurological problems before their first birthday.

The Canadian Paediatric Society and Health Canada recommend that breast-fed babies of vegan mothers receive a daily B_{12} supplement. For infants, the Canadian Pharmaceutical Association recommends 0.3 mcg daily, beginning in the second week of life and continuing until at least the second birthday. This B_{12} supplement is in addition to the vitamin supplements recommended for all breast-fed babies.

SEE PAGE 146

Medications

Chances are, any drug you take will pass into your milk. Fortunately, the average residue in breastmilk is less than 1 per cent of the mother's dose. There are few medications that cause a mother to give up breast-feeding, but if you're unsure whether to take a drug while nursing, discuss your concerns with your doctor, your pharmacist, or a drug information centre. One centre devoted to pregnant and breast-feeding mothers and health-care providers is the MotheRisk Clinic at The Hospital for Sick Children in Toronto (416) 813-6780.

Over-the-counter drugs

Most over-the-counter drugs are safe when used according to manufacturer's directions. However, it's best to check with your physician or pharmacist before self-medicating. For pain relief, acetaminophen rather than acetylsalicylic acid (aspirin) is recommended. For pain accompanied by inflammation, ibuprofen can be taken.

Prescription drugs

When you take prescription drugs, minimize your child's exposure to them by taking the medication after she has breast-fed, or just before she's ready to sleep. You should not breast-feed if you are taking any of the following prescription drugs:

bromocriptine, cyclophosphamide, cyclosporine, doxorubicin, ergotamine, lithium, methotrexate, phencyclidine.

Non-prescription drugs

Because there have been no studies on the effects of illegal drugs or so-called recreational drugs like marijuana on breastmilk, the MotherRisk program at The Hospital for Sick Children recommends that any women using drugs not breast-feed.

Herbal remedies

Many herbal remedies contain pharmacologically active ingredients. In fact, many prescription drugs come from herbs. If you're taking herbal remedies, stay within recommended dosages and monitor your baby for side-effects. Some herbal teas (those not containing alkaloid herbs) are considered safe while you're breast-feeding. But, as with any food or drink, avoid excessive intake. If the tea contains sage, for example, a large amount can reduce your supply of milk.

Special Breast-Feeding Considerations

Cesarean birth

A cesarean birth does not affect milk supply or lactation, but a baby may be slower to latch on until the effects of anesthesia wear off. However, if breast-feeding at birth is important to you, you can nurse immediately after a cesarean, right on the delivery-table. If you feel too queasy to breast-feed right away, you can still cuddle your newborn and begin feeding a little later.

Following a cesarean, the most comfortable feeding position may be lying on your side, with a folded towel protecting the incision. Flex your knees, perhaps with a pillow between them, to prevent straining the incision. Later, a comfortable feeding position may be sitting with a pillow on your lap to protect the incision, and holding the baby in the "football hold."

Your premature baby

Breast-feeding is considered crucial to the premature baby—some Canadian doctors say that breastmilk is like medicine to the preemie. As the mother of a premature baby, you face unique breast-feeding challenges. With the trauma of the early birth and the stress of seeing your tiny baby rigged to wires, you are understandably upset. If you are battling your own medical problems, your baby may have to be separated from you. Even if you can be with her, there may not be a private place in the NICU to pump your breastmilk or to feed her.

Initially, you may be asked to express your milk so it can be fed through a nasogastric tube that's inserted into the baby's nose and through to her stomach. As the baby gains strength, she will be encouraged to lick or nuzzle the breast. Before the baby can actually breast-feed, she must be able to coordinate sucking and swallowing.

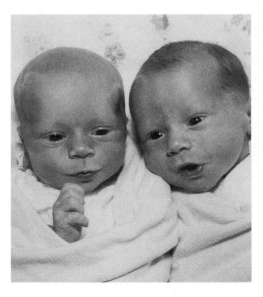

Your twins and triplets

Mothers of twins, triplets, and even quadruplets have breast-fed their babies. Mothers of multiples will have enough milk if they follow the basic rule: The more you nurse, the more milk you produce. In Canada, the mother of a single baby may feel she has to defend her decision to bottle-feed, while a mother of multiples may have to defend her decision to breast-feed.

Amid a frantic schedule of diapering, laundry, and perhaps caring for an older child, breast-feeding can offer a welcome chance to snuggle and rejoice in your double blessing. In the few weeks after birth, mothers of twins usually nurse one baby at a time. When the babies develop better head control and do not need as much positioning, it may be more convenient to nurse the babies together.

You can nurse twins. In fact, you'll save both time and money if you do.

Parents of Multiple Births Association of Canada (POMBA) estimates that breast-feeding saves parents of twins three hundred hours a year in time that would have been spent sterilizing and preparing bottles, and over $1,200 a year in formula costs. For parent-to-parent support, contact POMBA.

Your allergic baby

Babies are rarely allergic to breastmilk, but infants can react to the allergens in their mother's diet that pass into her milk. It's likely that your baby has a food sensitivity if, 15 or 20 minutes after a feeding, he breaks out in hives, has acute diarrhea or projectile vomiting, has difficulty breathing, or displays other allergic symptoms. If your baby experiences breathing difficulties or swelling of the lips or tongue, get immediate emergency medical help. For other allergic reactions, consult your doctor.

Commonly, an allergic baby is reacting to his mother's intake of cow's milk, other dairy products or eggs, and peanuts. Some doctors recommend that pregnant women and nursing mothers avoid or restrict peanut products. Other allergens that babies can be sensitive to include wheat, corn, citrus fruits, fish, seafood, and chocolate. Before eliminating foods, consult a dietitian or your doctor.

"When I first found out I was having twins, I went to the library and read a lot. I had breast-fed my two other children successfully, but I was worried how I would cope with two together. I thought I might not have enough milk for two. I worried that I would be breast-feeding 24 hours a day, and that it would be the end of my life. But it turned out so well that I breast-fed the twins until they were two-and-a-half. There's the assumption that you can't breast-feed twins, but you have two breasts and you have two kids. Well, it makes a lot of sense. It's efficient. But for triplets, well, I guess you'd have to be super organized."

MARGRET, MOTHER OF FOUR, TORONTO, ONT.

The Allergy/Asthma Information Association (AAIA) recommends breast-feeding a high-risk allergic baby (one whose parents have known food allergies) for a minimum of three months, and ideally for twelve months. The association maintains that, if your baby is sensitive to the tiny amounts of food components in your milk, he will likely be unable to tolerate most formulas. Breastmilk may inoculate your baby against some allergens or bolster his immunity against others.

Your adopted baby
It is possible to breast-feed an adopted baby, whether or not you have ever been pregnant. It can be difficult and it is time-consuming; but for the family committed to sharing the intimacy of breast-feeding, at least a partial milk supply can be created. Adoptive mothers can begin establishing a milk supply by pumping for about four minutes on each breast, several times a day, for up to two months before the baby arrives. Once your baby is in your arms, encourage her to nurse as frequently as possible.

When it is necessary to supplement your baby's intake with formula, you may wish to use a nursing supplementer (a gadget taped to the breast) so the baby receives the extra nourishment while nursing. While you are re-establishing or inducing lactation, closely monitor your child's weight and growth with a supportive physician. To help guide your way, read *Breastfeeding the Adopted Baby* (Corona, 1994) by Debra Stewart Peterson, who breast-fed all three of her adopted children.

Your baby with special needs
Babies with cleft lip/cleft palate, cystic fibrosis, celiac disease, neurological impairments, and other medical problems have successfully breast-fed. In some situations, the added health benefits of breastmilk are especially significant. For example, the immune benefits of breast-feeding are considered important for a baby with Down syndrome because of his greater susceptibility to infections. La Leche League Canada, which offers parent-to-parent support, offers the following publications: "Breastfeeding the Chronically Ill Child" and "Nursing Your Baby with Cleft Lip or Cleft Palate."

The Newborn

Bottle-Feeding

With the slogan "Breast Is Best" behind numerous campaigns to encourage Canadian families to choose breast-feeding, you may feel guilty about your decision to bottle-feed. But the choice is yours and, according to 1995 statistics, baby formula is still a popular choice. Twenty per cent of Canadian babies begin feeding from formula right after birth. By the age of six months, seventy-five per cent of babies receive formula either exclusively or in combination with breast-feeding.

Both you and your baby will enjoy the intimacy and tenderness of snuggling up together during bottle-feeding. Just as a breast-fed baby is cradled in her mother's arms near her heart, eyes, and voice, a bottle-fed baby needs the same closeness. Giving your baby a bottle is a time for you to prop up your feet and relax. It's a time when your baby feels warm, secure, and loved.

Choosing a formula

A commercial formula is the only suitable choice until your baby is between nine and twelve months of age. The Canadian Paediatric Society recommends iron-fortified formula. Cow's milk (including evaporated milk), goat's milk, and soy beverages do not provide adequate nutrition for infants and are difficult to digest. Cow's milk may cause intestinal bleeding and can strain a baby's immature kidneys.

Bottle–feeding, whether expressed breastmilk or formula, allows a father to connect with his baby in a special way.

Ask your doctor about the formula most appropriate for your baby. Milk-based formulas are the most commonly used in Canada. If you or your partner has a family history of milk allergy, a soy-based formula might be recommended. However, as many as 40 per cent of infants allergic to milk-based formula are also allergic to soy-based formula.

Will that be liquid or powder?

Commercial formula comes in three forms—powder or granulated, liquid concentrate, and ready-to-serve. When diluting the powder or liquid concentrate, be exact! Follow the dilution instructions on the label to the letter. If you add too little water, your baby can become dehydrated. If you add too much water, your baby won't get enough calories and nutrients.

Powder and liquid concentrate are less expensive than ready-to-serve. Buying by the case is usually cheaper, but you still need to budget $84 to $120 a month for formula for the first nine to twelve months of your baby's life. Avoid changing formula brands to take advantage of a sale. Babies can experience digestive disorders when their formula is changed. Consult your physician before changing your baby's formula.

Water supplements

Healthy bottle-fed infants do not need bottles of water. However, if the weather is oppressively hot or if the infant has diarrhea or a fever, the Canadian Paediatric Society recommends that the baby be offered 60 to 90 mL (2 to 3 oz.) of water. A baby with a fever may need even more. If your baby is under three months old, the water should be boiled for 10 minutes, then cooled.

Which bottles to use

There are two kinds: regular or those with disposable liners. Regular bottles give you more nipple options. You may need to try several before finding one that your baby likes. Glass bottles are easier to clean than plastic ones. Avoid opaque bottles or bottles in novelty shapes because they are hard to clean. Bottles with disposable liners are less kind to the environment and more expensive, but you only need to clean the nipple and the plastic holder.

"My husband would look at a baby bottle and say, "It looks clean, so it is." But it wasn't clean! It needed to be sterilized! I had a big bottle-steamer that fit on top of the stove. It was a 45-minute process every day. Every day it was scrub, scrub, steam, steam. It was a lot of work and very tempting to be neglectful, but I took the job seriously. When my children both outgrew the need to sterilize their bottles, I gave the steamer to Goodwill. I was so glad it was over. What a grind!"

LISA, MOTHER OF TWO, LONDON, ONT,

Preparing bottles

Health Canada recommends that you sterilize your baby's bottles, nipples, nipple covers, and other equipment used in preparing formula until your baby is three to four months old. Bottles may be sterilized in the dishwasher if it has a sterilizing cycle. They may also be placed on a rack in a pot of boiling water and sterilized for five minutes. Nipples and pacifiers should not be cleaned in a dishwasher; they can be placed in a jar with a perforated lid, placed in the pot standing upright, and sterilized with the bottles. Allow them to cool. Rubber nipples deteriorate over time so examine them periodically, and discard any that have softened or are cut or torn. Note that disposable bag liners are already sterilized. Make sure that you don't touch the inside of the liner while you're filling it. The Canadian Paediatric Society offers these guidelines for preparing formula.

➤ Wash your hands carefully and thoroughly.
➤ Use water that is boiled (for at least five minutes) and cooled to room temperature while covered with a lid.
➤ Wash the bottles thoroughly with soap and water, and remove all milk residue from the bottle and nipple with a brush.
➤ Sterilize the bottles by immersion on a rack in boiling water for five minutes.
➤ Allow bottles to dry before filling.
➤ If ready-to-feed formulas are used, pour in without dilution.
➤ If powder formulas are used, do not use your finger for levelling. Level carefully with a spatula or the back of a knife. Mix with warm boiled water according to label instructions.
➤ If concentrated formulas are used, dilute with cooled boiled water according to instructions.
➤ Promptly refrigerate the prepared formula.
➤ Use the formula within 24 hours of preparation. Discard unused formula remaining in the bottle.

Storage

Left-over formula powder can be kept in its container, covered, for up to one month. Left-over liquid concentrate formula can be kept in the can or a sterilized jar, refrigerated, for up to 48 hours.

When to feed

Don't expect a baby's hunger to correlate with your schedule. To avoid overfeeding or underfeeding, follow one simple rule: Feed your baby when your baby is hungry. Signs of hunger include sucking, smacking lips, searching with an open mouth, and bringing hands up to the face. Some babies will try to shove a chubby fist right inside their mouth when hungry.

Crying is another sign of hunger, but you don't have to wait for your baby to start crying before feeding her. In fact, if you wait until your baby is caterwauling, she'll have worked herself into such a state that you may have to calm her down before she'll be able to bottle-feed. As you grow to know your baby, you'll learn to recognize her early signs of hunger and have her bottle warmed and ready before she cuts into her frantic cry for food.

Range of Feeding Amounts

At birth:	6 to 10 feedings, each 60 to 120 mL (2 to 4 oz.)
2 to 3 months:	5 to 6 feedings, each 120 to 180 mL (4 to 6 oz.)
4 to 6 months:	5 to 6 feedings, each 150 to 180 mL (5 to 6 oz.)
7 to 9 months:	4 to 5 feedings, each 180 to 210 mL (6 to 7 oz.)
10 to 12 months:	3 to 4 feedings, each 210 to 240 mL (7 to 8 oz.)

How much to feed

Let your baby control the amount he drinks. He'll let you know when he's had enough by turning his head away, pressing his lips together, or by simply not sucking. You don't want to waste formula, but it's better to pour unwanted formula down the kitchen drain than force it on a full baby. You may consider increasing the amount of formula you give at each feeding if your baby seems dissatisfied, or cries and sucks his fist after a feeding. If this dissatisfaction persists, add another bottle every day.

Babies differ in size, activity level, growth rate, and feeding habits. The same baby can vacuum back his bottles one day, then be in a sipping mood the next. There are no firm requirements for how much your baby should drink, but Alberta Health offers the guidelines above.

Warming bottles

Until your baby is between ten and twelve months, you need to warm her formula, but only to body temperature. Cold drinks can cause cramps, diarrhea, and other discomfort. Test the temperature by sprinkling a small amount of formula on the inside of your wrist. It shouldn't feel either hot or cold. Once warmed, formula should be consumed within one hour or discarded.

To warm refrigerated formula, use an electric bottle warmer, or run hot tap water over the bottle, or put the bottle in a container of hot water until it's lukewarm (about one or two minutes). Shake it frequently as it warms. Always check the temperature of the formula before offering it to a baby.

Heating a bottle in a microwave oven poses risks because the formula heats unevenly or easily overheats, and has caused burn injuries in babies. If, however, you choose to use the microwave, remove the bottle top and nipple and put only the bottle in the microwave. Use only microwave-safe plastic or glass bottles. (Disposable bags may explode, and glass bottles that are not microwave safe can become too hot.) Heat only at

Medium and only for a few seconds. After heating, shake the bottle at least ten times and carefully check the temperature.

Dangers of prop feeding

To shave a few minutes off your busy schedule, you may feel tempted to prop up the bottle so your baby can feed himself. Don't do it. Not only will you both miss the intimacy, but your baby might breathe formula into his lungs or choke.

Putting your baby to bed with a bottle also makes him more susceptible to ear infections. When infants swallow while lying down, the formula may enter the eustachian tube, which connects the middle ear space to the back of the throat.

Your physician can help you with any concerns about bottle-feeding. Many formula manufacturers offer a cross-Canada toll-free service to answer your questions. Check for the number on the formula packaging.

Vitamin and mineral supplements

The Canadian Paediatric Society recommends that babies who are not breast-fed be given iron-fortified formula from birth. If you choose iron-fortified formula, your baby does not require an iron supplement. Your baby does not need any vitamin supplement, except on the advice of your physician, or if you live in northern Canada.

SEE PAGE 39

How to Bottle-Feed

➤ To prevent the baby from swallowing air, tilt the bottle to keep the neck full of milk.

➤ To develop your baby's eyesight, alternate holding the baby on your left and right arm.

➤ The hole in the nipple should let the formula run out at about one drop per second. If the hole's too small, enlarge it with a red-hot needle.

➤ Halfway through, and after every feeding, burp the baby. Place her over your shoulder or legs and gently rub her back until she burps. Do not hit her on the back. Don't be surprised if the shoulder you're burping her on suddenly feels wet. Regurgitation is common with burping. If after a couple of minutes of rubbing her back, your baby does not burp, don't insist. Or if she's drifted off to sleep while feeding, let her sleep. Don't wake her to burp her.

➤ After a feeding, rinse bottles to avoid formula build-up. Squirt hot water through the nipple hole to clean away any clogged formula.

Sleeping

In the womb, the fetus probably sleeps 20 to 22 hours a day, depending upon the stage of gestation, and he comes into the world carrying those sleep patterns with him. Immediately after his arrival, your newborn will probably be alert for about the first hour. After that, expect him to submerge into a deep sleep for most of the next 24 hours to recover from his arduous journey.

During his first week of life thereafter, a newborn might sleep an average of 16 hours a day. There is, however, considerable variation within that average—some babies sleep as few as 10.5 hours, others as many as 22 hours. Newborns regulate their own need for sleep, dozing for short periods ranging from 2.5 to 4 hours. They make little distinction between day and night and awaken two or three times a night.

Newborns sleep so much because, during sleep, their neurological systems work much better and grow much faster. And infants have a lot more growing to do than adults. Most newborns are happy to sleep their days away, and need no help at all dropping into slumber. Indeed, many new parents are surprised to discover the greater struggle lies in keeping their newborn awake—to feed or change him—than in getting him to sleep. If your newborn is not sleeping well, consult your doctor. Never give sleep medication to a newborn.

What Wakes a Baby

Generally, babies wake in response to pressing messages in their brains telling them they're hungry or uncomfortable. New babies don't have the capacity to store nutrition: they wake up simply because they run out of fuel. As they get older and their stomachs get larger, they'll be able to last for longer periods of time without refuelling. Babies are also driven by the eliminative process. In the early weeks, they are more likely to eliminate while asleep than awake. They move on from this early sleep pattern very rapidly. Even at one week of age, your baby may already have reduced his daily sleep time by a couple of hours.

A Newborn's Dreams

Human beings dream right from the start. Indeed, when a baby is first born, she dreams more than she'll dream later on. In the first week or so, she might dream during 30 to 60 per cent of her sleep time, compared to the 25 per cent of sleep time that adults spend in a dream state. Premature babies, in particular, spend most of their resting state in REM sleep, the stage of sleeping characterized by *rapid eye movement* and during which dreaming occurs. During REM sleep, a newborn does not exhibit the same physical stillness as do adults. It's not at all uncommon for a dreaming baby to stretch or make sucking motions and facial twitches.

How rapidly a person goes into a dream state depends upon body size, so your baby passes through her dream cycles much more quickly than you do. An adult lapses into the dream state every 90 minutes. No one knows for sure the duration between cycles for a newborn. But, says sleep expert Dr. Stanley Coren, author of *Sleep Thieves* and a professor of psychology at the University of British Columbia, "It happens very quickly. It's not unusual for the newborn infant to enter a dream state every 20 minutes or so, but it's changing so rapidly, that's just a snapshot."

The shorter sleep cycles that babies experience mean that their periods of light sleep occur more frequently than do those of adults. In fact, newborn babies have almost twice as much light sleep as adults do, which is what makes their sleep so easily disturbed.

The "Family Bed"

Whether or not parents should share their bed with their children is controversial—everyone knows some who do it and others who discourage it. Certainly expert opinions vary widely. Like most parenting issues, family-bedding goes in and out of vogue. But the practice has spent more time in vogue than it has out.

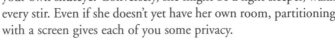

It's practical for a nursing mother to have her newborn beside her when the baby wants a late-night snack.

Parents and babies have slept together since the beginning of time. During the medieval era, everyone in the household clambered into the same bed at the end of the day, including the servants. It wasn't until the beginning of the twentieth century that most families provided a separate bed for their babies. Moving babies out of the parental bed fit with the temper of the times, since the prevailing wisdom was that mothers should not rock, cuddle, or kiss their babies lest they impede the development of their independence. The pendulum swung back again, starting in the 1950s, when some child-rearing publications began to suggest that it was acceptable for babies to share their parents' bed at times.

Today, opinions are split, usually depending on the age of the child. A nursing mother will catch some extra sleep by having her newborn beside her when she wants her midnight snack. Certainly, having a newborn's crib or cradle in your bedroom for the first several weeks is practical because she wakes several times a night for a feeding and a clean diaper. It has also been suggested that the family bed might help alleviate a new mother's postnatal depression because the presence of her newborn makes her feel fulfilled.

But once a baby begins sleeping through the night, you may find that everybody gets a better sleep if she has her own room. Babies can be noisy, restless sleepers and their fitful periods throughout the night may hinder your own shuteye. Conversely, she might be a light sleeper, waking at your every stir. Even if she doesn't yet have her own room, partitioning the room with a screen gives each of you some privacy.

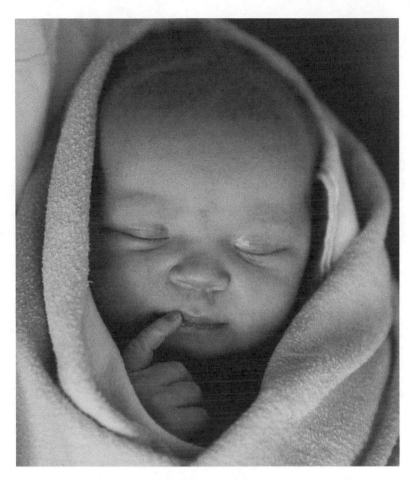

Put your newborn on her side or on her back to sleep, rather than on her tummy.

Some parents have a big family bed, open to any child wanting comfort and a cuddle. Many parents feel that their baby will develop a greater sense of security by sleeping with them than by sleeping alone in a crib. But the baby's safety is a major concern, especially up to the age of two. If either adult is a heavy or restless sleeper, he or she might roll over onto the baby. Parents should also be aware that there is risk of suffocation for a young child because of the bedding—pillows, down comforters, blankets.

Having a child in their bed at night will affect the renewal of the parents' sex life; and there is the possibility that, when the adults want their child to sleep in her room, they'll find that she can't cope with sleeping on her own. Once the child has graduated from crib to bed, some parents choose to comfort her by lying beside her in her own bed until she falls asleep.

Your decision about the family bed is entirely your own. Be flexible, and don't be afraid to admit that the choice you originally made didn't turn out to be right for your family. After all, you cannot know what works for you until something does.

The Newborn

Crying

If you have a baby, you have to be prepared for crying. While the amount varies widely, all babies need to cry. It's the way they communicate, the way they get the attention they need. Although it can be very frustrating to deal with a howling infant, it can help to know that your baby's tears fit some well-defined patterns. The patterns are remarkably consistent in all countries and all cultures around the world.

In the first three months, a baby will cry more than she will for the rest of her life. The amount of crying steadily increases, peaking at an average of three hours a day around six to eight weeks of age. But the period of crying time can vary from one hour to most of the day and still be within the typical range. Most of the crying takes place in the afternoon and evening, typically between 4 p.m. and midnight.

People once thought babies cried more in the late afternoon and evening because the mother was anxious or the father came home from work feeling stressed. Some claimed that mothers responded too readily to their babies during the day, which "spoiled" them and caused more crying at night.

Now the most widely accepted theory is that newborns have a built-in ability to screen out noises and sights from the world to ensure they get the rest they need. As their nervous systems develop, that screening ability begins to weaken, usually disappearing at about six weeks of age. Babies become more sensitive to the world around them and react in the only way they know how—by crying. Babies do most of their crying in the evening because that's what they are programmed to do.

Although babies tend to follow a set pattern, they usually cry for a good reason. Babies cry to tell you if they are hungry or thirsty, if they are too hot or too cold, if they are tired or frustrated, or if they have a dirty diaper. And the sound of their cry changes, depending on what the infant needs. Parents are remarkably quick to learn how to interpret these cries. Here are some of the most common types with suggestions for dealing with them.

Hunger
The most common cause of crying in the early months is hunger. The hunger cry is rhythmic, persistent, and demanding. Hungry babies may also suck on their fingers or hands. The only way to stop the cry is to feed the baby, either from the breast or the bottle.

Pain
This cry is more urgent, louder, and higher-pitched than the hunger cry. The baby will seem very distressed and might scream or shriek. There will often be long gaps in the screaming during which the baby seems to be holding his breath. The source of the trouble could include gas pains, teething, ear aches, or even an accidental prick with a safety pin. Check for

the source of the pain first and deal with it immediately. Changing a diaper, burping the baby, or making sure he is warm enough may be all that's needed. Picking up the baby and comforting him will soon bring an end to this kind of crying, once the pain goes away.

Boredom

Babies need lots of stimulation and, when they don't get it, they'll let you know. The boredom cry is low and rhythmical, full of sobs and moans. The only cure is to pick your baby up and play with her. Don't be afraid of spoiling her or starting a bad habit of demanding your attention. Attention and stimulation are basic needs, just as much as feeding is. The result of one fascinating study points this out clearly. Researchers changed half of a group of babies using clean diapers. With the other half, they removed each soiled diaper, but put it back on again. The babies in both groups stopped crying and seemed happy. The lesson?—handling and paying attention to a baby is a powerful method of dealing with his unhappiness.

Other causes

Sometimes babies cry because the parents get the timing wrong. A baby who is just about to nod off to sleep will not appreciate your efforts at play and stimulation. Cuddling will work a lot better. Try to avoid giving him a bath while he's tired, or changing his diaper if he's very hungry. Let the baby tell you when he is ready.

Many babies object to having their clothes removed. With practice you will get faster at changing the baby's clothes and reduce the amount of time he is unhappy. As he gets a little older, the act of undressing him will cease making the baby anxious.

It's common for babies to suddenly jerk themselves awake, just when you are sure they're finally drifting off to sleep. A baby's undeveloped nervous system makes sudden jerks and twitches very common. If it happens a lot, some experts suggest swaddling the child—wrapping him snugly in blankets—to keep him from jerking his arms or legs and waking himself. Some authorities do not agree with the practice. The best advice is to make sure your baby is comfortable and to see how he reacts to swaddling, if he has a tendency to jerk his blankets off during his sleep.

Certainly it's important to keep newborns warm—after nine months in the warm confines of the womb, they find it a bit of a shock to adjust to the big cold world. Keep the room warm for bath times, and make sure the baby is wearing enough to be comfortable, but do not overdo it. The latest research indicates that keeping a baby too hot may be a contributing factor to Sudden Infant Death Syndrome (SIDS).

SEE PAGE 106

Illness

Sometimes crying will indicate that your baby is sick. Here are a few of the warning signs to watch for: fever, flushing, listlessness, loss of appetite, unusual thirst, a loose or foul-smelling stool, glassy or watery eyes, and vomiting. The crying can be sharp and loud or weak and whining. The baby can be unusually sweaty or have an unexplained rash. Normally alert babies might start sleeping more than usual. These symptoms may occur alone or in any combination. Be especially alert if the baby's temperature reaches the fever mark or higher—that mark varies with the means of taking the temperature. Certainly, if you suspect something is wrong, contact your doctor.

SEE PAGE 284

Cutting Down on Crying

Although you cannot influence your baby's built-in crying pattern, you can do something about the *duration* of that crying. Dozens of studies over the years show that babies like motion. It's probably a result of being rocked in the womb as the mother moves and walks. Being carried in a sling on the mother's or father's body is the best kind of motion. Carrying also provides other comforts: warmth, body contact, exposure to a variety of sights and sounds and, in front packs, easy access to mother's breast.

There is plenty of evidence that babies who are carried often are babies who cry less. One Montreal study of infants in the first three months of life found that those who were carried a minimum of three hours a day cried two hours less than infants who were carried the typical amount of time in a normal day.

A quick response to your child's tears has also been proven to be effective. Studies have shown that, when parents make a point of responding quickly and consistently, babies find other ways of expressing themselves. Of course some friends and relatives won't approve. For years, people believed that a baby who got too much attention would begin to manipulate his parents. But now there is evidence that, for very young children, a speedy response may build a feeling of security. While it may seem like more work for the new parents, their reward may be less crying later on in their child's life. Don't worry if sometimes you cannot respond right away. Just try to be as consistent as you can.

Ron Barr of the Montreal Children's Hospital describes the "caregiving package" (a complex of calming behaviours) of the !Kung San, a group of hunter-gatherers in central Botswana. Their care of newborns provides an example of the positive results of carrying infants and responding quickly. The mothers carry their infants all the time in an upright position in a sling strapped to their bodies. The babies are surrounded by a wide range of noises and smells and are able to see what's going on around them. They are also able to breast-feed every ten to fifteen minutes and any cry or whimper elicits a response. The observation that, in a typical day, the babies cry 50 per cent less than the average Canadian baby suggests that carrying infants and responding quickly to their cries have positive effects for children. No one knows if it's the carrying that does the trick or if it's the sum total of all the caregiving tactics.

Colic

You have tried everything, but your newborn will not stop crying. There's no other sign that she's sick, you respond quickly, you carry her frequently, but almost every evening, the crying starts and does not stop for three or more hours. The chances are that your baby has colic. It's estimated that 15 to 20 per cent of all babies are colicky.

Most medical experts now define colic simply as an excessive amount of crying—the high end of the normal range, or more than three or four hours a day at least three days a week. Typically, this excessive crying starts when the baby is two to three weeks old and ends at three or four months of age, although in some cases it may last longer.

Colic is not a disease—in only about 5 per cent of cases is excessive crying caused by illness. Nor does crying alone suggest that colic indicates problems with the baby's colon or digestive system. Babies often pass gas and pull their legs up to their stomachs during bouts of crying that might be described as colicky. But if there are other symptoms such as diarrhea or vomiting, the crying may be the result of diet. Some children are allergic to cow's milk in formula or cow's milk protein passed on through the mother's milk, especially if there is a family history of milk allergy. Consult with your doctor who might suggest that you replace cow's milk for yourself and the baby for up to seven days to see if the crying behaviour changes.

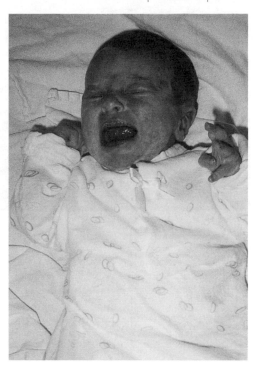

A baby's cry makes a parent respond as if to an electric shock.

"We ran the vacuum and he really quieted down. We had it on so much we thought we were going to burn the motor out.... So we just taped 90 minutes of the vacuum cleaner running and that did the trick!"

ROBIN, MOTHER OF ONE, WINDSOR, N.S.

There seems to be no link between colic and the sex of the child, the birth order or intelligence, and it does not run in families. One child can be an angel and the next can keep you up every night. There is nothing to indicate that a baby with colic will turn out to be a difficult child later in life. That does not mean it's easy to deal with. But there are a number of techniques that seem to help.

One of the most effective is movement. Some babies like to be carried in a sling or a pack, others prefer the rocking motion of a cradle. One

Alberta study showed that the most effective rhythm is one rocking movement per second, but see what works best with your child. Taking the baby for an outing in a baby carriage or stroller may also help.

White noise, an electronic noise with a constant intensity, is also very effective—even a dishwasher or vacuum cleaner can lull the baby to sleep.

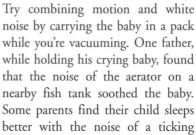

Between 15 and 20 per cent of all babies are colicky.

Try combining motion and white noise by carrying the baby in a pack while you're vacuuming. One father, while holding his crying baby, found that the noise of the aerator on a nearby fish tank soothed the baby. Some parents find their child sleeps better with the noise of a ticking clock—perhaps because it simulates the sound of the beating heart heard in the womb. Some companies market audiotapes of white noise that have been shown to help.

A favourite trick of experienced parents is to take the baby for a ride in the car. This combines movement with the white noise of the engine and the air rushing past, and it works in some cases. Just don't be surprised if the baby wakes up as soon as the car stops. Some companies have capitalized on this idea by selling devices that attach to the crib, imitating the motion of a car.

Sometimes wrapping the baby snugly in a blanket can help. Pacifiers work with some children; others won't accept them. Try different kinds, but avoid using them before you've established a regular pattern of breast-feeding, and avoid using them as a substitute for your own personal attention.

If your colicky baby does not respond to any of these measures, you may want to discuss medication with your doctor. However, most doctors are reluctant to prescribe medications for babies only a few weeks old because of the possibility of side effects or an overdose.

Dealing With Your Own Frustration

Colic does not result from bad parenting or from tension in the home. On the contrary, the constant crying creates anxiety in the parents. It's very hard to live with a colicky baby, even when both parents take on the job. One study showed that the sound of a baby crying makes a parent's body respond as if given an electric shock.

If you are feeling so frazzled that you fear you might hurt the baby, put him in a safe place and go to another part of the house until you feel in control again. If you cannot take any more, ask a friend or relative to look after the baby while you get out of the house. Consider calling a parent help line in your community, or make some time to join a parent discussion group and you'll see that you're not alone. And don't despair. The colicky crying period will end soon!

Tips for Handling Colicky Babies

There is no magic trick for calming a colicky baby, but here are a few suggestions to try, alone or in combination. Not all of them will work for your baby, and those that do work will not work all the time.

→ Hold her often and try to pick her up before the crying really gets going. A baby crying in high gear is harder to settle.

→ Try the "colic hold." Lay the baby face down along your arm, with her head in the crook of your elbow and your hand coming up between her legs. Use your other hand to hold her in place.

→ Baby massage (see page 61) is another possible means of calming your baby.

→ Put the baby in a pack and go for a walk.

→ Rock the baby in your arms.

→ Create white noise: vacuum cleaner, fish tank aerator, dishwasher.

→ Make recordings of white noise to play to your baby.

→ Go for a ride in the car.

→ Attach to the crib one of the commercial devices that simulate a car ride.

Communicating

With all the concerns about your newborn's crying, you might be surprised to learn that your baby is already starting to learn the basics of another form of communication—conversation. Babies do not usually begin using words until around their first birthday, but there is more to conversation than just words. The most basic skill is learning to attend, that is, to pay attention to the person speaking. Babies begin to do this soon after birth. They are fascinated by the human face. Watch how your baby studies your face. By looking back at you, a baby is already practising the art of attending and has taken the first step toward communication. Make sure your child has plenty of opportunities to interact with you in this way.

A baby's ability to listen also starts to develop early. Your newborn listens to you talk, even though he doesn't yet have the ability to connect the sight of your face with the sound of your voice. Notice how he will sometimes stop crying if you speak, or how he will appear to be excited if you talk to him as you approach his crib. Babies can't understand your words, but they do react to the tone of your voice. They feel reassured if you speak in soft, loving tones, but they're likely to burst out crying or cry out in fear or panic if you speak sharply.

Parents seem to know the best way to speak to their infants. The exaggerated, singsong voice most parents use not only gets the baby's attention but might actually help the baby to begin understanding the elements of speech. It's one way babies learn that voices rise and fall and have a rhythm all their own.

Basic Care

As the nervous parent of a newborn, you may be daunted by the apparent fragility of your heavy-headed, floppy-limbed baby. Take heart. It may take a few weeks, but soon you will be holding, comforting, and dressing your baby with the calm confidence of a seasoned parent.

Babies are resilient, but they prefer gentle handling. Most of all, they want to feel secure and supported. Don't let your baby feel that the earth is dropping away beneath her. Support her under the neck and hips at all times; talk to her and touch her to alert her that you're about to lift or move her. She'll let you know if you've handled her inappropriately—startled infants instinctively throw out their arms and legs, clutching for support.

Lifting up

Lift her head first and, as you lift, support her head and neck with one hand and her thighs and bottom with the other. To increase your baby's sense of security, make sure she always feels well supported. When you pick her up or put her down, give her a few seconds to register the new support, whether it is a car seat, a mattress, or your hands.

Laying down

Lay the baby's head down first. Move your hands and arms away gently, so you don't alarm her. Doctors now recommend "back to sleep," that is, that infants preferably be placed on their backs to sleep. They may also be placed on their sides with their lower arm forward to stop them from rolling over. These positions minimize the risk of sudden infant death syndrome (SIDS) in which a baby dies unexpectedly, usually while sleeping.

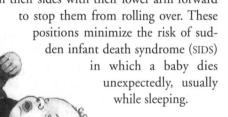

"Wearing" Your Baby

Baby slings—fabric pouches worn slung across one shoulder—are an excellent way to carry and calm infants. Although women in many cultures have used baby slings for centuries, some women have only recently discovered their convenience and comfort. It is considerably easier to snuggle a baby into a sling than the other kinds of baby carriers, and slings can also be used by fathers and other caregivers without major readjustments.

More and more mothers and child-development experts champion the benefits of "baby-wearing," or "marsupial mothering," giving it credit for accelerated parent-infant attachment, decreased crying and colic, and enhanced mental development. Whatever the psychological advantages, there are practical advantages to wearing your baby: It helps relax a fussy baby; it allows mothers to nurse discreetly, even while standing; it frees your hands to tend to another child, to make a meal, or to write a note.

You can also "wear down" your baby—that is, carry her until she falls asleep. You then slip out of the sling and put the baby to bed, leaving the sling on as a cover. Take care that she can't get twisted in the sling ties. As your child gets older, you can use the sling to hold her on your hip, or in a variety of ways—most slings come with detailed instructions.

Some cautions

➤ While getting used to wearing a sling, always support your baby with one hand. In time, you'll be able to have both hands free.

➤ Do not wear the baby while you're cooking at the stove, or while cycling or driving.

➤ Support the baby when you bend down or lean over.

➤ Don't drink hot beverages while carrying your baby in the sling.

➤ When your child is old enough to be balanced on your hip, be sure the top "rail" (edge) of the sling is pulled up over your baby's back as high as his shoulder blades. This will prevent him from arching backwards out of the sling.

➤ When your child begins reaching, keep an eye out for potentially dangerous objects that might be within her reach from the sling.

Baby Massage

Health professionals recommend skin-to-skin contact between mother and infant to promote attachment. There is now increasing evidence that gentle massage also helps both parents become more sensitive, responsive, and attached to their newborn. Massage stimulates the baby's circulatory system and benefits her heart rate, breathing, and digestion. American researchers have shown that full-term infants who received regular massage gained more weight and went to sleep more quickly, and that massage also helped premature infants increase their weight more quickly. Baby massage is an excellent way for fathers to connect with their infants as mothers do when they are breast-feeding.

Preparing to massage

➤ Make sure you are relaxed and your baby is receptive—perhaps after nursing or bath time.

➤ Plan to spend 15 uninterrupted minutes with your baby. Put on some soothing music; turn off the phone.

➤ Warm the room and your hands. Ideally, baby will be naked, although you can massage through clothing. If baby is naked, keep a towel nearby for accidents.

➤ You may use a mild baby oil or lotion to reduce friction against baby's skin.

➤ Use a light touch to begin, and gradually increase pressure as baby becomes more comfortable.

➤ Use fingertips and palms.

➤ Draw baby's attention to the part of the body you are massaging. As you stroke her face, for example, smile at her and say "Relax your cheeks." You will be helping your child learn to consciously release her tension, and associate your touch with positive feelings.

➤ Most newborns adore massage, but around four or five months, as they become more active, some no longer enjoy it. Take your cues from your child.

➤ Remember that there is no right or wrong way to massage your child, as long as you proceed gently and with patience.

Basic techniques for massage

Face: With the thumbs, make a smile on the upper lip and then the lower. Massage temples. Walk your fingers across the forehead.

Chest: With both hands together at the centre of the chest, push out to the sides, following the rib cage, as if you were flattening the pages of a book. Without lifting hands from the body, bring them around in a heart-shaped motion to centre again.

Arms: Lift each arm and stroke the armpit a few times. Gently squeeze and turn baby's arm, from shoulder to hand.

Stomach: Using the outside of each hand, make paddling strokes on baby's tummy, one hand following the other, as if you were a water wheel scooping water toward yourself. Walk your fingertips across baby's tummy from right to left.

Legs: Roll the legs between your hands from knee to ankle. Knead each leg, squeezing gently.

Back: Start with both hands together at the top of the back, at right angles to the spine. Move your hands back and forth, in opposite directions, going down the back to the bottoms, then up to the shoulders, and back down again.

Bathing

Although you should wash the folds and creases in your baby's body every day, you don't necessarily have to immerse her in a bath. It's a tricky task to hold a slick, squirmy infant with one hand while you reach for shampoo or facecloth with the other. A complete dunking can also be quite alarming to some newborns. The point is to remove the milk, urine, and feces that might have accumulated in all the creases during the day. It doesn't really matter how or when you accomplish the task. Bathe baby when you are both feeling relaxed and happy, even if that's first thing in the morning. Place supplies nearby ahead of time so that you don't have to let go of the baby to reach for them.

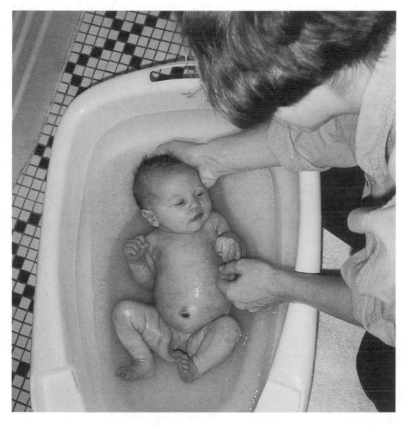

Bathe your baby when you are both feeling relaxed.

> Bathe baby in a warm room. Keep bath time brief to prevent chilling.
> Use warm water that feels comfortable on your elbow.
> Remove any jewellery that might scratch baby.
> Hold baby securely: use your left forearm or the crook of your left elbow to support the head. Grasp baby's right shoulder and armpit with the fingers of your left hand.

> Some mothers find it soothing to get into a bath with baby at the end of the day. Let her nurse there, and then support her on your thighs and knees while you wash her.
> If being naked or immersed makes your baby panic, you can top-and-tail her. Lay her on a towel and cover her, exposing at one time only the area to be cleaned.
> Don't use cotton swabs to clean inside ears and noses. You could severely damage the tender tissue. Mucus and earwax will work itself out in time. Wrap a clean facecloth around your little finger to cleanse the outer areas of the ears and nose. You can use cotton swabs outside.
> Soap is not necessary. If you want to use soap, make sure it is a mild formulation, not perfumed, and rinse carefully to prevent irritation.
> Dry baby thoroughly.

"Sometimes at the end of the day, when I was tired and she was crying, I would just get into the bath with her and let her nurse. She'd fall asleep on my breast. We stayed there for a long time, calm and quiet in the warm water. It kept me sane."

CHRISTA, MOTHER OF ONE, VANCOUVER, B.C.

Cord care

According to a recent study at Chedoke-McMaster Hospital (in affiliation with McMaster University Faculty of Health Sciences), the best way to care for baby's cord is to leave it alone. It will dry up and fall off faster, usually within eight to ten days, than if you treat it with alcohol solutions. Although it may look raw and tender, it is unlikely to cause your baby any distress. A small amount of blood spotting is not unusual; however, report any odour or discharge to your doctor or public health nurse. Dry the area after bathing and changing, and prevent diapers from rubbing the area.

Nails

Many babies are born with alarmingly long fingernails which can leave nasty scratches. Trim the nails with a baby-sized fingernail trimmer. Don't cover baby's hands with mitts or socks. It limits her ability to touch.

Excreting

You know you are truly a parent when you find yourself caring about the precise colour and composition of your baby's bowel movements.

Meconium is the name for the greenish-black sticky mucus that fills the intestines of babies in the womb. Ordinary digestion cannot occur until the meconium is eliminated, usually within a day of birth. If your baby has not passed the meconium by the second day (it is impossible to miss), alert your doctor or public health nurse. Your baby might have a blocked bowel.

When the meconium has been passed and feeding has begun, baby will pass so-called transitional stools over the next month. These stools range in colour from greenish-brown to bright green, and may be semi-fluid, or full of curds and mucus. This is normal for a newborn, whose digestive system is still adjusting to life outside the womb.

A normal stool for a breast-fed baby is mustard-yellow, with a creamy consistency and a yeasty or slightly sour smell. Bottle-fed babies excrete less frequently, and will have darker, more solid stools, with a less agreeable odour.

An exclusively breast-fed baby cannot be constipated. A formula-fed baby may become constipated, which is indicated by the infrequent and painful passing of a hard stool. Make sure you are mixing the formula correctly, and if you are, consider trying another brand. Offer frequent drinks of water. If the child remains constipated, consult your doctor.

A breast-fed baby with diarrhea will likely show other signs of illness such as fever. A bottle-fed baby with diarrhea could be ill, or could be reacting to the formula. Consult your doctor.

Diapering
Proper washing of cloth diapers and frequent changing will protect your baby from diaper rash. Newborns will go through eight to twelve cloth diapers per day. Buy at least three dozen diapers and four to six overpants.

Rinsing
Discard solid waste from either cloth or disposable diapers in the toilet. Breast-fed babies have loose stools and their cloth diapers do not require rinsing. But do rinse the cloth diapers of older babies in the toilet before soaking them. Cloth or disposable liners make it easy to collect and dispose of solid wastes before throwing out disposable diapers.

Soaking
Soak soiled cloth diapers in a solution of a bucket of water to a half cup of bleach for at least six hours. If you are on a septic system, use a cup of Borax. Drain this solution before washing.

Washing and drying
Double wash and rinse cloth diapers in the hottest water possible, using a high-quality detergent that does not contain whiteners, softeners, or heavy perfumes. If your baby has persistent diaper rash, try drying her diapers in the sunshine if you have access to a clothesline. Sunshine kills the yeasts that cause some diaper rash. Excessive drying causes diapers and overpants to wear out quickly. Air-dry overpants whenever possible. If ammonia odour is a problem, pre-rinse diapers with vinegar.

Dressing

➤ In the early days, stretchy one-piece front-fastening sleepers are your best choice because you do not have to slip anything over baby's head.

➤ You can lay the sleeper on the changing table or bed, lay baby on the sleeper, and gently pull the clothing on around the baby. The key is to pull the clothing, not the baby.

➤ If baby is nervous about being exposed to the air, drape a receiving blanket over her body.

➤ Do not dress baby in fabrics that you yourself would find uncomfortable next to your skin. Watch for reactions to certain materials, such as wool.

➤ Many parents favour sleeping bag-style sleepers for their infants. These sleepers keep baby warm, and have a drawstring bottom that allows easy access to diapers.

➤ Dress baby in one more layer than you yourself would find comfortable. Babies need extra warmth, but they should not be over-heated.

When dressing your baby, pull the clothing, not the baby.

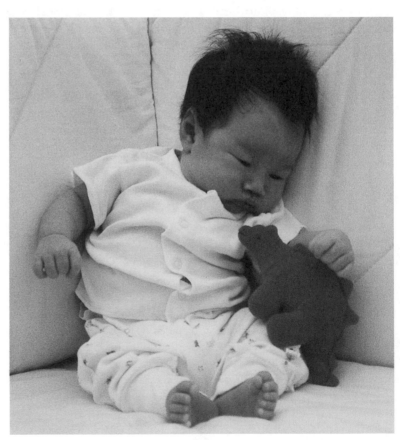

Outings

It will take your newborn weeks to adjust to life outside the womb. Proud as you are of her, don't rush her public debut. Let her settle in for at least a week. When the time comes for her first outing, gather all the baby paraphernalia before you snuggle baby into her carrier, stroller, or car seat.

Keep the first trip short, so as not to stress yourself nor to overstimulate the baby. There is nothing more alarming and exhausting than being stuck in a traffic jam with a hysterical newborn strapped into a rear-facing car seat in the back seat. No matter how short your trip or how soundly your baby is sleeping, never drive with your baby in a sling or baby carrier. Always use the car seat.

Newborns should be carefully protected from wind and cold. Bundle her well, and protect her face and extremities. Keep her close to your body for added warmth. In warm weather, keep newborns out of direct sun, and don't use sunscreen on children under six months. Protect your baby from stinging and biting insects by covering the stroller with a light receiving blanket or a cloth mesh screen.

Visiting the doctor

When you take your baby to visit your family physician for the first time, you should expect the visit to last 15 to 20 minutes. The doctor will weigh and measure the baby, including the circumference of her head, to begin tracking your child's growth and development. Almost all newborns lose 5 to 10 per cent of their birth weight the first week as a result of normal post-delivery fluid loss. Breast-fed babies generally lose more than bottle-fed babies. All babies are born with extra fluid and fat to tide them over until their mother's milk can supply the required fluid and nutrition. By the time they're two weeks old, most newborns have regained or surpassed their birth weight.

Your doctor will also examine your baby closely to rule out any medical concerns. While observing your relationship with the baby, she will invite your questions about any difficulties you may be encountering such as depression, feeding problems, or family jealousies.

Before your visit, make a note of your baby's routines—for example, the number of wet diapers a day, nursing every two hours, fussy between one a.m. and four a.m.—to share with your doctor. As well, jot down any concerns you may have. This will ensure you receive the reassurance or guidance you need to head off any problems that may be developing.

It's recommended that you make "well-baby" visits to your doctor during the baby's first week, then during the third or fourth week, and after that at two months, four months, six months, and twelve months. These correspond to the recommended times for immunization shots. Don't skip SEE PAGE 292 these early visits; give your doctor the opportunity to track your baby's physical and mental development. Some disorders which are not apparent at the first visit, such as a hernia or a dislocated hip, might be caught during subsequent visits.

The Newborn

How a New Mother Feels

Giving birth causes such major changes in a woman's physical and emotional life that it can take her some time to sort out the confusion of thoughts and sensations. It's difficult to understand at first whether what you're feeling is connected to the physical stresses of delivering and feeding a baby, the hormonal storm that rages through your system, your lack of sleep, or the natural stress that comes with starting a completely new role with major responsibilities.

"Becoming a mother was, to me, the most natural thing of all. You never know how you're going to be until you actually have the child in front of you, but there was no difficult hump for me in going from being childless to being the mother of someone. It's what I've always wanted to be, and now I'm there. All my wishes have been fulfilled."

DEBORAH, MOTHER OF ONE, TORONTO, ONT.

To acknowledge this confusion is not to suggest that your feelings are negative. You're probably also feeling great joy, a joy that you may never have experienced before, a tremendous closeness with your partner, and a thrilling sense of pride when you look at that wonderful new baby you've birthed. No matter how prepared you are, the next few weeks will carry all three of you along for the ride on an extraordinary roller coaster.

C'mon. Smile for daddy.

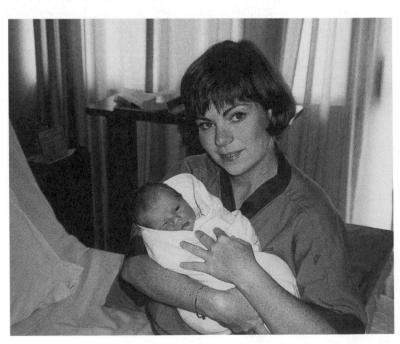

Getting Comfortable Physically

Forget about housework and put your thank-you notes aside. Sleep is Job Number One. Whenever your baby sleeps, you should rest, too. Try to make time for personal hygiene—although it sounds ridiculous, you may have trouble finding time to pull a brush through your hair. Showering is preferable to bathing at first, and you may even need help getting in and out of the shower.

If you delivered vaginally, you may be suffering some pain at the baby's point of exit, particularly if you had an episiotomy. A warm sitz bath with mineral salts can provide relief. So can a shower of warm water from a squirt bottle each time you go to the bathroom. (If little clots of blood fall into the toilet bowl, that's perfectly normal.) It's worth investing in a foam "donut pillow," so you can sit down more comfortably. If you had a C-section, treat the scar with warm, soapy water, but don't rub a washcloth on the incision.

Your bladder control may be diminished. Practise Kegel exercises (squeezing your vaginal muscles) and urinate often. If you have hemorrhoids and can take a warm bath, do so. Otherwise, be kind to yourself with stool softeners, lots of fibre, and plenty of fluids. Your breasts need special attention after delivery, whether or not you're breast-feeding. If your breasts are painfully engorged, try ice packs. If you have hot, red marks on your breasts, you may have a blocked duct: Call the doctor. SEE PAGE 83

Overall, don't ignore your physical needs. Your body has just been through a huge change. Help it to recover by getting rest, eating well, drinking plenty of fluids, taking showers, and exercising, even if it's just a walk around the block to get a breath of fresh air.

"I wanted to prove to the world that I knew what I was doing. When I got home from the hospital I had a lot of trouble peeing, but I thought that was just normal after having a baby. It got worse and worse, until I was dreading having to pee and then I'd cry and cry. But I still thought it was normal, and I was just being a wimp. Then I took the baby in for her check-up a week later, and the doctor said 'And how are you doing?' and I told her about the peeing. And she said, 'Why didn't you phone me? You've got a terrible bladder infection. I could have given you something to clear that up in a day.' So the lesson I learned was, listen to your body. Listen to your intuition. If something's not right about you or your baby, tell the doctor right away."

JULIE, MOTHER OF TWO, VANCOUVER, B.C.

Coping Emotionally

Just acknowledging that the next few months will bring a wide range of new emotions means that you've taken the first step toward surviving them. In the span of one hour, a new mother can experience more emotions than she did in the previous two months: joy, rage, ambivalence, ecstasy, despair,

The Newborn

aggravation, bewilderment, bliss—and everything in between. Don't berate yourself every time you feel some emotion other than joy.

Exhaustion, the main complaint of new mothers, is a major contributor to low spirits. Even if you get the same total hours of sleep as before, the frequent interruptions make your sleep less effective. The best coping strategy is to sleep whenever your baby sleeps. If you don't nap easily, at least lie down and relax when she's down.

Accept also that you will feel unsure of your abilities from time to time, particularly in the early weeks. Confidence will come with experience—and from the insights and advice you glean from other parents. If you're feeling trapped by your new role, try not to abandon everything from your old lifestyle. Indeed, the parents who give in completely to the restrictions imposed by caring for their children are the ones most likely to become frustrated. You have to surrender some of the spontaneity, but you can still go out to the movies or for dinner—mostly with your baby, but sometimes without. How much your lifestyle changes depends on many factors, but mostly on how adaptable you and your partner—and your baby—are.

Baby Blues

Twenty-four to thirty-six hours after delivery, the sudden and dramatic drop in a new mother's levels of progesterone, estrogen, and other neural, thyroid, and adrenal hormones combines with a similar nosedive in endorphins. You may experience what's called baby blues or postpartum depression. Baby blues is the term used to describe the temporary reaction new mothers have to these hormonal changes and to the lack of sleep during their baby's first month. Episodes of baby blues are generally intense, but short. They might spring from a disappointing experience a woman suffered during delivery, such as a sense of losing control. They might include feelings of self-doubt and mild depression, but between 50 and 70 per cent of the women who experience baby blues find that they recover within seven to ten days.

"Right after my children were born, I wound up hemorrhaging and had to go back to the hospital where I suffered a week-and-a-half of incredible emotional turmoil. Added to that were the infertility treatments I'd been on for the previous two years and the extra high my hormones were at because of the multiple pregnancy. When all that stuff was over and I'd had these babies, boy did I crash. No one had prepared me for that. I felt extremely overwhelmed, I didn't understand that they wouldn't always feed twelve times a day. I was very tearful, very easily sent from an equilibrium to disequilibrium. I was stuck, couldn't see beyond where I was. We'd been trying to have children for seven years. All of a sudden, we had these two babies, and I was so depressed I didn't want them. How could I tell that to someone?"

PAT, MOTHER OF TWO, TORONTO, ONT.

Postpartum Depression

Postpartum depression (PPD) differs from the baby blues in severity and symptoms. It generally settles in between one and nine months after delivery. Sometimes the overlap of feelings leads to a misdiagnosis as the baby blues, but PPD is a more complex reaction and results in a pervasive melancholy and an overwhelming sense of exhaustion. You find that your interests plummet and feelings of helplessness and hopelessness prevail.

Research indicates that PPD occurs in 10 to 28 per cent of all women who give birth, regardless of other socio-economic or cultural factors. Women most at risk are: those who have a history of emotional problems, including an earlier case of PPD; those with a high-needs baby; those who have experienced a major stress in their recent past; those who have a low family income or a lack of support, particularly from their partner.

> **Antidepressants may help rebalance a brain chemistry that's gone out of whack.**

The symptoms of PPD that a new mother's partner and family should watch for include: high anxiety; hyperactivity or manic activity; sadness that lasts for two weeks or more; feelings of detachment; confusion or difficulty in making decisions on a day-to-day basis; feelings of inadequacy; sleeplessness; loss of appetite; loss of sexual desire; uncontrollable crying; and hallucinations or paranoia. In its severest form, postpartum depression leads women to experience suicidal feelings, delusions, and a marked detachment from reality. This kind of psychosis affects 2 per cent of the women who develop PPD, and it requires hospitalization.

In less extreme cases, antidepressants have been shown to rebalance a brain chemistry that's gone out of whack with depression. They won't change the stresses in a new mother's life, but they can help her to cope with them. For some, there's a time lapse of several weeks before feeling the full benefit of the medication, but antidepressants are not habit-forming. Although there is much controversy around the possible impact on the infant who is breast-feeding, there are varying treatments you can pursue. It's important to discuss your feelings with your doctor who can work out the best treatment for you in your particular situation and with your unique needs.

Most important to the recovery process of the woman suffering PPD is to acknowledge that she might be at risk and to ask for help from her doctor or a PPD support centre. There are more than a dozen support centres across Canada which offer a variety of programs. Postpartum Adjustment Support Services–Canada (PASS–CAN) will send an information package ($5) to any mother who requests it, (905) 844-9009, and it has links to PPD support groups in communities across the country. If there is no support group in your area, call Public Health or the local Canadian Mental Health Association office about possibly setting up such a group.

Make Time for Mom

A baby can be so all-absorbing that you forget you still need your own life. To focus on your own needs, ask yourself these questions:

→ Are you getting out of the house? Even a quick walk around the block—with baby or without—can clear out some cobwebs.

→ Are you accepting help? When a friend calls with an offer to baby-sit, don't get off the phone until you've scheduled a night.

→ Have you had an hour to yourself recently? While it's your partner's turn with the baby, have a bath, read a book, or work in the garden.

→ Are you making time for your appearance? You may decide to shed your high-maintenance hairstyle, but don't give up the routines—a monthly trim, new clothes in season—that make you feel good about yourself.

Redefining Your Role with Your Partner

Sweet, pure and joyous though children may be, there is some question whether they enhance the ties between a man and a woman. In fact, research suggests that a child tends to detract from the marital satisfaction of his parents, particularly for his mother. And the decline in marital satisfaction is almost constant, from the child's birth right through to his flight from the nest.

> **A baby forces couples to confront new areas of disagreement.**

A baby forces parents to venture into areas where they might have different opinions from their partner, opinions that were never relevant before. Discovering these differences can be less than pleasant and represents a whole new range of decisions to be negotiated. But Ann Duffy, a professor of sociology at Brock University, is quick to point out that the drop is evident in *marital* satisfaction—not in *life* satisfaction. "People get other gratification from joint parenting. How they rate their marital satisfaction is one thing, but they can still be very happy with their lives." And the secret for rising above the statistics, the experts agree, is for parents to share the parenting experience with one another—no matter how stressful that experience may be.

How a New Father Feels

Even after participating in the plans and activities over nine months of pregnancy, it never fails: Men become fathers rather suddenly. Until that baby arrives, your role has been to support your partner and to watch and wait. Then the baby arrives and everything changes. Now there's a tiny person whom you can hold and marvel at. You may feel worried about your baby-care skills and fearful of how your lives will change, but at least now your baby is a physical reality. You can finally get started at being a father.

Father's "Baby Blues"

It's not unusual for fathers to suffer a low emotional period in the first few weeks after birth, although not to the same extent as mothers do. Some fathers who take time off from work to be with their partner and new baby for that first intense week find it very hard to go back to work and be separated from their family. They may also feel resentful of the special bond that is growing between mother and child.

Although breast-feeding is recognized as the best form of infant nutrition and important for mother and infant, fathers may perceive it more negatively; if so, it might inhibit the development of the father-infant relationship. A 1990 academic study revealed that a father's concerns about breast-feeding include the lack of opportunity to develop a relationship with his child, feelings of inadequacy, and being separated from his mate by the baby.

A father may also feel pressure to maintain the family income, particularly if his partner left her job or reduced her earnings to have more time with the new baby. Combine these feelings with an alarming lack of sleep and a sense of loss over an old lifestyle and you have a recipe for a serious case of the blues.

Fathers and Breast-Feeding

To be more involved in the breast-feeding process, fathers can:
- → get the baby and bring him to mom in the night.
- → settle him down after a feeding.
- → cuddle in beside the feeding couple.
- → burp the baby after feeding.
- → wake the baby up, if he falls asleep while feeding.

Getting Adjusted

Be warned: the first few days at home with your partner and new baby will be utterly exhausting with lots of responsibility placed on your shoulders. Your partner and baby may be home from the hospital just twenty-four hours after the birth, and you may be the primary caregiver for both of them, unless you've arranged for help from a family member or a friend.

If your partner had a cesarean, the recuperation period for her will be more painful and lengthy than for a vaginal birth. One of your roles will be to monitor your partner for the early stages of postpartum depression or even the normal hormonal letdown that occurs after childbirth. Sometimes it's the partner who recognizes the symptoms before the mother does.

"Becoming a dad was something I resisted for a long time. It seemed huge and it scared me. But since the birth of our baby, I'm happier than I've ever been. I'm calmer, more at peace. Wish I'd done it sooner."

ADAM, FATHER OF ONE, TORONTO, ONT.

Spend as much time as you can with your new baby in those first few weeks. Whatever picture of your impending baby you had in mind will probably be revised several times in the weeks following his arrival. Who knew the kid could cry so much? What's the deal with the shape of his head? And how am I expected to function on so little sleep? No doubt you will love your baby, and no doubt your love will grow, but there's a learning curve for both of you—father and baby.

In some ways, fathers may have even more difficulty than mothers in adjusting to life with a new baby. Many new fathers have not even held an infant before, let alone been responsible for raising one. And fathers generally don't get the same amount of time to form an attachment with their child as mothers do.

In many families, the new father is the family's primary breadwinner, even if it's just temporary. On top of that, men have to take on an expanded role at home, sharing in the care of the new baby and providing relief for a partner who is getting even less sleep than he. They may also have to pick up the housekeeping slack and assume responsibility for older children. All told, it's like taking on another full-time job. It's critical to stay calm and trust that you'll grow into your new role.

Redefining Your Role with Your Partner

The primary and universal complaint of new parents is that they are exhausted; the second, that they don't have enough time alone together. There may also be some friction because they aren't in sync sexually. The thought of sex with the woman who recently delivered his child may be off-putting for some men. But other men find they have enhanced feelings for their partners after the miracle of birth.

In the former case, the new father has to overcome anxiety about considering the mother of his child as a sexual creature again. In the latter case, a man might feel rejected by a partner who doesn't share his interest in

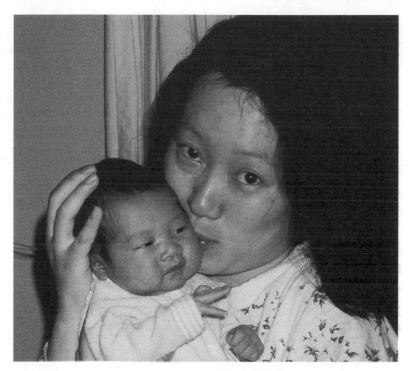

A new baby turns a couple into parents and changes the relationship into a family.

renewing sexual activity. But she is the same woman she was before she became a mother, just busier and more pre-occupied. Whether there's a baby in the next room or not, human beings are sexual people. Recognize that making love may never be as spontaneous as it used to be, and figure out how to make sex a part of your life again. Grab every opportunity for non-intercourse sexual intimacy—hugging, touching, cuddling. It's normal to delay resuming your previous sexual frequency, but if disinterest persists beyond three months or so, you might seek the advice of a therapist.

Thriving As a Family

It's hard to imagine how a tiny baby who does little more than sleep, eat, and cry could have such a huge and instant impact on the lives of his parents. But in that moment of birth, your life together is altered forever. The two of you had a certain kind of relationship with its daily routines, its patterns of ups and downs, and now you have another.

When a baby turns a couple into parents, he changes the dynamics of their relationship with each other. Many couples will tell you that nothing heightens the love two people share more than the addition of a child. But a baby also forces the two of you into areas where your opinions will differ on subjects that just never mattered before. You may find yourself disagreeing and having to negotiate on everything from how many covers the baby needs in bed to how best to show your love for your new baby. You will make discoveries about each other that may surprise or upset you.

Most conflicts in new-parent relationships centre around the issue of time—there's never enough of it. There's not enough time to get adequate sleep, which leaves mother and father irritable with one another. Related to that is a profound sense of a loss of closeness, even when there is time for one another. Accept that the spontaneity of your pre-baby days is gone and start actually scheduling time for each other.

➤ Be alert to possible couple time. Even new parents have the odd half-hour of peace. Put it to use: Reconnect with one another.

➤ Spell each other off. Each of you needs a reasonable break from the strains of parenting. You'll be calmer and your relationship will be less stressed.

➤ Accept help. Offers from grandparents and baby-crazy friends who can step in for an hour and give the couple some time alone should never be declined.

➤ Enjoy your baby together. You don't always have to escape your new role to enhance your partnership. Mutual enjoyment of the life you created is the best treatment for surviving the disruption your baby has brought with him.

Before their first child arrives, a man and a woman may be unaware of how their partner will respond to the demands of a baby. Trusting another person to keep an appointment or to not betray your relationship is entirely different from trusting someone to do right by your child. A baby calls for a much deeper trust in one another than you may ever have experienced before. Learning to live up to this ultimate—and mutual—challenge of caring for another life is an ongoing process of trusting one another. As you meet your baby's needs and share the job of protecting her, you'll discover a new appreciation of each other's strengths and weaknesses.

A New Grandparent's Role

When a baby comes into the world, she does more than transform two people into parents—she transforms four other people into grandparents. With that metamorphosis, comes an extraordinary opportunity to cultivate existing relationships and to develop new ones.

A new mother is bound to see her own mother in a new light the moment she steps into her shoes. Even if you don't agree with some of the choices your mother made in raising you, you'll likely gain a new perspective on why she made them. Your relationship with your father will also undergo a change. Some grandfathers have more time to become involved in the lives of their grandchildren than they had with their own kids. It can come as a surprise to a new parent to discover a doting, jubilant grandfather in place of a stern or distant father. This may be the time that your relationship with your partner's parents, too, becomes stronger, as both sets of grandparents are drawn into the circle that your baby's arrival has created.

Just as there may be tension between you and your partner about what's best for your baby, there may be similar tension between parents and grandparents. You might expect that grandparents will keep their advice to themselves or, if they don't, that you can shrug it off as advice from another time. But you will receive advice, much of it conflicting, from many different sources. As a parent, you have to sort through that advice and decide what's best for your baby. But don't be surprised if your mother's advice is just the ticket. You need your own mother's trust in your ability to be a good parent, whether or not you follow her advice. And you need to trust that whatever advice and help she offers comes from a passionate love for her new grandchild.

A grandparent's role in a child's upbringing is a very special one. The opportunity to grandparent a new little person is a gift that was earned through many years of parenting. Don't deprive your parents of your baby, nor your baby of your parents. And rejoice in the new dimensions all of your new roles add to the relationships that were already in place.

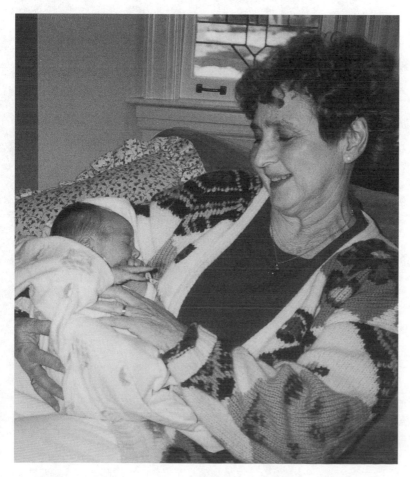

Grandparents love the opportunity to cuddle a newborn again.

The Newborn

The First
Six Months

3

The first weeks of your baby's life may have passed in a blur—meeting his physical needs, adjusting to a disrupted sleep schedule, and getting used to the presence of a new little creature in your house. But as your baby begins to settle, you will enjoy more and more alert time together. As you get to know your child better, you'll each begin to understand his emotional needs. Babies are little sponges, soaking up a steady stream of cuddling, playing, snuggling, and smiles. As parents, it's your job to give your baby as much emotional care as he needs.

You can't spoil a young baby with too much attention. The opposite is true. Babies who do not receive emotional support or who don't have at least one special person to whom they can attach themselves tend to develop more slowly, even if they are well cared for physically. Babies are completely dependent on their parents for everything, so if you show them that they can count on you, they'll develop their sense of security.

One of the best ways is to respond quickly to your infant's needs. Since babies express most of their needs by crying, that means a parent should respond to their cries as quickly as possible. Well-meaning friends and relatives might tell you the baby is just exercising her lungs; they might smile knowingly when you jump up to check on your crying child; or they might say the baby has her mother (or her father) wrapped around her little finger. But the research is clear: If you respond quickly, your baby will develop into a happier, more relaxed child.

Giving your baby lots of close, warm attention teaches her how to love others. There are also rewards for you. Parents become the centre of their infant's universe, the people on whom she lavishes her special attentions. And some time between one and two months, your infant will bless one of you with her first toothless smile. And you will be the parents of the sweetest baby in the world.

Feeding and Nutrition

During the first month, many mothers abandon breast-feeding because they run across a problem they can't solve. In Canada, the Number One reason mothers stop breast-feeding in the first few weeks is their perception that their baby isn't getting enough milk. But if a mother nurses frequently, this should not be a problem. The more the baby nurses, the more milk the mother makes.

Breast-Feeding Problems

Sore nipples, engorgement, or fatigue convince other women that they should stop. Here are solutions to all these problems. If you need more hands-on help, call your hospital or family doctor for a referral to a lactation specialist. These experts can show you or tell you how to solve a breast-feeding problem.

"I had fully expected to breast-feed my son when he was born. I never expected it would be difficult. I went in with my eyes closed. But when he tried to nurse, he would push the nipple out. He was losing so much weight that they had to gavage him—they put a tube down his throat into his stomach and they poured formula in. The nurses told me not to watch because it wasn't going to be pretty, but I felt responsible so I stayed. One nurse basically said, 'You're a bad mother. You should give him a bottle.' On the fourth day, I gave him a bottle. His eyes just opened up and he drank a full four ounces. There was no way he would take the breast after that.

Before my daughter was born, I went to the library and took out eighteen books on breast-feeding. I nursed my daughter for thirteen months, when she self-weaned. She was a much more content baby. The breast soothed her. Having fed both ways, I know that breast-feeding beats bottle-feeding in every way. I've learned that, when you breast-feed, you have to expect that there may be problems, and know how to deal with them. I'll never know if I could have breast-fed my son."

SERENA, MOTHER OF TWO, CALGARY, ALTA.

Cracked and sore nipples

The key to preventing sore nipples is to ensure that your baby latches on correctly. Nipple pain will decrease once you and your baby have developed a proper latch.

To soothe sore nipples after each feeding, rub a few drops of colostrum or hindmilk into your nipples. (Hindmilk has antibacterial properties.) Expose your breasts to air and light as often as possible. Use a blow-dryer on a low setting for several minutes to improve drying, circulation, and healing.

Soap can irritate your nipples. When you're bathing, you'll find that water is sufficient to wash your breasts. Beware of products that promise a quick cure.

Nipple creams are not recommended. The Canadian Institute of Child Health (CICH) notes that there are no studies showing topical applications to be of any benefit, and the institute points out that the vitamin E and unpurified lanolin in some of these products can be harmful to your baby.

Nipple shields can significantly reduce your milk supply and the infant's milk intake, and interfere with suckling. If you choose to use shields, have your baby weighed regularly to ensure that he's gaining weight adequately.

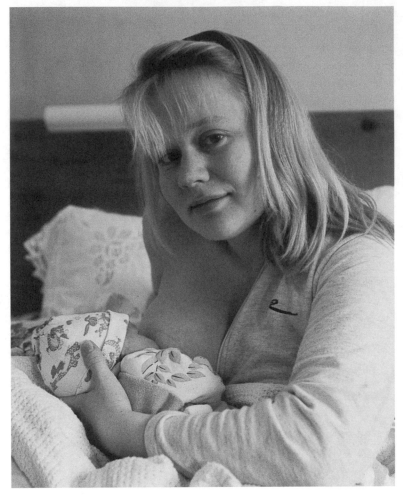

The more the baby nurses, the more milk the mother makes.

Flat or inverted nipples

If you have flat or inverted nipples, you may have heard that you won't be able to nurse. Don't believe it! Babies breast-feed, they don't nipple-feed. If your baby is able to latch on correctly, receiving a good mouthful of breast, then flat or inverted nipples will not likely cause a problem. Before feeding, gently roll your nipple between your thumb and forefinger to help the nipple stand out. As for breast shells for inverted nipples, a recent multi-centred trial found that they only overcomplicate the breast-feeding process.

Leaking

Your milk may start flowing when you're at home and you hear your baby waking up. Or, less conveniently, your breasts may start to leak in the boardroom while you're giving a presentation. Some women can stop the flow by folding their arms and pressing down on their breasts. Others wear print rather than solid-colour tops for camouflage.

Breast pads can help prevent leaks from showing, but they should be changed when they get wet or even moist if you want to prevent sore nipples or infection. Pads made from cotton or paper or cotton flannelette are best. Avoid breast pads that have plastic or waterproof liners because they don't allow air to circulate to your nipples.

Breast infection
If your breast is hot, red, and painful and you have flu-like symptoms of fatigue, chills, and a fever, you may have a breast infection, called mastitis. It occurs in 1 to 5 per cent of nursing mothers; its cause may be less frequent nursing, cracked nipples, or inadequate milk drainage.

Be assured that there's nothing wrong with your milk. In fact, for a more rapid recovery, you should nurse more frequently. Offer the baby the painful breast first, varying the baby's position to ensure drainage. Acetaminophen can reduce pain as well as fever. Applying warm wash cloths to the breast may also offer some comfort. Consult a physician if your symptoms persist for six to eight hours—antibiotics may be necessary.

Plugged milk duct
If you notice a small, hard lump that's sensitive to the touch and may be red, you might have a plugged milk duct. The obstruction may occur because the breast has not been fully drained for a long time or because there has been pressure on the duct. Untreated, a blocked milk duct can cause an infection.

Take a hot shower or apply hot compresses, gently massaging the area in the direction of the nipple. Feed your baby every two hours, always starting with the affected breast. Vary your feeding positions to facilitate milk flow. If the lump persists after two days, consult your doctor or lactation consultant.

Breast-feeding in public
A 1995 study by Health Canada revealed that embarrassment to mothers and their partners is a common reason why women choose either not to breast-feed or to stop nursing. Breast-feeding advocates argue that women need not feel ashamed of their bodies; certainly, nursing in public doesn't mean that you flaunt your breasts. To be discreet, choose two-piece outfits with tops that can be lifted to nurse. Go for extra privacy with a jacket or cardigan, drape a shawl over your shoulder, or use a nursing bib.

Working and Breast-Feeding
A common reason for a new mother to stop breast-feeding when her child is between four and six months is that she's returning to work. But if you don't want to give up the closeness of breast-feeding, it's possible to both work and continue nursing.

To do so, you'll probably need to "express" your milk. Expressing helps you keep up your milk supply, prevent engorgement, and have breastmilk to offer your baby the next day. While you're at work, it's usually best to express your milk about every three hours. You need a place where you can feel relaxed and enjoy some privacy. Some women use a private office, others an out-of-the-way washroom or the health room.

As soon as you're reunited with your baby at home, sink into a comfortable chair and let your baby latch on—nursing is a perfect way to reconnect. In fact, you may want to nurse more than usual when you're at home. Nurse your baby in the morning before you get dressed, so she's content while you prepare for the day. Before you leave, nurse her again.

"My son was what you would call a high-needs baby. He needed to be held and carried a lot. There was an intense attachment, he wouldn't go to anyone, including his father. When my son was six weeks old, I hadn't slept in six weeks.

He was such a big baby, he would nurse for two hours at a time. I would just pop in a video and sit on the couch for hours. I lost count of how many times a day he would nurse. He nursed all through the night, too.

Once I accepted that he was going to nurse a lot, things got better. I took him everywhere. My breasts aren't that big so I could breast-feed subtly in public. It was just during the latch-on that anything would show. My husband and I would be out for dinner, and it would be dessert before the waiter really realized that I had been breast-feeding all along."

JILL, MOTHER OF TWO, DELTA, B.C.

When you get home, set aside thirty minutes to nurse and get reacquainted before attending to household chores. Expect to nurse more often during the evening and through the night.

On the days you don't have to go to work, you can nurse your baby as usual. If you've been expressing milk at work, your milk supply will be sufficient to satisfy your baby. When you return to work after a weekend, you may find that your breasts are fuller than usual on Monday because of the added stimulation over the weekend.

But you may not have to follow the standard work week. Women have shown a lot of ingenuity in incorporating breast-feeding into their work schedule. Some women move their office to home. Some work more frequent but shorter shifts. Others drop into their child's daycare for feedings. Still others opt for breast-feeding when they're home and formula-feeding by a caregiver while they're at work.

Whatever you choose, over a period of time both your milk production and your baby will adapt to your new schedule. To learn more about breast-feeding and working, read *Of Cradles and Careers*, a book by Kaye Lowman published by La Leche League, or *The Working Woman's Guide to Breastfeeding* (Meadowbrook, 1987), by Nancy Dana and Anne Price.

Baby's First Food

Breastmilk or formula milk remains the major part of a baby's diet until she's between nine and twelve months of age. Most babies do not need additional food before six months of age, but some mothers start to supplement breastmilk or formula as early as four months of age. How do you know when your baby is ready for her first mouthful of Pablum?

She will let you know—loud and clear. A baby ready for more than milk is hungrier than usual. The breast-fed baby drains both breasts at each feeding and needs more frequent feedings than a month ago. The bottle-fed baby consumes 1 L (32 oz.) of formula a day—and wants more! Other signs of readiness include sitting up with support, showing she has control of her head and neck muscles; lifting her head and supporting her upper weight on outstretched arms when placed on her stomach; and a weight of at least 6 kg (13 lb.).

> A baby ready for more than milk is hungrier than usual.

When it's time for more than milk, Pablum (fortified infant cereal) is the best first food for your baby. You may be told that feeding cereal to your baby will help her sleep through the night, but there's no evidence for that, and it's not a good enough reason to start her on solid foods. The reason to begin feeding cereal is to satisfy her hunger and encourage her eating skills. And for the breast-fed baby, fortified infant cereal is a way to augment her iron supply.

Meeting baby's iron needs

After birth, a baby's iron reserves gradually deplete. A baby who is raised solely on breastmilk maintains good iron reserves until four to six months of age. A baby raised on iron-fortified formula maintains good iron stores while on the formula.

From birth to twenty-four months of age, your baby's brain goes through major stages of growth, and iron is an essential nutritional mineral in its development. Our bodies need iron to form the red blood cells in hemoglobin, which carries oxygen in the bloodstream to various tissues in the body. Inadequate iron nutrition in his first six months may result in both poor physical growth and impaired learning ability.

Both preterm babies and babies from low socio-economic backgrounds are at high risk of iron deficiency. A study of infants from low-income families in Montreal, who were between ten and fourteen months of age, found that 24.3 per cent of them had iron deficiency anemia. In Canada, iron deficiency and iron deficiency anemia are prevalent even among those not considered to be at risk. It's estimated that 3.5 per cent of six-month-old babies and 10.5 per cent of eighteen-month-old toddlers have either an iron deficiency or iron deficiency anemia.

Choosing a cereal

Adult cereals are not nutritionally formulated for babies, and their thick, lumpy texture may cause choking. You just can't beat infant cereals for infants. They're fortified with easily absorbed iron and are enriched with calcium, phosphorus, vitamins B_1 and B_2, and niacin.

➤ Begin with single-grain cereals with added iron. Do not give your baby mixed grains until you are sure she is not allergic to any of the grains combined in the cereal. Rice is a good first choice because it's the least likely to cause an allergic reaction. Good second choices are barley or oatmeal.

➤ Select infant cereals without added sugar. Sugar isn't necessary and it might encourage your child's sweet tooth.

Allergy alert

Allow at least four days after introducing each new food to note possible reactions that might suggest a food sensitivity or intolerance. But if, within a minute or even within twenty minutes after a feeding, your baby breaks out in hives, has acute diarrhea or projectile vomiting, has difficulty breathing, or displays other allergic symptoms, it's likely that your baby is allergic to the new food. Get immediate emergency medical help, and consult your doctor. If these symptoms occur in a much less severe form after ingesting the new food, either over the next few hours or up to forty-eight hours, he may have a sensitivity to the food. Record the reactions and consult your doctor—less severe reactions to new foods are more manageable.

How to Feed

Since breastmilk or formula milk is still your baby's most important food, offer her the cereal only after you have nursed or bottle-fed her. A baby under six months of age is still too young for a highchair, so cradle her in your arms as you would for breast- or bottle- feedings, but hold her slightly more upright or use an infant seat.

Put a bit of cereal, diluted to almost liquid consistency, on the end of a baby spoon. Put the spoon to her lips and let her suck the cereal from it. Don't put the spoon in her mouth or she won't be able to use her highly honed sucking skills. The introduction of spoon-tip-feeding helps your baby learn how to guide food to the back of her mouth for swallowing.

Babies are instinctively afraid of new foods and prefer familiar foods. Some babies need to try cereal eight or ten times before they happily accept a spoonful. Food rejection is completely normal and may well be an adaptive mechanism to prevent babies from eating harmful substances. You can help your baby accept cereal by mixing it with a familiar taste. If you're nursing, mix the cereal with breastmilk; if you're bottle-feeding, mix it with formula.

How Much to Feed

The tiny amount of Pablum your baby needs will make you feel like you're feeding a baby bird. Manitoba Health offers the guideline that four- to six-month-old babies receive 15 to 30 mL (1 to 2 tbsp.) of cereal morning and evening. But that's only one guideline—follow your baby's feeding cues. If he's not hungry, he'll close his mouth, turn his head away, or even fall asleep. If he's hungry, he'll appear excited by the prospects of Pablum. He might wave his chubby hands in the air and kick off his socks. Or he might lean forward and flash you his heart-melting toothless grin.

Pablum and The Hospital for Sick Children

As you reach for your baby's first box of infant cereal, you're reaching through Canadian history. Pablum was developed at The Hospital for Sick Children in Toronto by doctors who had what, in the 1920s, was an outlandish idea. Drs. Theo Drake and Fred Tisdall, with their mentor Dr. Alan Brown, believed a healthy diet for children could head off disease.

In Canada at the time, babies were being fed cereals made from two types of wheat, farina and semolina. The cereal was easy to digest, but it was also mostly starch. The nutritious part, the bran and the wheat germ, had been processed out and used as livestock feed. Meanwhile, babies and children were dying of rickets, diphtheria, typhoid, and diarrhea.

Although the doctors didn't yet know the vitamin requirements of babies, they did know which foods were nutritious. They mixed recipes of wheat meal, oatmeal, cornmeal, wheat germ, bone meal, dried brewer's yeast, and alfalfa and tried out different combinations on the babies at Sick Kids. The babies loved the cereal, and they obviously prospered on it.

The doctors finally settled on one recipe of the above ingredients, and Pablum was marketed in 1931 so that all Canadian babies could benefit from it. Until the patent ran out 25 years later, royalty income from sales of the baby cereal went to the hospital's Pediatric Research Foundation. The Foundation funded the research that devised procedures to repair congenital hip dislocation, lateral curvature of the spine, and the heart defect that led to "blue babies." Reorganized as the Research Institute in 1954, it is one of the largest pediatric research institutes in the world.

Choosing Childcare

If you're among the 80 per cent of new mothers who return to their jobs when their maternity benefits expire, then finding good childcare is a top priority for you and your partner. The majority of new moms re-enter the work force when their baby is less than four months old, making infant care the most sought-after childcare in Canada. Unfortunately, it's also the most difficult to come by.

Licensed and Unlicensed Care

In Canada, the majority of children, 44 per cent, are cared for by their parents; 28 per cent are cared for during the parents' work day by other family members; another 23 per cent of working parents use a baby sitter. The remaining 5 per cent of parents use licensed childcare services or perhaps a nanny.

Childcare services, licensed by provincial governments, are offered at centres and in private homes. Some centres may be located in a school or a church. Others are privately owned and operate in a rented space, perhaps in a shopping plaza. Licensed caregivers must follow a set of government regulations covering everything from the number of children permitted in the centre or home to the type and frequency of foods served during the day. In licensed daycares, a copy of the license and inspection reports, as well as menus and activity programs, will be posted on a bulletin board or you can ask to see them. Long waiting lists for licensed care, up to eighteen months for infants, are common. In many small towns and farm communities, licensed care may not even be available.

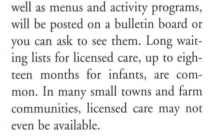

Each province and municipality sets its own licensing standards for daycare centres.

Not-for-Profit and For-Profit Centres

In your search for daycare you will also come across two descriptions of centres: not-for-profit and for-profit centres. Within the child-care field there is great debate over which is better. Most child-care experts prefer not-for-profit centres because parents have a say in the centre's day-to-day operations. Parents often sit as members of the centre's board of directors. Not-for-profit centres may also be subsidized by government, trade unions, or employers. The subsidy, whether it's rent-free space or cash donations, gives the centre more leeway in discretionary spending on toys and educational equipment. Staff tend to be paid higher salaries, leading some experts to speculate that these centres attract the best child-care workers.

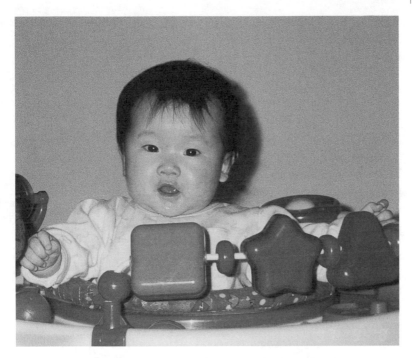

Good daycares offer amusements and activities for even their youngest charges.

But don't cross a daycare off your list just because it's for-profit, because many are every bit as good as their not-for-profit competition. A good centre, regardless of status, will attract good employees. One indication of how good a centre is will be the staff turnover. When the turnover is frequent, there's usually a problem. Unhappy staff are not going to make great caregivers.

Regardless of whether the centre is privately or publicly owned and operated, the first thing you must do is to book an appointment for a visit. Just dropping in is not a good idea. Without an appointment, the manager of the centre may not be able to do anything more than hand you a pamphlet and an application. Although some daycares have full-time supervisors, most require the supervisor to spend part of the day with the children, pitching in when a staff member takes a break, or a child needs extra care.

Workplace centres

In larger cities, some employers offer workplace childcare in a centre that may be on site or nearby. Clearly there are some advantages for a mother in being close to her baby during the day. At lunch you can visit and nurse or help feed your baby or just drop by for a cuddle. Being able to visit when you want goes a long way to reassuring both parents that your baby is being well cared for.

There are, however, some disadvantages to workplace care. Your baby will be joining one of you on the journey to and from work. If it's lengthy, the trip to and from work could pose a problem, especially in bad weather when a cranky infant and bumper-to-bumper traffic test your patience. If you must drive, the baby will be exposed to a higher risk of injury should you be in a car accident. You'll also miss the unwinding time that many people need to separate themselves from work and prepare themselves for home.

What to expect when you visit

Because of its financial support and location, each daycare centre will look different. Generally, the best-equipped daycares are located in colleges and universities where they operate as model teaching centres. For most parents, however, these centres are few and far between and rarely located near their home or office. If you're lucky enough to live or work near one, don't hesitate to get on that waiting list.

Walking into the infant care room and seeing the cribs lined up can be disconcerting for many people. With all the cribs together, the infant room can take on the look of a factory, a far cry from your baby's own colourful nursery. But look a little closer. Many of the cribs will have bedding brought from home and brightly painted walls decorated with cartoon character cut-outs. What counts is that the staff be appropriately trained and that the ratio of children to staff be adequate. The minimum ratio for infants is 3 to 1; for preschoolers 6 or 8 to 1; for 5-year-olds, 10 to 1. There should also be enough staff to maintain the minimum ratios during lunch and breaks all day long. Observe the staff to see how they interact with the children. They should cuddle the babies, talking and singing to them, and more. Even for infants, activities that stimulate their senses and their minds are important.

What to look for

Spend a little time here. Watch how the staff pick up the babies. How long do they allow a baby to cry before she is cuddled? Do the staff have rocking chairs to sit in and cuddle each baby? Are the rockers placed somewhere safe, far from crawling infants. Are all the babies asleep at one time? Each baby has her own inner clock and it's unlikely all will fall asleep at the same time. If this happens, ask why. If your baby doesn't need as much sleep as others, you may find her ready to play at 2 a.m. because she slept all day at the daycare.

Watch staff change and diaper the babies. Staff should be safety-conscious and keep one hand on the baby at all times, while changing him. All the necessary equipment—diapers, wipes—should be close at hand. A separate wash cloth or disposable wipes should be used each time. The change table itself should have a protective cloth or covering on it that is changed for each baby. Staff must also wash their hands with soap and water after each diaper change.

In the infant room, or on a bulletin board located near the entrance to the centre, look for the day's or week's activity sheet. It provides a rundown of how the infants will spend their day. Look for age-appropriate toys. Toys should be washed daily to prevent the spread of germs. There should also be a safe place for infants to lie and learn to roll, crawl, and eventually walk. The floor may be carpeted, but carpets are great sources of hidden dirt. Cushioned mats that can be easily cleaned are best.

It goes without saying that the infant room, like all others in the daycare should be childproofed. Check for gates on doorways, safety latches on child-sized cupboards, and attached shelves that prevent a curious climber from having a pile of toys topple on her.

Do the daycare staff have rocking chairs to sit in and cuddle each baby?

Finally, when your tour is over, ask about the centre's philosophy of childcare. For example, how is misbehaviour in older children handled? Time-out, separating the child from her peers for a short period, is one method of dealing with behaviour problems, but ensure there is no physical punishment. Also ask about the qualifications of the staff. It's important that most staff have an Early Childhood Education certificate issued by a college. The training they receive can mean the difference between adequate care or great care.

Illness

Your baby is going to get sick. How frequently depends on his exposure to other children and their germs. The infant room should be kept separate from the toddlers and pre-schoolers to reduce the infants' exposure to colds and viruses.

Most daycare centres do not allow parents to leave sick children. If your baby has a fever or shows other signs of illness, you'll be asked not to leave her at the daycare centre. It's not fair to risk infecting the other children.

Should your baby become ill during the day, staff will call you to come and take her home. If you absolutely can't do it, make arrangements with a family member or friend to respond to the sick call. Before that happens, think about who might be able to help out in an emergency. Put this person's name on the list of people who have permission to pick your child up from the centre. Without parental permission, the centre will not release the child.

Cost

Infant care is the most costly of all childcare. Expect to pay from $780 to $1280 a month in a licensed centre. Some families with low incomes qualify for a subsidy, which means the provincial government pays a portion of the fee. If you think you might qualify, ask about subsidy qualifications. Many centres have a limited number of "subsidized spaces," and they have long waiting lists.

Home Care

A homey setting where the values and food reflect your culture may be just what you're looking for. Some private homes are licensed, most are not. Some caregivers issue a tax receipt, others do not. A licensed home will be inspected, but the frequency and thoroughness of these inspections vary from province to province, community to community. Don't rely on a license or certificate as a guarantee of good care. Unlike a daycare centre, which employs a variety of staff, home daycare usually has only one caregiver, and that person will have complete control of your baby.

What to look for

The only regulation governing the standard of care that must be provided in a private home is that the caregiver look after no more than five kids not her own. But this rule is broken often. On your visit to the home, count the children in the sitter's care. Be sure to ask if there are any school-age children who may not be in the home at the time of your visit, but who will be present before and after school. These children, too, will need attention from the sitter when they are there.

> To keep your baby healthy, the caregiver should wash her hands after each diaper change.

Checking out a private home poses its own dilemmas. You want the home to be neat and clean—after all, babies put anything and everything in their mouths. But a too-tidy home may indicate that the caregiver spends time cleaning her home while she's caring for your baby. If your baby is the only one in the sitter's care, she might clean during his nap times; but if there are more than two children in her care, ask yourself who is minding the children when she's vacuuming or cooking supper for her own family.

Questions to ask

When you visit a private home daycare, ask the caregiver how she divides her time. How will she prepare bottles or lunch for the children and keep an eye on them? Visit each room of the house. Has it been childproofed? Ask the caregiver where she stores household cleansers and medicines. Get her to show you. Look for the obvious: gates on stairways, tools and exercise equipment stored in a locked room, small toys that belong to older kids out of baby's reach; a diapering centre close by the room where the children spend most of the day. Are all the supplies close at hand? Rules for cleanliness still apply. The standards in a home-care setting should be no different than in a licensed centre. To keep your baby healthy, the caregiver should wash her hands in hot water with soap after each diaper change. Bottom wipes should not be shared. Disposable wipes may not be environmentally sound, but in a home-care atmosphere they are preferable.

The interview

Most of us are nervous in interviews, but chances are the caregiver has been through it all before. To a qualified caregiver, the questions you ask will seem normal, not nosy, so don't be shy. Think about what you want to know before you conduct the interview. Write down your questions, and take along paper and pen to jot down notes as the two of you talk. If you are interviewing several caregivers, the notes will come in handy for remembering who said what.

You may also question a potential caregiver about health screening as it relates to communicable diseases, except AIDS. You may feel uneasy asking for information you wouldn't normally question, but remember she will be spending considerable time with your baby and his well-being depends on you and your decisions.

Questions You Should Ask

When you're interviewing a caregiver, be sure to meet the rest of the family. Even though you aren't hiring her teenage daughter or husband to care for your baby, there's a good chance they'll be in the home while your baby is there.

- ➤ How long have you been looking after children?
- ➤ What do you like about this job?
- ➤ How will the children spend their day? Tell me what a typical day is like.
- ➤ Will the children spend time outside playing? Will you take a walk outside with the baby in his carriage?
- ➤ Where will the baby be when you're preparing meals or bottles?
- ➤ When the baby cries, what do you do?
- ➤ What do you consider misbehaviour?
- ➤ What is your policy on misbehaviour?
- ➤ What do the children eat for lunch and snacks?
- ➤ Will the television be on during the day? If so, for how long and what type of programs will be watched.
- ➤ When do you do your housework?
- ➤ Will there be anyone else, older children and their friends or a spouse, home during the day?
- ➤ Will you or anyone else in the house be smoking? If you smoke outside, who will be watching my baby?
- ➤ Do you have any first aid training?
- ➤ Should a child become ill in your care, what is your procedure?

Ask a potential caregiver to describe what your baby's typical day will be like in her home.

Checking references

Ask for and check references from several parents who have recently left their child with the caregiver. If the parents are strangers to you, they may feel reluctant to give you a lot of detail, but when something's not right, it will be conveyed in their conversation. Talk to the caregiver's neighbours. Explain to them that you're planning to leave your baby with the woman next door. Ask them what kind of care she offers. Do the children seem happy? Does she take them outside for walks or to play in the backyard? Is she calm and collected around children, or does she lose her cool when things go wrong?

Illness

Anyone who spends time with children is likely to get sick. When your caregiver is too ill to look after children, you will need back-up care. Make arrangements with the caregiver to notify you (even if it means a wake-up call at 5 a.m.) if she's too ill to look after the baby. You'll need time to call your back-up caregivers or notify your employer that you won't be in to work.

It's also likely that your baby will get sick. Find out what the caregiver's policy is on sick children. Some accept a child with a cold or the flu, others may not want to jeopardize the health of other children in their care.

Cost

Fees for care in private homes vary widely across Canada, but expect a range from $75 to $200 per child per week.

Hiring a Nanny

Keeping your baby at home and bringing the care to him means you don't have to wake a sleeping infant, dress and feed him for the trip to the daycare centre or the caregiver's house. Baby can sleep peacefully while you get yourself ready for work. Providing one-on-one care for an infant is one of the key reasons many parents choose to hire a nanny who will come to their home.

A nanny is generally considered to be someone who lives in your home. Some nannies may have received child-care training, usually in a foreign country. But many young women want to travel to a foreign country, to improve their English skills, and to find a position as an *au pair* with a family. Some women take jobs as nannies in order to immigrate to Canada; they must first be employed for two years to become eligible for landed immigrant status, so they will look for a long-term commitment from you.

One difficulty in hiring a nanny directly from another country lies in checking references. Although it's possible to make inquiries and check out references, it can be time-consuming and costly in long distance telephone bills. Private agencies that match nannies with potential employers do some of the legwork, but you pay a finder's fee for their service. It's important to note that, should you sponsor a nanny from another country, you need lead time of approximately six months to complete all the government documentation. Citizenship and Immigration Canada offers a kit, "The Live-In Caregiver Program," for parents wanting to employ a non-Canadian nanny.

You may find it simpler to hire a nanny who has already worked in Canada and has local references you can check. To find a nanny, ask friends and neighbours if they know of one who is ready to leave the family she's with, check newspaper classified ads for nannies looking for work, or place your own ad. Child-care resource centres are also a good place to begin a search. Read the bulletin boards carefully and consider posting a copy of your ad there.

Some families choose a nanny because they're looking for someone who will also clean house, run errands, and do the cooking—in short do everything the parents might do if they were home. But it's unrealistic to expect a stranger to fill your shoes. Before you hire a nanny, set out a list of her most important duties—they should all centre around childcare. Don't expect her to be maid and chauffeur, too.

Live-in help has lots of advantages. If you work shifts or stay late at the office, you can count on the nanny to be home. Children who are cared for at home are exposed to fewer viruses so they're sick less often. Even when they do get sick, a live-in nanny will be there to take care of them. If you have more than one child, a nanny can be an economical alternative to enrolling two children in daycare. But remember, she's going to be living in your home. That means you'll be giving up space and privacy.

Who's minding nanny?

One of the objections to nannies is that, in a one-on-one situation, there is no other adult present in the home to make sure that the caregiver is doing her job. You'll need to plan spot-checks. You and your partner may want to stop in at home at different times of the day to see how things are going. One woman who did that got an unpleasant surprise. She discovered her eight-month-old daughter peacefully asleep in her crib. The nanny, however, was nowhere to be found. She had put the baby down for a nap and gone out shopping.

Becoming an employer

As soon as you hire a nanny or caregiver to work in your home, you become an employer, subject to many of the same rules and regulations that govern any employment situation. Revenue Canada requires you to report your employee's income, making all the proper deductions in a timely fashion. The paperwork may be an annoyance, just one more task for you to do in an already hectic schedule, but it's essential.

Hours of work and wages are set by the provincial Ministry of Labour. Most provinces require employers to pay nannies at minimum wage. In Ontario, for example, minimum wage is $6.85 an hour. Depending on where you live in Canada, you may also have to pay an employer's health tax. And don't forget vacation pay and statutory holiday pay. The deductions you make on behalf of the nanny are determined by Revenue Canada. Prior to the end of the first month of employment, you must visit a Revenue Canada office and fill in an application. You will be assigned a business number. After you file your first tax remittance, Revenue Canada will automatically send statements to you each month to fill out and pay by the fifteenth of each month.

A nanny rapidly becomes part of your children's extended family.

Cost

The sample is based on Ontario's minimum wage of $6.85 an hour and a work week of 44 hours, the maximum time you can have an employee work before you must pay time-and-a-half.

Sample Distribution of a Typical Nanny's Weekly Pay in Ontario

Weekly wage:	$301.40
Deductions:	
Canada Pension Plan	6.85
Employment Insurance	8.74
Federal taxes	42.15
Net Pay:	$243.66
Room and board	$85.25*
Nanny's take-home pay is:	$158.41

* This is the maximum you can charge for a private room and 21 meals a week, and you cannot charge for meals she does not take.

In addition, employers resident in Ontario have to pay worker's compensation (gross earnings x .215) and match the Canada Pension Plan and Employment Insurance contributions deducted from the nanny's salary.

Safety tips

Maybe you can't turn your home into a daycare, but it's worth taking a safety lesson or two from licensed daycares. To begin with, write out your street address and telephone number. Should a caregiver have to make an emergency call, she may become confused and forget the house address. Also list all emergency information at each telephone in the home. Include the numbers to call for police, fire, and ambulance. The list should include the full names and job titles of both parents, a number where each can be reached and the name of both employers. Add to the list the names of baby's doctor, and family members or friends who can be called in an emergency.

Post a menu detailing feedings and make sure the nanny knows how to operate a microwave. However, formula should not be heated in a microwave because it heats food or liquid from the middle out; what tests warm on your wrist can, in fact, be dangerously hot for your baby.

Childproof your home and backyard. Spend some time with the nanny showing her the neighbourhood, including the location of parks and libraries. Discuss where she is permitted to take your baby and let her know that you want to be informed beforehand of outings. One mom discovered her baby was making a cross-town trip on the streetcar several times a week. When the nanny was asked about it, she explained that she took the baby with her to visit friends who lived several blocks away.

Introduce her to the neighbours. Let her know who in the neighbourhood is likely to be home during the day if she runs into a small problem and needs assistance. Last of all, set down the house rules. While you can't regulate her life outside of working hours, it's important that she show up for work cheerful and well rested. Above all, be sure she knows her job description—what you expect her to do and to *not* do.

Basic Care

In just a few short weeks, you and your baby have grown accustomed to each other. He recognizes your voice and touch, and has let you know how he likes to be handled. During your baby's first six months, his basic care still revolves around cleaning, diapering, and dressing. The difference now is that you have both acquired the necessary confidence to enjoy a little more physical interaction. Use the time you spend washing and grooming your baby to communicate with and socialize your baby through games. Every baby loves Peekaboo and This Little Piggy. You'll also make up your own games as you go along.

Bathing

For many babies, bathtime is a party—they love to stretch and splash in the warm water, often soaking the attending parent in the process! If you are fortunate to have a water-baby, try to time the daily bath before the evening feed; he will be thoroughly exercised and relaxed and ready for a long nursing session and sleep. Babies who are timid at bathtime will probably do better with a morning bath, when they are feeling relaxed and refreshed after a good sleep. Don't try to bathe a terrified baby—continue spongebathing until he is feeling a little more secure.

When washing your baby, don't try to pull back your son's foreskin or wash inside your daughter's labia. You risk tearing the tender membranes and causing serious infections. Be aware that it may take some time before the foreskin of your son's penis fully retracts.

Although you can bathe a newborn in a bathroom or kitchen sink, you will quickly need to move on to a baby tub. Put the tub at hip height on a level, non-skid surface. And be wary of the day when your little one suddenly decides to roll over, right out of your hands and face first into the water. Keep the water level shallow enough that he can easily lift his head above the water. Infants can drown in as little as 4 cm (1.5 in.) of water. Never leave your baby unattended in the bath.

When baby has outgrown the baby tub or leaves more water outside it than inside, he's ready to move into the family bathtub. You might begin by placing the baby tub in the unfilled big tub, so he can adjust gradually to the big walls and echoing noises. When filling the big tub, always turn off the hot water first to prevent any scalding hot water from dribbling out of the faucet and on to baby. You might like to get in with the baby at first, or let a trusted older sibling join him in the bath, but be warned—many babies relax their bowels the minute they hit the warm water.

Diapering

Diaper rash can be a stubborn problem for some babies and their parents. It ranges from a minor red rash to a raging inflammation complete with open sores and pustules. Diaper rash is caused by the organisms that break down the urea in the baby's urine. Many things contribute to diaper rash: inadequately sterilized diapers, insufficiently rinsed diapers, excessively wet diapers, and inadequate cleaning of baby's bottom.

Babies who are prone to diaper rash will do better in sun-dried cloth diapers than in highly-absorbent disposables, which combine moisture and warmth to create an ideal breeding ground for the organisms that cause diaper rash. If you apply a barrier cream, you will have to clean off and reapply the cream at every change. But diaper rash will heal itself if you leave baby's bottom bare and open to the air. Unfortunately, this is not always the most practical solution. If you must keep baby in diapers, make sure you meticulously clean and dry his bottom every time you change him, and don't use powders.

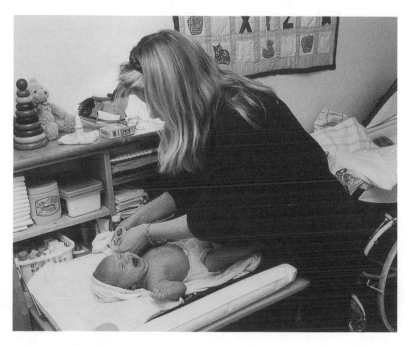

An organized "change centre" lets you get that wet diaper changed quickly.

Teething and Dental Health

At around six weeks of age, babies' salivary glands increase their volume of secretions and they starting spitting and blowing raspberries. At about three months, they start drooling, sucking on their hands, and chewing on convenient shoulders. Teething proper begins in the next few months. If you suspect your young baby is teething, run your finger along the front edges of her gums. Swollen ridges are the tip-off of imminent teeth.

When your baby's first teeth erupt, sometime after the sixth month, you can wipe the teeth with a clean cloth or a soft baby toothbrush. Toothpaste is not necessary, and in fact is not recommended until children have learned to rinse away the excess toothpaste instead of swallowing it. When a child swallows toothpaste, she may ingest too much fluoride, which can adversely affect her teeth.*

* SEE PAGE 148

When baby starts drooling and chewing on convenient objects, rub your finger along her gums to check for imminent teeth.

SEE PAGE 159

Early teethers

It's uncommon, but not unheard of, for a baby's teeth to come through in the very early months of life. Indeed, some babies are born with one or two teeth already in place. If these teeth aren't well anchored in the gums, doctors may recommend having them pulled to avoid the risk of choking if they come loose. These early teeth may be pre-teeth; having pre-teeth does not mean that primary teeth won't start to arrive at the usual time of six months. But more often they are primary teeth and, when the child is older, dentists can fashion temporary dentures as stand-ins until their permanent successors begin to take over starting about age six.

Nursing bottle caries

One risk to your child's teeth is a condition known as "nursing bottle caries," caused by putting your baby to bed with a bottle of milk, juice, or any other liquid besides water. The sugars in these drinks cause decay, and new teeth, which take time to harden completely, can decay rapidly. If you see dull white spots or lines in your baby's teeth, especially along the gum margin, your child is at risk and you should see your dentist immediately. Never dip your baby's soother in honey; increasing the risk of caries is less serious than the risk to children under twelve months from honey's possible contamination with clostridium botulinum spores.

Visiting the Doctor: Vaccinations

During the first six months, you should visit your baby's doctor at regular times so she can record and assess the baby's physical development. Within the second month, you should also begin an immunization program for your baby that will continue throughout his life. If your local public health unit offers a regular immunization clinic in your neighbourhood, you may not have to visit your doctor. But do keep a record of the vaccinations your child receives.

"I found the vaccinations very stressful. Finally, I asked my husband if he would take the baby for his shots. It didn't seem to upset him as much. I really think the baby picked up on my tension. His dad was much more relaxed about the whole thing. We never had any problems with the vaccines."

ROSALYN, MOTHER OF TWO, WHITE ROCK, B.C.

Within living memory, diseases such as polio once killed or maimed thousands of Canadian children each year. In Canada today, an aggressive national immunization program has resulted in the control or elimination of polio and other childhood diseases. Most children are routinely immunized against measles, mumps, rubella, polio, diphtheria, pertussis (whooping cough), *haemophilus influenzae* type b which causes bacterial meningitis, and hepatitis B. Although some parents are hesitant about—or refuse—immunizations for their children, it's essential that parents understand the risks of not immunizing their children. The Canadian Paediatric Society's publication *Your Child's Best Shot: A Parent's Guide to Vaccination*, 1997, offers information about the vaccinations and the diseases they are designed to prevent. An immunization program is only effective with the full support and cooperation of the public it aims to protect.

Health Canada offers a recommended schedule for childhood vaccination, but your province may have different guidelines. Your doctor or a nurse should show you how to hold your child during the vaccination, which may cause brief discomfort. The site of the injection may be tender for a few hours, but your baby should be feeling fine within twenty-four hours. A topical anesthetic is usually reserved for needs more serious than a vaccination, but some doctors may recommend a dose of acetaminophen one-half hour before the injection to reduce the pain or after to reduce fever.

SEE PAGE 292

Why You Should Immunize

Here are the reasons why it's crucial to have your child immunized against serious infectious diseases.

1. Vaccines are safe.

The benefits of vaccines far outweigh the risks. Vaccines are manufactured in licensed laboratories according to stringent standards. The majority of adverse vaccine reactions—sore arms or a mild fever— are minor. A more serious reaction, even a death, occurs so infrequently that it's almost impossible to make an accurate assessment of the risk to your child. However, the government can and will recall vaccine lots if there is the slightest suspicion about the quality or safety of the vaccine. Still, researchers are seldom able to corroborate a link between vaccines and bad reactions.

2. Vaccines are effective.

Even in Canada, where most children are immunized, there is a failure rate. No vaccine is 100 per cent effective, but most childhood vaccines are 85 to 90 per cent effective. For reasons related to the individual, not every child develops immunity, so some children will still be susceptible to the vaccine-preventable infectious diseases. However, they are more likely to experience a milder form of the disease than if they had not been immunized. When there is an outbreak of one of these infectious diseases, only 10 to 15 per cent of the immunized children will be at risk, but all the children who were not vaccinated will be at risk.

3. Vaccines continue to be necessary.

Widespread vaccinations have reduced most vaccine-preventable diseases to very low levels in North America. However, some of these diseases still run rampant in other parts of the world. An unprotected population could be at risk of contracting diseases that travellers unwittingly bring back. A few cases of one disease could quickly grow to epidemic proportions without the protection of vaccinations.

4. Vaccines are not linked to Sudden Infant Death Syndrome.

The Institute of Medicine in the U.S. reports that "all controlled studies that have compared immunized versus non-immunized children have found either no association with, or a decreased risk of, SIDS among immunized children, particularly with DPT (diphtheria, pertussis, tetanus) vaccine," and concludes that there is no evidence to "indicate a causal relation between this vaccine and SIDS."

5. One unvaccinated child does make a difference.

Your unvaccinated child becomes the weak link in the protective chain that bars disease from your community. Don't let disease get a foot in the door: Immunize your child.

Sleeping

As new babies grow, they spend less and less time sleeping. By the end of the first month, most babies are sleeping fifteen hours a day and are alert for two- or three-hour stretches. By six months, most infants are sleeping just twelve to fourteen hours a day.

You may find yourself frustrated by your baby's sleep patterns, but don't try to alter them. Your baby needs to set her own sleep and waking schedule, says Canadian sleep expert, Dr. Stanley Coren. If you try to change her to suit your needs, you'll risk making her pattern more inconsistent and slowing her progress towards adopting the twenty-four-hour circadian rhythm, the twelve-hours-on and twelve-hours-off schedule of day and night that humans naturally follow.

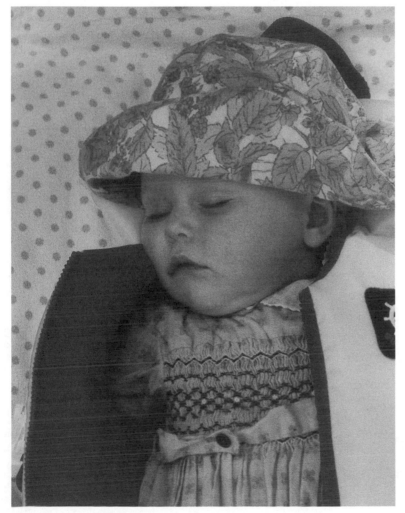

Babies still need 12 to 14 hours a day of sleep, and they catch a few winks whenever they feel the need.

Infants are not born with an innate sense of circadian rhythm. Indeed, their early rhythm is based on "ultradian" cycles, anything shorter than twenty-four hours. Between two and eight weeks of age, babies are on a sleep cycle of roughly four hours of sleep followed by thirty minutes of activity, although this pattern constantly shifts. By about three months of age, the neurological systems of babies have matured enough that you can expect them to combine two sleep cycles into one period of sustained sleep. However, this cycle won't necessarily occur at night. It's not until about four months of age that a pattern of more activity during the day and more sleep at night becomes better established.

From three months of age to one year, a baby will usually require regular daytime sleep periods, lasting from one to two hours, or longer if you're lucky. Babies generally enjoy one nap in the morning and another in the mid-afternoon, although for some energetic infants, naps are forgotten shortly after the newborn stage. Left to their own sleeping habits, babies begin to develop much more regular cycles and to have longer sleep episodes at night. Their sleep will have less REM (rapid eye movement) time, or dreaming, but it will generally be a sounder and deeper sleep with less frequent nighttime stirrings.

Is That the Baby?

If your baby is awake and you'd rather he wasn't, check these possibilities first:

→ wet diaper
→ hunger
→ dry air
→ stuffy nose
→ teething pain
→ too hot or too cold

Sleep Problems

By adult standards, all babies sleep badly. They awaken regularly and are frequently reluctant to return to sleep. But what some parents see as a sleep problem is just the naturally short sleep-wake cycles of young babies. It's important for parents to recognize this and to compensate for their own sleep loss whenever their baby is dozing.

If your baby is older than four months and still doesn't distinguish day from night, you can encourage the process by providing more stimulation during the day—talking to your baby and playing—and minimizing stimulating activities at night. For daytime naps, some parents put their babies to sleep in a carriage or a portable cradle in a less quiet place; for nighttime sleep, they place the baby in her crib in a quiet room with dimmed lights.

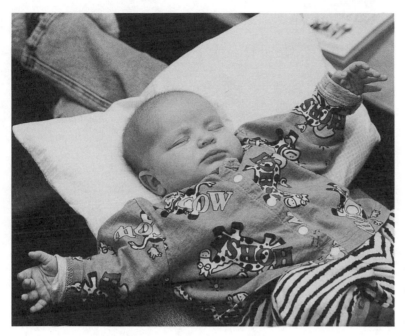

By adult standards, all babies sleep badly. They awaken regularly and are frequently reluctant to return to sleep.

Allergies

Cow's-milk allergy is the cause of some infants' sleep troubles. About one in every six babies has a genetic predisposition to this allergy, whose symptoms range from bloating and irritability to vomiting and profuse diarrhea. SEE PAGE 44

Colic

About one in every five babies experiences colic. You'll probably know SEE PAGE 57 whether your baby has colic when he's between two and three weeks old, which is when the pattern becomes predictable. Colic is one of the most common causes of disturbed infant sleep.

Babies who have colic don't go to sleep easily, and they wake frequently. They seem considerably more aware of—and distracted by—their external environment than their non-colicky counterparts. Take heart: Colicky babies are almost always vigorous, healthy creatures who gain weight well. Colic usually disappears between three and four months of age, as quickly as it appeared.

Should you let her cry?

You thought your baby would be asleep by 8 p.m., but at 10 p.m. she's still fussing for no reason apparent to you. Should you let her cry it out? The short answer is No when the baby is less than six months old. Child-care experts agree that very young babies can't distinguish between needs and wants. Their cries are vocal solicitations for any number of needs, some that are obvious, like a clean diaper, and others that are not so easily discerned, like comfort and love. They shouldn't be ignored.

Sudden Infant Death Syndrome (SIDS)

Sudden Infant Death Syndrome, the sudden and unexpected death of apparently healthy infants, is the leading cause of death between the ages of one month and one year. In Canada, SIDS claims the life of about four hundred infants a year, approximately one out of every one thousand live-born babies.

SIDS is not caused by external suffocation, nor by vomiting or choking. It's not contagious, and it can't be predicted. It is sometimes also referred to as crib death or cot death, because the babies die in their sleep. No one knows why a baby who seems healthy can suddenly die without evident cause. Health experts, however, make these recommendations for the care of a normal, healthy infant:

- Breast-feed the child from birth to six months or longer.
- Ensure he is cared for in a smoke-free environment.
- When putting him down to sleep, place him on his back or side until he learns to turn from back to tummy on his own.
- Ensure the infant is dressed and covered in a manner that avoids overheating, even during an illness.
- Avoid using sheepskin, pillows, soft bedding, comforters, and positioning devices in his crib.

Establishing a Schedule

Although your baby's sleeping and feeding schedule may still be a little erratic, you can start some routines that will have some positive effect now and will pay off later by making your life much easier. It's never too early to establish a schedule for your little one.

A regular sequence of events is particularly important at the end of the day. A bedtime ritual is indispensable for encouraging sleep—have a parade of predictable events such as bathtime, story time, and a last feeding. Keep the nighttime feeding very quiet and low-key, to prepare your baby psychologically for sleep. Dim the lights, speak and sing softly.

Sleeping through

For most parents, the first time their baby sleeps through the night is a major milestone. This much-heralded event occurs on average at three months of age. About 10 per cent of infants sleep through the night at one month of age, and an equal number won't sleep through until about six months of age. But it's important to realize that these statistics refer to *the first time*, not when the child sleeps through the night as a regular occurrence. Take note: *Sleeping through* refers to a sustained sleep period of at least five hours.

Crying

If you've had a rough two or three months dealing with your baby's crying, the good news is that the worst may be over. Babies, even the fussy ones, cry less around twelve weeks of age. That doesn't mean that you won't have any more sleepless nights, but you will find that the crying tends not to last as long as it did. It will also become easier to stop the howling once it begins. Nobody knows exactly what brings about the change, but researchers think that, by the time infants reach this stage, they feel less frustrated because they have more control over their bodies. They're also beginning to develop other ways of communicating—looking at what they want, smiling, and vocalizing.

The crying also becomes easier to interpret. When you're trying to figure out what your newborn needs, it might seem like "one cry fits all." But by the time the baby is two or three months old, you'll hear distinctive cries for each of the baby's moods. It's by this age that your infant will be using the boredom cry—a lower-pitched, whimpery sound. This cry tends to rise and fall rapidly, trailing off at the end. It is often an early warning that the baby is going to launch into a real crying storm if you don't give him some attention soon.

This is also the time that babies first show an emotion we usually associate with older children—anger. The anger cry is a full-throated bellow. You will recognize the rage when you hear it. Babies use the anger cry when you walk away from them before they are ready, when they want something they cannot have, or when they want you to stop bothering them.

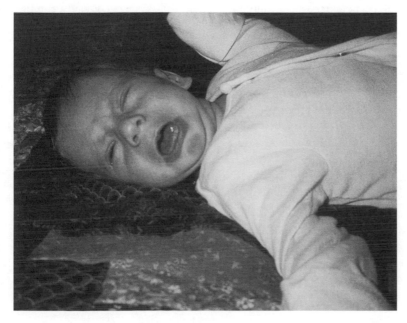

The challenge for parents is to determine what message their child's crying is commmunicating.

Soothing Your Crying Baby

Babies in their first six months of life cry for all the same reasons that new-borns do. The big difference is that they are becoming better at soothing themselves and the main way they do it is through sucking. Babies have a need to suck, not just for food, but to feel at peace. If your baby has not already discovered his hands, help him out. When the baby is in a quiet mood, help him put his fist to his mouth or offer him a pacifier.

Medical experts are much less concerned about the use of pacifiers than they once were.

You will likely hear conflicting advice on the subject of self-soothing versus pacifiers. One school holds that a pacifier is at least preferable to finger-sucking because it can be monitored and controlled.

Medical experts are also much less concerned about the use of pacifiers than they once were. There is plenty of evidence that if a baby's need for sucking is met early, and if parents do not simply use a pacifier to replace other kinds of soothing, the baby is unlikely to depend on it for long. There is just one word of caution. Babies who are already crying in earnest or who are in the middle of a good colicky wail will not be calmed by a pacifier. Sucking is most effective before the baby's crying is out of control.

But because it's unsafe to tie a pacifier around a child's neck, you may find yourself scrambling all over the house in the middle of the night looking for it. Not every child accepts a pacifier; some find other means of comforting themselves—whether by thumb-sucking, hair twiddling, blanket stroking, or some combination. At least, they always have these soothers at the ready. Often, there is little the parent can do to discourage a comfort habit: Many children begin sucking their hands or stroking their ears within days of birth.

If your child's habit is not causing him harm—for example, if his hair twiddling is not irritating his scalp—don't worry about it. Be pleased, in fact, that your child has found a resourceful way to soothe himself. Most children outgrow their comfort habits by the time they are three or four years old. Sometimes they will give up a habit for a time, and then begin again when they suddenly find themselves facing a new stress such as the birth of a sibling or starting preschool. Once the child enters daycare or school, peer pressure usually finishes off the habit. Be aware that your constant nagging on the subject may serve to reinforce it.

Chronic thumb- or finger-sucking after age five can seriously damage the formation of your child's teeth and palate. Consult with your doctor and dentist for advice on how to manage the problem.

Sounds are also effective. When your baby begins a fussy cry, you may find that a music box, a gentle voice, or other soft sounds can quickly stop it. If the crying has intensified, loud music or white noise works better. Babies in the second half of their first six months are also very

responsive to faces. Sometimes, just seeing your face up close is enough to cut short a grumbly cry.

Remember, too, that if your baby is particularly active and alert, he may also be easily bored. Do not wrap him up too tightly; he needs to be free to move his arms and legs. And let him be around you as much as possible— if your baby can see you or, better still, hitch a ride in a sling or a pack as you go about your day, he will have plenty to keep his growing mind active.

The Dangers of Losing Control

If you ever feel that, with the baby's sustained crying, you might lose control and shake him, put him down carefully in his crib and get away from him. An infant's head is large compared to the rest of his body, and his neck is relatively weak. A shake, even a mild one, can induce bleeding inside the skull, which can cause brain injury, blindness, mental impairment, and epileptic seizures.

Go to another part of the house and take some deep breaths. Cry or scream to release the tension. Call a friend or neighbour for help, or call a support line or your doctor. Don't return to your baby until you have regained control or have found help.

Communicating

Communication encompasses so much more than just words, and before you hear actual words from your baby, you will begin to interpret her "language." Like adult language, this communication involves taking turns, dealing with personal emotions, and understanding other people's emotions.

Even in her first few days, your baby begins to develop the ability to respond to your tone of voice and to your facial expressions. By two months, she begins to use sounds, to link them to the way her parents respond to her. When a baby's cries of hunger bring her parents to feed her, she learns that with her voice she can begin to take some control over events.

In the first two months, the baby begins to babble and coo, often to express pleasure. When parents respond to the baby's babbling with baby talk of their own and look into their infant's eyes, they are beginning to teach her how to take turns in a conversational exchange. By about three months, parents make a subtle change in the way they talk to their babies. A mother might say, "How are you?" then pause as if waiting for the answer. That's the baby's cue to respond by babbling or laughing or just smiling.

Another important change happens about the three-month mark. As the baby's ability to focus her eyes improves, she starts to fix on interesting objects, especially brightly coloured toys. At this point, parents can pick up the object the baby has spied, bring it close to her and begin talking about it. A parent might pick up a doll, wiggle it, and say, "Look at the dolly." This helps the baby make a connection between an outside object and language—the real basis of communication.

Nothing is as important to the infant's developing mastery of language as just talking to her. Researchers say it must be "directed talk"—about things or actions on which the child has already focused. It may seem intimidating to have the responsibility of helping your baby learn vital communication skills in the first six months of life—along with all the basic daily care of feeding, burping, bathing, laundry, health checkups, and outings. Don't worry. Researchers say that most parents progress through their child's stages of communication at just the right speed without even being aware that they're doing so.

Experts cannot agree on whether we have a built-in ability to teach language skills to infants or whether we learned from our parents. Whatever the answer, most parents' instinctive responses to their child's attempts at communication seem to work without extra training. But there are a few things you can do as part of "directed talk" to focus your baby's developing communication skills. Make conversation a part of everything you do with your baby. Respond when he makes noises and gestures—because he's practising his side of the conversation, you have to do your part. Ask questions just as you would with an older child who is capable of answering.

Such exchanges give your baby a chance to respond any way he can—with a look, a frown, or a giggle.

You may show him books, read a story, and talk about the pictures as you turn the pages. Don't expect a baby to take more care of a book than of a rattle. However, it's not too early to begin developing awareness that being read to is part of quiet time. And listening is an important aspect of all communication.

"I used to prop the baby up on the table while I was folding laundry or making dinner. And she would watch me and we would chat... well, I would chat, and she would just sit there and smile and dribble. But I think it made us both feel more connected."

JULIE, MOTHER OF TWO, BOWEN ISLAND, B.C.

Although most parents listen eagerly for their child to say his first word, experts suggest they should watch for a more important development. Your baby should be learning to pay attention to you when you speak and to show pleasure and excitement over sounds. If by the age of three months your child seems indifferent to your conversation or doesn't seem to have the idea of taking turns making sounds, talk about it with your doctor who may choose to test her hearing or assess developmental progress. A child's inattention to sounds might signal a developmental problem, or it could be a sign of hearing problems. Keep in mind that even deaf babies babble and make noises in the same way as hearing infants, but at the age of six months they fall completely silent. Parents are usually the first to spot a hearing problem in their child.

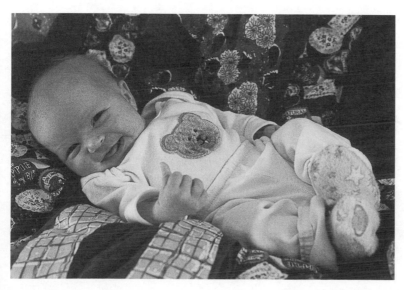

Your baby will invite you to "converse" with her long before she can utter a word.

The First Six Months

Playing and Learning

One of the wonderful opportunities given to new parents is the chance to play with their babies and to observe them while they play alone. A baby's play has a serious purpose. During play, your baby develops his physical, cognitive, emotional, and social skills. Play is also critical to the formation of his identity and personality. But by its nature, play is voluntary and spontaneous, not imposed by you as a parent. You can make suggestions about play, but often your child will invite you to play. Play gives you and your baby an opportunity to get to know and grow with each other.

How Play Develops

From birth your baby has the potential to explore and find out about the world through her body and her senses. Play starts shortly after birth with the stimulation of your baby's senses during those first brief periods of bright-eyed, quiet alertness when your baby is very responsive to sights, sounds, and movement.

"When Georgia was three months old, she saw her feet. She kicked them and they moved. Her eyes were like saucers. I don't know if she sensed that she was connected to her feet."

SUSAN, MOTHER OF THREE, TORONTO, ONT.

Research shows that babies are more interested in the human face than any other object. Babies are also especially attracted to the sound of the human voice. Most of all, a baby recognizes and responds in a special way to his mother's voice. So, in the beginning, you are more fascinating to your baby than any toy.

Entertaining play can begin with face-to-face interactions. A baby loves to look at your face and will respond even more to your exaggerated facial expressions: a big smile, wide eyes, an open mouth, frowns, yawns, or dancing lip movements. You can mimic your baby's expressions back to him, and soon he will imitate your expressions. Mirroring and exaggerating your baby's expressions will make you both smile, and the exchange helps develop your baby's awareness of himself as a separate entity.

The sound of your voice talking, singing, or cooing as you make entertaining faces will delight your baby even more. He will eventually respond with smiles, wriggles of delight, squeaks, squeals, coos and other sounds of his own. A mother can instinctively use her voice and facial movements as instruments to strike a variety of notes and make playful, rhythmic music for her baby. By stimulating the senses of sight and sound at the same time, she ensures the baby will be more actively engaged and learn more than if only one sense is stimulated. So vocalizing, touching, and smiling together provide a richer experience for you and your baby.

Although you are the star performer at the centre of your baby's world, there are many ways to engage his senses. The senses of sight, sound, taste, touch, and smell are the first windows through which your baby gets to know his environment and the most important people in it. By encouraging the development of his senses, you stimulate his cognitive or intellectual growth.

You can create a lively environment for your baby with stimulating sights and sounds. Babies are attracted to strongly contrasting patterns, like checker-boards and stripes, and designs that are bold and bright. Decorate your baby's room with this in mind when you are selecting wallpaper, quilts, and playthings.

Take your cues from your baby about how much stimulation is right for his particular temperament. When he's had enough, he'll look away or turn his head. If a baby is over-stimulated, he may cry.

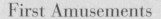

First Amusements

Hang a mobile above your baby's crib and put pictures where he can see them. You can cut faces out of magazines, make colourful drawings of your own, and show him pictures from books.

Rattles, squeaky toys, music boxes, musical mobiles and other similar toys will all catch your baby's interest. You can tell whether your baby is listening by watching him search for the sound with his eyes. He will be fascinated when a toy that he touches makes a noise.

SEE PAGE 117

Your baby may be captivated by common household sounds: the hum of a vacuum, a blender, or an electric razor; splashing water; the sounds of bells or chimes; and the soft tinkling of a piano, the strum of a guitar, or background music.

Take your baby to see the sights and hear the sounds of the world outside your home. On outings, point out and name people, animals, cars, trees, and other objects of interest.

Motor Development

By the second and third month, your baby's hands start to open up and you can begin hand play. By the third or fourth month, she will begin to make random swipes at objects placed within her reach and to grasp rattles and other toys. Toys like rattles, which make sounds as they move, help your baby make the connection between what her hands are doing and what her eyes are seeing. She will also play with her hands, watch what they're doing, and begin to realize that they belong to her.

As her hands and eyes start working together, she'll gradually be able to reach with some accuracy for objects and to explore objects with her hands and mouth more purposefully. By the fifth or six month, your baby will be able to transfer toys from hand to hand, play with blocks, and manipulate objects.

As your baby gradually uncurls, learns to lift her head, and begins to use her legs and arms more freely at two or three months, she will discover the joys of physical play. Lay your baby on her back on a mat so she can kick. Put an object to one side of her to encourage her to start rolling over.

Your baby will play with her hands and begin to realize that they belong to her.

Your baby may also begin at three months to lift her tummy off the ground, to push with her feet and fingers, to squirm, to wriggle, or move around. Put an enticing toy just beyond her reach and she may struggle to move toward the object.

At about four months, help your baby learn to sit up by pulling her gently to a sitting position and propping her up in a stroller or adaptable chair or infant seat. This gives her an expanded view of the world and builds the muscles necessary for sitting up and balancing without assistance, which she may be able to do by six months. You can help her to learn better balance by placing toys in front of her so that she reaches for the toys and develops her trunk muscles. When a baby can sit alone, she becomes more adept at playing alone.

When your baby seems ready, pull her to a standing position in her crib or playpen, or on your lap. A baby loves to stand on your lap and bounce, which develops her leg muscles so that she will eventually be able to pull herself up and stand by herself.

Social and Emotional Development

The early face-to-face playing is the model for your baby's future interactions and relationships with other people. You and your baby will gradually learn how to play and to just be with each other. If play is loving and fun, your baby learns the shared feelings of joy, curiosity, thrills, fright, surprise, and delight that are the stuff of friendship and love. Play is a wonderful outlet for expressing and releasing positive, joyful feelings as well as negative ones, like fear or anxiety.

As your baby achieves developmental milestones such as smiling, swiping or swatting, grasping and sitting, provide him with positive reinforcement—hugs, cheers, claps, and other forms of encouragement. Learning and development are stimulated by positive gestures, and this will build your baby's self-esteem and self-confidence.

Although it is through your baby's play that you can measure your child's development, take care not to use playing as a test of progress. Your baby will sense the pressure and will pick up the message if you're not satisfied. This kind of exchange undercuts his self-esteem and may inhibit or stifle his development. If you give your baby encouragement and the room to grow, he will develop emotionally and socially in his individual way.

The Connection between Playing and Learning

By reaching for a toy, a baby is developing the specific skill of hand-eye coordination. And when he is successful, he gains confidence, which is a vital foundation for developing other skills. One of the greatest benefits of play for a baby is that he learns how to be an effective learner and to enjoy learning, which provide the foundation necessary for continuing to learn.

Play is a great confidence-builder because an infant enjoys the results so much. In play, a child develops a sense that he can do things and make things happen. Studies show that the more children play, the more they learn, as researchers have found through developmental tests. So play helps to build a positive self-concept and enhances self-esteem.

Play helps a child develop the skills that are essential in thinking, in problem-solving, in developing language skills, and in acquiring the skills of social interaction. Play can enhance creativity, as well as concentration and attention. It allows the child to learn and develop mastery of his body.

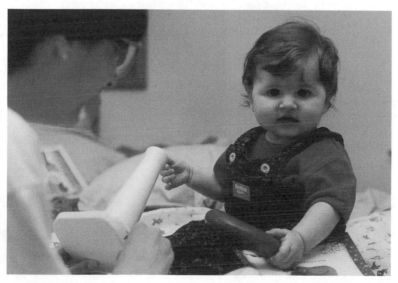

By six months of age, with enough practice and muscle development, babies learn to balance themselves well enough to sit up.

Parents as playmates

As a parent, you might initiate play. You can also be the model for different play activities, so that your infant learns by imitating you. Join in when your child is playing, or simply observe and supervise so that the infant is in charge. Let your infant take the lead whenever he can, and you follow. Be ready to quit when your child is ready. The child plays as long as he's learning or having fun and then he ends it. Follow his wishes. The best play of all occurs when you and your baby respond in turn to each other.

The parent may facilitate a child's play, taking a more or less active role when appropriate. But even when you are simply observing, make comments or encouraging sounds to let your baby know that you enjoy what he's doing.

Games Babies Love

Games teach your baby a wide range of social, physical and mental skills, and babies find them endlessly amusing. Choose games that you enjoy too. Your mutual enjoyment will be infectious.

Musical mittens

Toys that make noise will arouse your baby's interest as he tries to connect the source of the sound with his ears and his eyes. To play "musical mittens," take some brightly-coloured mittens and sew a tiny bell securely onto each one (a bell that could be easily pulled off poses a choking risk for your child). Put the mittens on his hands. He will soon discover that when he waves his hands, the mittens make a tinkling noise.

Sing along with Dad

Most babies like the sound of your singing, no matter what the rest of the world thinks. Lullabies and nursery rhymes are always a hit. Get some CDs or tapes to remind you of the words and the melodies. Sit your baby on your lap and bounce him to the rhythm of a nursery rhyme. Lift him up into the air, wiggle him to the beat, and bring him back down to a safe place on your lap for the finale.

What's in the cupboards?

Your baby loves to have things to grab and hold, to feel and play with different shapes and textures. Along with rattles and other toys, let him explore household objects such as spoons, pots, pans, cans, plastic or paper cups, and empty shoe boxes—after you've first ensured that the area is childproofed.

Safe Toys

Use a tube from a toilet paper roll, or a toy-testing tube (less than 4 cm, 1.5 in.), to check toys that may pose a choking hazard. If the toy fits inside, it is too small for a baby to play with.

Some kids' toys are noisy. Research shows that repeated exposure to toys that squeak, go bang, honk or have a siren can permanently damage a child's hearing. A child's inner ear is more sensitive to noise than an adult's, so if it sounds uncomfortably loud to you, it's probably much too loud for your child.

Peekaboo forever

Peekaboo is a standby that never fails to amuse. Cover your face with your hands, a blanket, or a piece of clothing. Say, "Where's mommy?" Uncover your face and say, "Peekaboo, I see you!" And don't forget hand games like Round and Round the Garden, Patty-Cake, and The Itsy-Bitsy Spider.

Blockbuster

Babies love the infinite possibilities of blocks. Watch your baby pick up blocks, transfer them from hand to hand, bang them together, drop them, and stack them.

Mirror, mirror on the wall

Mirrors give babies a change of view. Use a metal safety mirror rather than a glass one. Hang it near the crib or changing table, but out of the baby's reach.

Fly, baby, fly

This exercise will benefit both of you. Lie on your back with your knees and feet up. Lift your baby up so that his torso and legs are resting on your shins. Hold his arms at your knees to support him and look at each other's faces. Raise your knees and lift his arms into the air so that he's "flying," but still securely held.

Thriving As a Family

You've gone from focusing exclusively on your own and each other's needs to being consumed by the needs of your baby. During this time, some men keenly feel the loss of their partner's attention, particularly the temporary loss of their sexual affections. It's entirely natural for a new mother to become quite consumed with her baby, to the possible exclusion of the baby's father. And it's just as natural for a new father to envy the amount of time and attention his wife gives the baby, or the affection she displays. Mom and baby seem forever cuddled together while the baby nurses and the father feels left out, a third wheel.

Indeed, some women feel similar resentments when they watch the attention their partners shower on the new baby. Dad comes home, gives mom a quick hello, and then spends all his time talking and cooing with the baby. If the mother was working outside the home before the baby, she may also envy her husband's freedom to leave the house while she stays at home.

Sharing Your Feelings

Dad can be the one to tuck baby into bed after she nurses.

Each of you may be so busy and so overcome with all the new emotions that you believe your thoughts and feelings are obvious to your partner. But the baby has not magically transformed you into mind-readers. You should give voice to your feelings, talk out your concerns and your problems. Of course, mom needs to spend much of her day nursing and holding the baby. Of course, given what her body has just been through, her interest in sex may be low for awhile. Of course, dad needs as much time with his baby as he can.

But it's still important for couples to tell each other how they're feeling, to let their partner know when they feel excluded. Find ways to include each other. Dad can learn baby massage or be the one to tuck baby into her bed after she feeds. Mom and dad can share the evening playtime with their baby instead of leaving it up to one or the other.

During this period of adjustment, each of you will become accustomed to your new role and be able to reapportion your affection to one another as well as the baby, and you'll be able to rekindle your sex life. Ultimately, it's a question of balance between your relationship, the novelty of your baby and your baby's neediness, and your growth as a family.

Sharing the Load

The way that parents show their love for their child, particularly when the child is a baby, is not by what they say but by what they do. All the attention that you and your partner give the baby—the changing, the feeding, the playing, the rocking—is how your child learns that he's well-loved.

All that attention takes time, which is why many couples begin their discussion with the topic "Who does what?" in their post-baby world. A recent study showed that, before a child arrives, male and female partners each spend 40 hours a week on paid employment and 20 hours a week on work in the home. When the woman returns to the work force after the birth of a child, her hours per week jump to 90—what some call the double-day—while the man's total hours stay at the original 60. It's not hard to imagine the kind of resentment, not to mention exhaustion, that disparity in time will create. Take a close look at how the two of you share the load.

If You're a Single Parent

Single-parent families, even more than two-parent families, need support. Single parents should take help wherever they can find it, whether through informal systems like family and friends or through more formalized routes like local single parents groups. It's particularly critical to do so during the early months, when the tasks of caring for a new baby can often seem overwhelming. Equally important for single parents is a dedication to making or finding time for themselves, away from their children, on a regular basis. Accept all baby-sitting offers from trustworthy family and friends whenever they're extended.

"One night, a couple of months after my separation, my son Laurent became quite sick. I called a hospital and, after I described his symptoms, the nurse said to bring him right in. He's my oldest, which meant I would have had to leave the two youngest at home, alone, in the middle of the night. I didn't know what to do. I just thought: It's so hard to be alone."

IVANA, MOTHER OF THREE, ETOBICOKE, ONT.

Despite all the work, and sometimes the guilt, of raising children on your own, there are some positives to single parenthood. Many single parents feel their relationship with their children is much closer than it might have been otherwise. There is no co-management and, therefore, no parental battles. And, for all the times when you alone are to blame, there are just as many times when you alone deserve all the credit.

Keeping Your Baby Safe

One of the first things you'll be aware of as a new parent is that you start to see the possibility of danger for your child in situations that would have looked innocuous to you just a short time ago. That's good—it means that your antennae are up.

One of our prime responsibilities as parents is to keep our children from harm and that means learning how to prevent injuries. Experts don't talk about "childhood accidents" any more; they talk about "preventable childhood injuries." That's because studies have shown that the majority of injuries, which are the leading cause of death for children under age nineteen, are preventable. The following tips provide what you need to know about injury prevention for a baby.

General Home Safety

If you haven't already done so, get a fire extinguisher, hang it in a handy spot, and keep it serviced. Install smoke alarms in a central location on each floor of your home. Don't put an alarm in a bathroom or too close to the stove in a kitchen, because harmless smoke and steam vapours will reach it. If it sounds its shrill alarm just because you've had a hot shower, you may be irritated enough to deactivate it, then forget to reactivate it. But putting the alarm near the kitchen door is a good idea, because an unattended pot on the stove could start a fire.

Also install an alarm in any bedroom whose door is closed at night. If a fire starts in the wall of a bedroom with a closed door, an alarm in the hall may not activate until after the smoke has overcome someone sleeping in the bedroom.

> **Get a fire extinguisher, hang it in a handy place, and keep it serviced.**

Remove dust from smoke alarms every six months by vacuuming them, and test the battery by waving a stick of incense or a candle under it. Pressing the tester button may only tell you whether the battery is charged, not whether the unit is working. Consider installing carbon monoxide detectors also, especially if you have a fireplace or wood stove, an oil or gas furnace, and gas appliances. The units should be installed near sleeping areas.

If you rely on well water or a source other than city-treated water, test it twice a year for coliform bacteria as well as fluoride and nitrate levels. Take a water sample in to your public health unit or ask for a water-testing kit.

When planning the baby's room, place the crib away from radiators and the cords of window blinds. Don't string anything across the crib, and hang mobiles out of reach. If you're using a diaper pail, choose one that has a secure compartment for the deodorizer or don't use a deodorizer at all.

Buy two first aid kits, one for the car and one for home. Ready-made kits from an established organization such as St. John Ambulance provides a good model to start with. Make a list of emergency phone numbers and post a copy by every telephone in the house. This list should include: poison control, police, fire, doctor, taxi, ambulance, and 911 or its equivalent in your area. Also post your own address and telephone number, in case an emergency makes the baby sitter or a visitor forget the information, and the phone numbers of grandparents, neighbours, friends, and workplaces.

The Car

Motor vehicle collisions are the Number One cause of death and injury for young children, according to the Infant & Toddler Safety Association. The safest location for an infant car seat is in the middle of the back seat. However, there are times when parents prefer to put the baby in the passenger seat beside them. In this instance, the Infant & Toddler Safety Association recommends that the passenger seat be pushed back as far as possible away from the dashboard.

A baby should never be placed in the passenger seat if the car is equipped with a passenger-side air bag. In a collision, the impact of an air bag is potentially lethal to a baby or small child. Also some passenger-side seat belts are not designed to hold infant car seats. Check your manual.

SEE PAGE 126

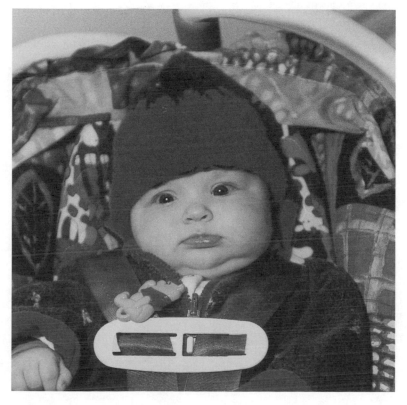

Never place a baby in the passenger side of a car equipped with a passenger-side air bag.

Introducing Your Pet

Some dogs and cats may react jealously to a new baby and, therefore, may be a danger. There are ways to prepare your pets for the baby's arrival, but even with preparation, never leave a pet alone unsupervised with your baby. In the first weeks after the baby arrives home, you need to assess whether the pets will behave appropriately or whether you will need to find them another home.

➤ Play a sound-effects tape of a crying infant to acquaint your dog with the noise. You may be able to borrow one from the library.

➤ Bring a blanket with the baby's scent on it home from the hospital before you bring home the baby.

➤ Encourage the dog to sniff the baby in your arms.

➤ Give your dog positive attention while the baby's with you: He'll learn that nice things happen when the baby is around.

➤ Keep dog biscuits in your pocket and give the dog one every time you leave the baby's room. He'll learn to follow you out.

➤ Teach your dog a new command: Gentle.

➤ Mothers who are breast-feeding should not change kitty litter. because they may contract a mild infection from the litter that could pass on to the breastmilk.

➤ Keep cats out of the baby's sleep area and away from baby's equipment or toys.

Teaching a pet appropriate behaviour around your baby may take time and patience.

Safety Rules to Remember

➤ Read the labels on all baby medication.

➤ Hold a baby while you feed her. Don't leave her with a propped-up bottle.

➤ Keep one hand on the baby while changing her on a change table.

➤ Always keep the sides of the crib or playpen up and locked in place.

➤ Don't tie a pacifier or a necklace around a baby's neck.

➤ Be wary of clothes with hoods and drawstrings.

➤ Use only sleepwear that is flame-retardant.

➤ Use only cold-air vaporizers

➤ Never put a baby on a waterbed. (The mattress has too much give, and an infant can't lift his head away for air.)

➤ Don't drink hot liquids when holding an infant.

➤ Don't use pillows in a crib.

➤ Always use restraint straps on infant seats and strollers and the like.

➤ Never leave a baby in an infant seat anywhere high, and especially not on a couch or bed. If the seat tips, the baby's face might be pushed into the bedding or mattress.

➤ Always supervise an older sibling around the baby.

➤ Never leave a baby alone in the bath or on the change table.

➤ Turn the hot water heater down to 48°C (120°F) from the usual 57–60°C (135-140°F) .

➤ Don't throw your baby up into the air or drop her onto a bed as a game.

➤ Don't give a baby a balloon to play with. The loud bang when it breaks can hurt her tiny eardrums, and the thin pieces of material that remain could suffocate or choke her.

Baby Gear

The arrival of a new baby brings you joy—and mountains of stuff! Some of it is essential, much of it is useful, but you'll find some items just take up space and you'll gladly unload them at your next garage sale.

What follows is advice for making wise choices on some of the big-ticket items that you'll need in the first six months of your baby's life. The essentials are a crib, a high chair, a stroller, and a car seat. Buy the best you can afford, because you'll use these items every day for the longest time. For more information on products, contact the Infant & Toddler Safety Association (ITSA). It offers safety fact sheets on many types of products.

The Nursery

The crib

Cribs range in price from $150 to several hundred dollars. Because their specifications are strictly regulated, the higher prices don't mean that the crib is safer, just that the crib has more styling or features. Avoid buying a used crib, unless you're very sure it's in good condition and was manufactured after October 1, 1986, the date of the most recent government safety regulations. Look for an adjustable mattress support and a drop-siderail that you can manoeuvre quietly, using two separate actions. If you plan to keep the crib against a wall, you may only need a single drop-rail.

The mattress should be new unless you're certain the secondhand one was well maintained, was not stored in an attic, basement, or garage, and you have the manufacturer's label information and warranty card. Look for a firm, flat mattress ($40-$160) that makes a solid sound when you knock on it. If it sounds hollow, the firmness probably comes from being wrapped in cardboard and you might surmise it was made with cheap materials. Some newly designed mattresses have corners that pop up so you can change the sheets without taking the entire mattress out.

The change area

The change area can be as simple as a washable pad on the floor. Avoid plastic change pads—they don't launder well. Waterproof nylon is better. Other options are a stand-alone change table ($130–$400) that can be used later for toys or for the laundry room; a changer that's incorporated into a dresser or fits on top ($150–$300); or a small table with a change pad hooked on top ($30) that can function as a bedside table or desk later. Changers that fit on top of the crib tend to be too small and are useful only if you have very limited space. Whichever change option you choose, make sure it's the most comfortable height for you.

Nice-to-have

Cradle or bassinet (about $70) to keep your newborn close. Make sure it has a firm, snug-fitting mattress, and a stable base. If it has folding legs, they should lock securely. Cradles should have slat spacing no wider than 6 cm (approximately 2.5 in.) and some means of limiting and locking the swing mechanism.

Nursery monitor ($50–$70; $300 for a video monitor). Hang onto your nursery monitor; it's handy when older kids are bed-bound with illness.

Comfortable chair or rocker. A glider rocker is highly recommended. Avoid squeaky wicker.

At-Home Necessities

The *high chair* ($40-$220) should have a wide, stable base and an adjustable deep-rimmed tray that can be operated with one hand. It should also have adjustable waist-and-crotch straps of leather or fabric. If you have very little space, choose a folding high chair with a good locking mechanism so it won't collapse. If it also has a removable tray and is adjustable in height, you'll be able to use it as the baby gets older when you can slide the chair up to the table—provided the chair arms fit under the table.

The feature of a reclining seat may not be useful; if the baby can't sit up, you won't use a high chair anyway. It's best to avoid chair seats that hook on to tables. They don't work safely with all tables, and babies can more easily reach what's sharp and what's too hot.

A *bathtub* ($10–$30) should have a reclining back rest, drainage holes, and a no-slip surface. If it's meant to fit over your bathtub or sink, measure your equipment first. You might try a terry cloth bath-frame instead, or simply wash your baby on a towel placed in the sink.

A good infant seat has a sturdy non-skid base and easy-to-use straps.

Nice-to-have

Infant seat: ($25–$60). Look for adjustable angles, portability, a sturdy non-skid base, washability, and easy-to-use straps. Some seats have built-in vibrators or are rockable. If you have one of the newer multi-use car seats or baby swings, an infant seat may not be necessary.

Automatic baby swing: ($85–$145). Look for a wide stable base, non-skid feet, a quiet motor with a long running-time between battery changes or winding, an adjustable reclining seat, and open access; if there is no bar on top, there's less risk of hitting the baby's head. Because this item is useful only while the baby is not active enough to tip it over—until about seven months of age, you may prefer to borrow one.

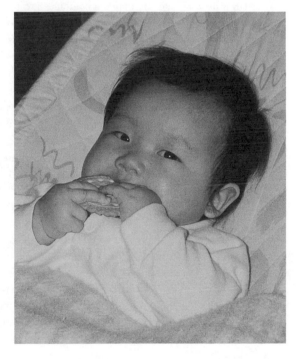

The First Six Months

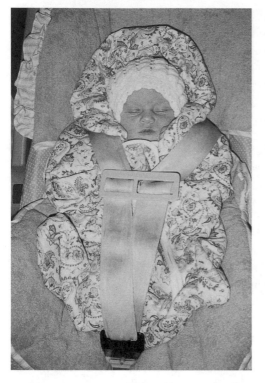

The best car seat to buy is the one that you will use properly every time.

Out and About

Car seats

A car seat is one of the most important products you will buy for your child. He will use one from the day he makes the trip home from hospital until he weighs at least 18 kg (40 lb.) or reaches a height of 101 cm (40 in.). With all the use and abuse the item takes, it's worth finding the best you can afford.

First and foremost, the car seat must meet Canadian Motor Vehicle Safety Standards (CMVSS)—check for the label and buy in Canada. If you are borrowing or buying second-hand, be certain that the seat has not been involved in a collision and is not on Transport Canada's Notice List. Don't use a seat that's over ten years old. After that, it's up to you.

The best car seat to buy is the model that you will use properly every time. An infant-only seat ($45–$105) is the most convenient during the first few months. It is designed to be used facing the rear of the car and protects babies from birth up to 10 kg (22 lb.) or 66 cm (26 in.). It can be used until your baby is between four and six months of age. Its major advantages are portability and convertibility; many models convert from carrier to rocker to baby-feeding chair. For newborns, a five-point harness is essential; an easy-carry handle, a shade canopy, and a stay-in-the-car seat base are helpful extras. A head cushion that supports the baby's head and a protector for your car seat are also worthwhile additional purchases.

Some parents choose to skip the infant seat, because as soon as the baby gets too tall or heavy, they need the larger car seat. These parents might go for the convertible seat ($75–$150), which is used rear-facing until the child is over 9 kg (20 lb.) and can sit independently for long periods. Then it can be placed so that the child, up to 18 kg (40 lb.), faces forward. You might look for a car seat that has washable upholstery, a T-shield, and a retractable belt that adjusts automatically to snowsuits and growing children.

Choose a model that's easy to use—the best is the one that you are comfortable adjusting and that works well with the seat belts in your vehicle. If possible, try a pre-purchase test of the seat in the store, filling it with a large doll or stuffed animal. Then test it in your car to see that it fits properly and that your seat belts hold it securely. Once you've made the purchase, keep the manufacturer's instructions handy, and fill out and mail in the registration card so that you'll be notified if there's a recall.

Strollers

With their high-tech ergonomics, suspension and braking systems, and a multitude of options, strollers can prove as difficult to choose as a car. You may want to direct some thought and money into this item because you'll probably use it for a few years and for more than one child. Decide where you'll likely stroll—through the woods or the local mall? Will you be putting it into and taking it out of a car trunk often? Or will you have to lift it on and off the bus? There's a stroller for every kind of stroll and for every budget—they range in price from nineteen dollars to several hundred dollars. Remember to take a test drive before you buy!

Look for dual rear-wheel brakes, swivel wheels with a secure locking system for moving over grass or gravel, a folding mechanism that locks in place so it won't fold up when you don't want it to, washability, an adjustable-reversible handle, and a harness that completely encircles your baby's waist. ITSA notes also that rubber tires last longer than plastic; nylon or rubber are less likely to crack in the cold; double tires wear better than single tires; balloon tires have the best shock absorption; and larger tires are more durable.

All buckled in and ready for a test drive in the stroller!

All-terrain strollers and umbrella strollers are also available. The latter is convenient and inexpensive, but it doesn't offer good positioning for very young babies. Prams can be big and awkward, but they're great on bumpy winter sidewalks, and they hold a lot of groceries. Look for inexpensive prams at garage sales or consignment shops.

Nice to have

Baby carriers have come a long way from the one-position-only kind that were popular a few years ago. Many front-carriers ($25–$60) are used until your baby is four or five months old or weighs 6–7 kg (13–15.5 lb.). They are designed to let him face forward or back.

Backpacks (about $70) may be used from about 5 months of age up to 3 years of age or 19 kg (40lb.). With a backpack, you can carry a baby and a whole slew of extras. Think carefully, though, before you buy one of the backpacks with wheels—are you really likely to take the pack off and pull it? Will the terrain be suitable for wheels? Try the carrier on first, ideally with the baby inside. Look for one that's comfortable, easy to use, and made of a fabric appropriate for the weather.

An Infant's Point of View

Much of my world is difficult to fathom because I am so helpless at the beginning. With physical closeness and careful observation, you'll soon understand me well.

My Body

- I'm born with a wrinkled, curled-up body, a scrunched-up face, no eyelashes, and maybe a little acne. But I hope you think I'm beautiful.

- I weigh between 2500 g and 4300 g (5.5 lb. to 9.5 lb.), and I'm 46 cm to 56 cm (18 in. to 22 in.) long. I'll lose a little weight during the first few days, but I'll regain it within a week.

- I may be bald or I may have a full head of hair, most of which will likely fall out in four or five months. I'll also lose whatever body hair I'm born with.

- If I'm dark-skinned, I may have clusters of dark pigment spots at the base of my spine. They will eventually disappear.

- I have a strong, natural urge to suck, but I might need a few tries before I get the knack of breast-feeding.

- My sense of smell is at least as good as yours, and my sense of taste is good, too. I'm partial to the sweetness of breastmilk, which is a complete diet for me for the first four to six months.

- I hear very well and could hear even before I was born, although for the first three months I usually can't tell where the sound is coming from.

- For the first two months, I can focus on things within 33 cm (13 in.), but only very large objects, and even those I can't focus on very well until I'm about three months old. When I look at your face I see mostly the edges— your chin, hairline, ears, and eyeglasses.

- For the first two months, I see only very strong colours—red, green, and blue, but not yellow. The stronger the contrast in a picture or mobile, the better I can see it. I can't distinguish one pastel from another for the first six months, so I won't notice if my blanket is pink or blue.

- I look helpless, but I have many reflexes: I automatically grasp your finger; I flex my foot and curl my toes when you touch my foot; I start "stepping" when you hold me and let my feet touch something solid; and I fling out my arms and legs when I'm startled. Most of these reflexes will disappear by six months.

- I make some interesting noises: I gurgle, snuffle, squeak, and grunt.

- The black stump of my umbilical cord falls off after one week or as late as the third week.

- I sleep as much as 22 hours a day or as little as 10 hours. My tummy is only the size of my fist, so I'll need 8 to 12 feedings every 24 hours for the first few weeks. I'll double my birth weight in five months.

My Body, continued

- I might have several loose bowel movements a day, or only one every few days.

- My eyes can change colour any time during the first year, usually around three months.

- My development goes from the top down. At three months I can control my eyes, tracking a moving object. Then I begin to hold my head up myself. By the fourth month I can push myself up onto my arms when I'm lying on my tummy. Between four and six months I can roll over from my tummy or my back. I can sit with support from you or pillows, although I might topple over when I reach for a toy.

My Feelings

- I have definite likes and dislikes right from Day One. I might prefer to be tightly swaddled or to have my arms free. I might like to be around lots of people and activity, or I might prefer quiet.

- I cry, but not too lustily until after the first week or so. I don't shed real tears until I'm about three or four weeks old.

- I'm pretty much focused on myself and my own needs for the first three months.

- I don't have much self-control. If I'm hungry and you make me wait, I'll get very agitated over the delay.

- I cry more and more over the first six weeks, at which point my crying reaches its height. Even if I'm perfectly healthy, I might cry for several hours a day because I'm hungry, wet, tired, bored, overexcited, lonely, uncomfortable in the same position, or even alarmed by the movements of my own waving arms.

- By three months, or even sooner, you may be able to discern the differences among my various cries.

- I tend to get more tense as the evening wears on. To relax into sleep, I need to suck, to be rocked, or to cry. I need some extra cuddling and soothing words from you to help me through it.

- I love lots of attention from you. Although I can't see you clearly at first, I know it's you by your smell and your voice, so hold me close and talk to me.

- When I know you're near, I may get so excited that I show it with my whole body, jerking my arms and legs.

- Since my sense of touch was the first of my senses to develop in the womb, I'm quite sensitive to it. Having my head stroked, my back gently rubbed, and my body cuddled all bring me pleasure.

My Feelings, continued

- When I'm happy to be with you and other people, I look with interest. When I've had enough and the stimulation is starting to overwhelm me, I'll turn away.

- I have a variety of facial expressions, including ones that make me look giddy, grumpy, or downright comical, but for the first two months they're not a reliable indication of my emotional state.

- My first toothless smiles, while charming, are mostly involuntary reflex actions, where I smile fleetingly at nothing in particular. In the second month I start to smile at people and things in general. After four months, I have a much more specific smile, with my biggest one reserved for you.

- If you're having a conversation with someone else and then turn to me and suddenly stop talking, I'll become confused and distressed. I'll be happier if you continue your normal, friendly chatter while you look at me.

- After three months, I start to anticipate exciting events like feeding time. I'll kick, wave about, and breathe heavily.

- By three months, my love affair with you is starting to peak. I might even break off from feeding to gaze up at you with longing. If I look as though I'm studying your face, it's because I'm beginning to see you more clearly.

My Mind

- I'm learning all the time. I probably take in more information during these six months than in any other six-month period of my life.

- Within a few weeks I can imitate sounds and movements, differentiate among sounds, and begin to categorize what I'm learning.

- Some parts of my brain—the ones that control my basic bodily movements and functions—are fully "wired" at birth. But all my early experiences help to form the trillions of connections (synapses) that are responsible for fine-tuning my motor skills and for the development of my language abilities.

- From Day One, I respond to the sound of human voices, but I pay more attention to high-pitched voices (especially my mother's) that use lots of repetition.

- By the second month, I recognize your voice. I have a "conversation" with you by responding to your words with smiles and gurgles and a lot of kicking and arm-flapping.

- My attention span starts out fairly high, and I can stare at something for minutes at a time. After three months it decreases, and a certain toy or picture might hold my attention for only a few seconds.

My Mind, continued

- At three months, I "discover" my hands, gazing at them in wonder. I might be able to get one of them in my mouth.

- By the third month, I start to swipe at objects, but since my hand-eye coordination isn't very good, I often miss.

- I'm gradually learning that I can make things happen. The first time I shake a rattle, I think the noise is an accident. Soon I figure out that my own arm movement is responsible for the rattle noise.

- By three or four months, I start to recognize my own reflection. I'd love an unbreakable mirror as a toy.

- I enjoy a change of scenery. I'd like it if you taped up some boldly coloured pictures at my eye level, and changed them often. Posters or magazine pictures will do fine.

- My memory is very short to begin with. If something or somebody disappears from view, I assume it's gone forever.

- At two or three months, I "talk" with soft cooing noises like *ooh* and *ahh*.

- After five months, I start to make sounds with consonants like *da*, *ma*, and *ba*, but don't think I'm saying *Dada*, *Mama*, or *ball*. It will be a few months before I attach any meaning to these sounds.

- Around six months, I start to babble, stringing sounds together. I use a slightly lower voice to babble to a man than to a woman.

- By five months, when I discover the pleasure of sucking my toes, I'm ready to enjoy the game, This Little Piggy Goes to Market.

- I need you to use my name a lot, so I can learn to recognize it and begin to form an identity.

- Between four and six months, I purposely reach for an object, whether it's a toy or a cup of hot coffee, so keep me safe.

- When I'm fussy and demand your complete attention, I'm not trying to manipulate you or get you under my control. I'm not capable of such willful motives. I simply need you.

My World

- I'm a sociable creature right from the beginning. I like having people around who love me and pay attention to me.

- During the first two or three months at least, my patterns of sleeping and eating don't conform to the rest of the family's.

- I like being held, and I adjust my body to fit into the embrace of the person holding me.

My World, continued

- Since I use my body to understand the world around me, I need some skin-to-skin contact.

- I begin to socialize with you by bobbing my head, imitating your facial expressions, and wriggling my body.

- Even if I don't stop crying when you pick me up, it doesn't mean I don't want to be held. There could be something else bothering me, and I may need you even more.

- After six weeks, I smile not just with my mouth but with my cheeks, my eyes, and my whole body.

- I want you to hold me close while I'm feeding. Please don't leave me alone with a bottle.

- If you interact with me, talking and smiling and moving me around, I stay more alert while I'm awake.

- Don't hold me only when I fuss. Hold me when I'm content, wide awake, and ready to interact with you.

- The more responsive you are to me, the more I coo with long, high, melodic sounds.

- I start making noises, like clicking my tongue or coughing, to get your attention and initiate some social contact with you.

- Although I love company, I may also need some quiet time to myself. I'll let you know, by turning away or crying, when I've had enough of people.

- Around four months, I begin to show an interest in a toy or stuffed animal, but nothing replaces the fun I have with you.

- I might become interested in solid food as early as four months, especially when I realize that eating is a social occasion.

- I enjoy longer and longer interactions with you, as you sing to me, play finger games, and exchange smiles and sounds.

- By five months, I'm giggling, and I might have a full, lusty belly laugh.

- Toward six months, I become more aware of my environment. I explore your face with my hands, pulling your hair, patting your face, or grabbing your glasses.

- As I become more aware of the thrilling pleasures of the world around me, I'm easily distracted and may be temporarily harder to feed.

- If you spend a lot of time with me, it won't spoil me. It will reassure me that I can depend on you to stay close and take care of me.

Six to Twelve Months

4

In the second half of her first year, the baby who was so helpless just a few months earlier becomes an explorer and an adventurer. Her newfound ability to crawl or scoot across the floor takes her to new and wonderful places. She experiments with everything she sees, pulling books down off shelves, throwing clothing about, and methodically plucking tiny objects off the floor and popping them into her mouth.

You might think that a little being who is testing her independence in this way might also be less emotionally dependent, but the opposite is true. A baby at this age forms even stronger bonds with her parents and care-givers, those who have lavished attention on her in her earliest months. She wants to be with you all the time and devote herself completely to you. Enjoy it. Don't worry that you might spoil your child. You won't. If you're reserved about showing your emotions, try to lower your inhibitions. Your baby is looking for lots of emotional interaction and attention from you.

There is an awkward side to all this attachment and loving. At about eight or nine months of age, babies develop separation anxiety. They cannot stand it if you leave the room, sometimes even for a minute. They howl and collapse into tears if you leave the house. Some days it's easy to handle. You can arrange for your baby to accompany you as you go about your daily routine. Other times it seems like a chore, and you might begin to resent your baby's need for constant attention. If you're working outside the home, the separation in the morning can be painful for both mother and baby. If the baby's father and other caregivers lavish much love and attention on her and accept her adoring attention back, that will help her to feel more secure without mom.

When your baby gets the close, loving attention she needs, she will be happier and more relaxed. First she learns that she can count on your love, then she goes on to form other loving relationships.

Feeding and Nutrition

By now, you and your baby are a comfortable and efficient nursing team, and you've been amazed and gratified by how your child has flourished on your breastmilk. How long you continue to breast-feed will depend on several factors. Do you enjoy breast-feeding with its wonderful physical closeness? Are you ready for the bit of freedom that might come if your partner could give the baby a bottle while you're out?

If you're planning to return to work soon, you might have considered weaning your baby. You may also feel subtle pressure from family and friends that it's time to wean. "Are you *still* breast-feeding?" is the question often asked of mothers when they are nursing older babies. In fact, you are in the minority, but breast-feeding advocates are trying to change that. The Canadian Paediatric Society recommends that mothers breast-feed until the baby is at least six months of age. But in Canada, three months is the median age at which babies are weaned. By six months, only 25 per cent of Canadian babies are being breast-fed exclusively.

If breast-feeding works for you, don't mess with a good thing, no matter how many times you're asked when you're planning to wean. Breastmilk continues to be the best food for your baby until he is a year old and, even after one year, your baby will benefit from the continuing emotional connection and physical comfort that breast-feeding provides.

Some babies self-wean. Between six months and a year, the number of feedings will gradually diminish, but a baby isn't ready to wean until he's over one year of age, eating a variety of solids, and drinking from a cup. If he is self-weaning, he will gradually lose interest in breast-feeding, one nursing session at a time.

But what if your baby suddenly loses interest in nursing and he's under a year old? Maybe it's as simple as his having a stuffed nose, temporarily preventing him from nursing easily. Or it could be teething. It could be that you've changed underarm deodorant, and he finds the new scent offensive. Or perhaps nursing has become a stressful time with lots of interruptions for you both. Make any changes you need to help him return to nursing and, if nothing seems to help, try nursing him when he's almost asleep. Some babies who won't nurse when they're awake will nurse when they're drowsy or even while sleeping.

If you decide to wean, realize that you can do it in stages. You've become skilled at increasing your milk supply to meet your baby's needs, so you can gradually decrease your milk supply by continuing with some breast-feeding and replacing others with bottle-feeding, using a commercial formula if your baby is younger than nine to twelve months, or drinks from a cup. If you decide to lead the weaning process, it's more comfortable for the mother and easier on the baby if the weaning is gradual, preferably over more than three weeks. To prevent engorgement of your breasts, give your baby a cup or bottle to replace one nursing, then the other.

Nursing a baby with teeth

Teeth seldom pose a problem. Your baby can't bite while she's sucking because her tongue covers her lower gum. If biting occurs, it's usually at the end of a nursing session after your baby is full. Look for a mischievous twinkle in her eye. A prompt, firm *No!* usually stops the inclination to bite.

"My son went through a biting stage when he was around seven months old. He wouldn't really bite down hard or draw blood, he'd just draw his teeth along the nipple. I had advice from another mother, a mother of five. She said that when it happened, to immediately sit him down and say "No!" This had worked for her, and I think I only had to do it twice. And that was that."

MICHELLE, MOTHER OF THREE, KEMPTVILLE, ONT.

To wean your baby, you can gradually reduce your milk supply by replacing some breast-feedings with bottle-feedings.

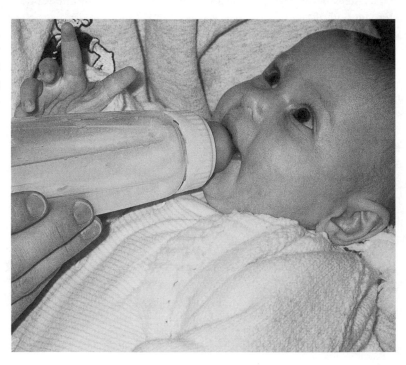

When Your Baby Won't Wean

According to your schedule, it's time to wean, but your baby's on a different schedule. When you offer the bottle, he screams for the breast. A baby who is reluctant to take the bottle or who can't figure out how to get the milk out of the bottle can make weaning a difficult transition for the whole family. Try these tips to help smooth the way.

- → Have the father, baby sitter, or anyone other than the mother hold the baby and offer the bottle. Many babies won't take the bottle if they know they can nurse.
- → Make the bottle as similar to the breast as possible. Run warm water over the bottle nipple to warm it to body temperature. Make the bottle smell like mom by wrapping it in her nightgown. Fill the bottle with expressed breastmilk rather than formula. Feed the baby in a nursing position.
- → Offer the bottle when the baby is moderately hungry, not when he's frantic for food.
- → Don't force the bottle nipple into the baby's mouth or he'll push it out with his tongue. Hold the nipple near his mouth, and he'll naturally guide it into his mouth.
- → When offering the bottle, soothe the baby by singing, rocking, swaying side to side, or walking.
- → Slip the bottle into the baby's mouth while he's sleeping, and he may unconsciously suck on it.
- → Don't leave the bottle in the baby's mouth while he's in his crib.
- → Experiment with different nipple types and hole sizes for one that the baby will accept.

Bottle-Feeding the Older Baby

Sometime between nine and twelve months, your baby can be switched from formula to cow's milk, which will be a little easier on your budget. If your baby is eating a variety of other foods (12 tbsp. a day) at nine months of age, you might start him on cow's milk rather than formula. But be sure your baby receives adequate iron from foods other than formula. Proper iron intake is crucial to his brain development and growth. Cow's milk is not a good source of iron, but iron-fortified formula is. Consult with your physician to decide if your baby is ready to give up formula. Before switching to milk, your baby should be:

- → between nine and twelve months of age.
- → eating iron-rich foods such as meats, peas, and iron-fortified cereal.
- → eating foods rich in vitamin C which helps iron absorption.

Until your baby is two years old, he should have homogenized milk, not 1%, 2%, or other fat-reduced milk. Fat-reduced milks don't contain enough calories and essential fatty acids for optimum growth and brain development, and the protein and sodium contents are too high for a baby's developing kidneys.

Limiting milk

Once your baby is drinking homogenized milk, don't overdo a good thing. He may still develop an iron deficiency if he fills up on milk and leaves little room for the foods that provide iron. The Canadian Paediatric Society recommends a maximum daily milk intake of 550–650 mL (18–20 oz.) for babies nine months and older. To ensure your baby receives adequate iron from foods, offer the bottle *after* he eats.

Weaning from the bottle

At the age of one, your baby may be ready to take his fluids in a cup. Introduce the cup at mealtime, but don't feel you have to eliminate the bottle altogether if your baby still enjoys it. Sucking on a bottle relaxes and soothes a baby, as well as feeds him. The need for sucking doesn't decrease until after age two or three. If your baby wants to crawl on to your lap for a bottle at naptime, enjoy it as a time of closeness for both of you. Just don't let him walk around with a bottle in his mouth, have juice in a bottle, or go to bed with a bottle. If these activities become habits, they will put his SEE PAGE 100 teeth at risk of tooth decay from "nursing bottle caries." There's no urgent need to wean your baby off the bottle. When your baby is ready to give up the bottle, he'll toss it across the room.

A high chair is a safe place for baby when you try out new foods and utensils.

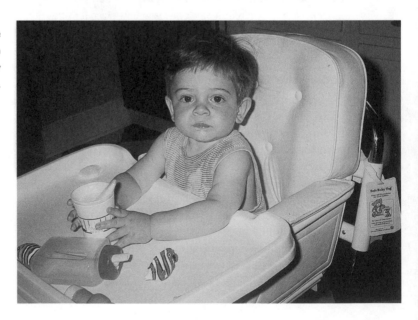

Introducing Table Food

At about nine or ten months, babies are ready to leave puréed foods behind and move on to chopped or finely cut family food. Most babies are quite eager to get in on what the rest of the family is having for dinner. As your baby adjusts, make meals a combination of puréed baby foods and table food, gradually shifting to all table food by his first birthday.

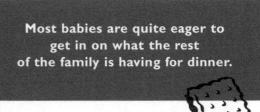

Most babies are quite eager to get in on what the rest of the family is having for dinner.

Don't impose your own diet rules on your baby. For your own health, you may follow a high-fibre, low-fat diet. But a baby under age one doesn't need fibre, and babies must have dietary fat. Don't start watching fat and cholesterol until your baby is over two years old.

Me do it!

One day, your baby is going to grab the spoon and insist that he can feed himself. As he smears puréed carrots on his highchair, dumps plums on the floor, and throws pasta across the room, keep in mind that your baby is too young for table manners. He's still figuring out where his mouth is. To ensure that he receives adequate nutrition, take at least two spoons to his high chair. As he swirls one spoon around his Pablum, use the other spoon to shovel the peas into his mouth.

Introducing Vegetables, Fruits, Juice, and Protein Foods

Once your baby has mastered infant cereal and is about seven months old, it's time to add finely puréed vegetables and fruits. Introduce these foods the same way you did cereals. Start a new food, then note any reactions, immediate or over the next few days, that might indicate she is allergic to the new food. Don't push food on your baby or trick her into eating. Pretending the spoon is a plane zooming in for a landing inside your infant's mouth may amuse her enough to open her mouth, but it doesn't help your baby attune to her hunger cues.

When introducing a food, realize that babies have an innate tendency to reject new foods. If your baby recoils at her first spoonful of squash, don't assume she hates squash for all time. She's just not used to it. You may have to introduce squash as many as eight or ten times before she decides that squash is her favourite food.

First vegetables, then fruit

Start with vegetables. If you start with fruits, which appeal to a baby's preference for sweetness, your baby may reject vegetables. The vegetables least likely to cause allergies include carrots, squash, and sweet potatoes, but since the first two have nitrates, you might limit the amount you provide. The fruits least likely to cause allergies include bananas, peaches, and pears.

Once your baby is eating well from a spoon, offer juice in a lidded cup or a teacher beaker. Apple juice is the least allergenic. Until your baby is eighteen months old, offer no more than 250 mL (8 oz.) of juice per day. If she drinks more, she won't have room for adequate amounts of breast-milk or formula.

"We always made a point of giving our children what we were eating, and we were eating from all over the map. We found they would eat almost anything—pork curry, fried chicken, Thai foods. They'd just scarf it down. The key thing was that we were not going to make two separate meals."

BRAD, FATHER OF TWO, BOWEN ISLAND, B.C.

Finally protein foods

At about eight months, your baby is ready for puréed meat or tofu. The meats least likely to cause allergies include beef, veal, lamb, and poultry. When you introduce your baby to eggs, start by giving him only a hard-boiled yolk. Babies under age one should not be given highly allergenic foods like egg whites, fish, or nuts. A child with a family history of allergy should be restricted for longer. Continue to check with your family physician up to age three.

Your baby is too young for table manners. He's still figuring out where his mouth is.

Guidelines for Feeding

Until your baby is nine months old, breastmilk or formula is the most important nourishment. Offer milk first, then food. After nine months, offer food before milk.

Age Seven to Nine Months

Early morning:	Breastmilk or formula
Morning:	Breastmilk or formula
	15 to 60 mL (1 to 4 tbsp.) cereal
	15 to 60 mL (1 to 4 tbsp.) vegetables or fruit

Afternoon:	Breastmilk or formula
	15 to 60 mL (1 to 4 tbsp.) cereal
	15 to 60 mL (1 to 4 tbsp.) vegetables or fruit
	15 mL (1 tbsp.) meat

Evening:	Breastmilk or formula
	15 to 60 mL (1 to 4 tbsp.) cereal
	15 to 60 mL (1 to 4 tbsp.) vegetables or fruit
Late evening:	Breastmilk or formula

Age Ten to Twelve Months

Morning:	60 to 120 mL (4 to 8 tbsp.) cereal
	60 to 120 mL (4 to 8 tbsp.) vegetables or fruit
	Breastmilk, formula, or homogenized milk

Afternoon:	60 to 90 mL (4 to 6 tbsp.) cereal
	60 to 120 mL (4 to 8 tbsp.) vegetables or fruit
	15 to 45 mL (1 to 3 tbsp.) meat
	Breastmilk, formula, or homogenized milk

Evening:	60 to 90 mL (4 to 6 tbsp.) cereal
	60 to 120 mL (4 to 8 tbsp.) vegetables or fruit
	15 to 45 mL (1 to 3 tbsp.) meat
	Breastmilk, formula, or homogenized milk
Late evening:	Breastmilk, formula, or homogenized milk

Making Your Own Baby Food

Babies eat puréed foods for just a few months, so making your own baby food is more like a brief fling in the kitchen than a labour of love. Sometime between nine and twelve months of age, your baby will be ready to move from puréed to finely chopped foods.

There's a clear cost advantage to making your own baby food, especially if you use local vegetables and fruits in season. The Saskatoon Community Health Unit estimates that homemade baby food costs 30 to 50 per cent less than commercial baby food. By making your own baby food, you can introduce a wider variety of foods than are commercially available. But making baby food is not for everyone. It takes time you may not have. And if it annoys you to have someone spit out the food you've carefully prepared, you're better off serving commercial baby food. Don't worry if you decide not to make your baby's food. Remember, you have eighteen years of feeding to go.

"When you have four kids, you have to cut corners somewhere. I used to make baby food from pumpkins. It was really cheap, and pumpkin has lots of vitamin A. I don't know if people know how easy it is to make baby food."

BETH, MOTHER OF FOUR, SNOW LAKE, MAN.

Home-cooked nutrition

Home preparation gives you complete control over what goes in your baby's mouth. But homemade baby food is only as nutritious as you make it. If you overcook, for example, home-prepared baby food scores fewer nutrients than the baby food you buy in the store. You'll want to use the crispest green beans, the rosiest apples, but what you don't use is equally important. Do not add:

- salt—it can tax your baby's immature kidneys and encourage a taste for salty foods.
- spices or herbs—babies prefer plain food.
- margarine or butter—they're unnecessary.
- sugar, molasses, honey, or corn syrup—sweeteners can lead to dental and weight problems later.

It's especially important not to add corn syrup or honey, including pasteurized honey. They may contain botulism-causing bacteria that pose a serious risk to a baby's immature digestive system. Honey and corn syrup should not be given to infants under age one.

What you need

When you prepare baby food, it's important that your work area and equipment be impeccably clean. Wash your utensils and the washable parts of equipment in hot soapy water, rinse them in your hottest tap water, and air dry. Or wash them in a dishwasher. Before handling food, remember to wash your hands.

You probably already have the equipment you need to make baby food. To make banana baby food, all you need is a fork to mash a banana. Here's how to use other common cooking utensils to make baby food.

➤ If you have a finely meshed sieve and a spoon, you can prepare many fruits and vegetables. First, mash cooked foods with a fork or potato masher and then press through the sieve with a spoon. Mix to desired consistency with water or cooking liquid.

➤ Blenders are excellent for fruits and vegetables, but tend to shred rather than purée meats. Excess exposure to light, heat, and oxygen destroys nutrients, so minimize the blending time. Cut food into small pieces before placing it in the blender, and blend no more than 500 mL (2 cups) of fruit or vegetables at a time, or 250 mL (1 cup) of meat. Add water or cooking liquid, as needed, to make a smooth consistency.

➤ A food processor will purée all foods into a smooth consistency, including most meats.

➤ You can use a manual food grinder to prepare meats as well as fruits and vegetables. A baby-food grinder or mill is inexpensive and useful for single servings. It's also small enough to tuck into your carry bag. Simply put cooked food into the mill and turn the crank. Mix in water or cooking liquid, as needed, for a smooth texture.

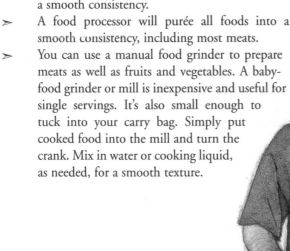

Making vegetable baby food

➤ Choose fresh or unsalted frozen vegetables. Canned vegetables are not recommended because they contain salt.

➤ Good choices for home preparation include peas, green and yellow beans, sweet potatoes, parsnips, white potatoes, asparagus, zucchini, and pumpkin.

➤ You may want to delay introducing spinach, cabbage, beets, broccoli, cauliflower, turnips, squash, and carrots until your baby is at least seven months old. These vegetables contain substantial amounts of nitrate, and nitrates can be toxic in babies because they have difficulty eliminating them. You can reduce the nitrate content when you prepare these vegetables by choosing freshly picked or frozen vegetables and purée the cooked vegetables with fresh water rather than the cooking liquid.

➤ To prepare fresh vegetables, wash them thoroughly before peeling them.

➤ Cook all fresh and frozen vegetables before puréeing or mashing.

➤ To conserve nutrients while cooking, leave food whole, when possible, or cut into large pieces, and have the water boiling before you add the vegetables.

➤ Cook vegetables in a small amount of water and only until tender-crisp. Steaming or microwave cooking are ideal. Cook frozen vegetables without thawing according to package directions, disregarding any seasoning suggestions.

➤ Purée vegetables while they're still hot.

➤ When puréeing, add cooking water (except from nitrate-containing vegetables), if necessary, to make a smooth consistency.

Making fruit baby food

➤ Choose fresh, unsweetened frozen, or dried fruit. Fruits canned in water or fruit juice may also be used. Avoid using fruit canned in syrup with high sugar content.

➤ Good choices for home preparation include apples, pears, bananas, peaches, apricots, plums, prunes, papayas, mangoes, and avocados.

➤ Avoid fruits like strawberries, raspberries, and pineapple because of fibre or seeds.

➤ Wash fresh fruit thoroughly, then peel.

➤ Bananas, papayas, mangoes, and avocados can be served raw. Simply mash with a fork or purée in a blender. If needed, thin with juice or water.

➤ To conserve nutrients while cooking, leave food whole or cut into large pieces. Cook fruit in a small amount of water and only until tender-crisp. Steaming or microwave cooking are ideal. Cook frozen fruit without thawing, according to package directions, disregarding any sweetening suggestions.

➤ Purée the fruit while it's still hot.
➤ When puréeing, add unsweetened fruit juice or cooking water, if necessary, to make smooth consistency.
➤ Cook all other fresh and frozen fruit before puréeing or mashing.
➤ Canned fruits do not require cooking.

Making meat and other protein baby foods

➤ Choose lean cuts, either fresh or frozen.
➤ Good meat choices include chicken, turkey, lamb, beef, pork, liver, and veal.
➤ Good fish choices include halibut, sole, flounder, and haddock.
➤ Legumes and tofu are good alternate protein choices.
➤ Not suitable for babies under one year of age are wieners, sausages, ham, salami, bologna, bacon, corned beef, and canned fish. They contain high amounts of salt, fat, spices, and chemical preservatives in some cases.
➤ Use low-fat cooking methods; either braise, roast, stew, or boil. Avoid frying.
➤ Cut meat into small pieces to decrease processing time.
➤ Purée meat while it's still hot.
➤ Add water or vegetable liquid, if necessary, to create a smooth consistency. If your cooking equipment is unable to grind meat to the desired texture, use the commercially prepared baby food.
➤ To prepare legumes for a baby, cook them well, then press them through a sieve to remove fibrous husks.

Storage of homemade baby food

Once you've made your baby food, serve it immediately or put it into the refrigerator or freezer. Leaving the food at room temperature increases the risk of contamination. If refrigerating it, cover the container with foil, plastic wrap, or a tight-fitting lid. Store it in the refrigerator for no longer than one or two days. If freezing it, you can keep puréed fruits and vegetables for three months, meats for one month. There are two methods of freezing baby food.

Food-cube method

1. Sterilize the utensils.
2. Pour a serving of puréed food into each cube of an ice-cube tray.
3. Cover the tray and put it in the freezer.
4. When the food is frozen, pop the cubes out of the tray and store them in a freezer bag.
5. Prevent the destruction of the vitamins in the food by using a straw to suck as much air as possible out the freezer bag before you seal it.
6. Label and date the bag, and store it in the freezer.

Plop method
1. Sterilize the utensils.
2. Take a spoonful of puréed food and drop or plop it onto a cookie sheet. The size of each plop should be the size of one serving.
3. Cover the plops with plastic wrap and put the cookie sheet in the freezer.
4. When they're frozen, remove the plops and store them in a freezer bag.
5. Prevent the destruction of the vitamins in the food by using a straw to suck as much air as possible out the freezer bag before you seal it.
6. Label and date the bag, and store it in the freezer.

Serving homemade baby food

Serve refrigerated food the same way you serve refrigerated commercial baby food. To serve frozen food, take a serving from the freezer bag just before you're ready to serve it. Thaw and heat it in a double boiler, in a custard cup in hot water, or in the microwave oven. Before serving, stir food well and check its temperature. Never refreeze puréed food once it has thawed.

The Vegetarian Baby

If you are a vegan, offer a variety of foods following Canada's Food Guide to Healthy Eating. Substitute tofu or well-cooked vegetables for meat. The daily diet of your older infant should include:

- ➤ soy formula or milk
- ➤ iron-enriched cereal
- ➤ whole-wheat bread
- ➤ cooked puréed vegetables
- ➤ tofu or tahini (sesame seed paste)
- ➤ fruit

Vitamin and Mineral Supplements

Vitamin D. The vegan's baby needs vitamin D and B_{12} supplements in the dosage recommended by your doctor until at least the child's second birthday. A breast-fed baby should continue with 400 IU of vitamin D daily until she's drinking 200 mL (7 oz.) of formula daily, or until she is between nine and twelve months and drinking 500 mL (2 cups) of milk. Both formula and pasteurized milk have vitamin D added. If your family lives in the Far North and your baby is breast-fed, increase your baby's dosage to 800 IU daily during the winter months. Formula-fed babies in the Far North need 400 IU of vitamin D daily during the winter months.

Iron. If you choose not to breast-feed, the Canadian Paediatric Society recommends you use iron-fortified formula from birth. With formulas or cereals that are iron-fortified, your baby does not need an iron supplement. If you do breast-feed and your baby is not eating iron-fortified cereal or other foods that contribute iron by six months, he is at risk of developing an iron deficiency. If your baby is inactive, pale, irritable, not hungry but overweight or unusually thin, talk with your family physician to determine the cause and whether your baby needs an iron supplement.

Multivitamins. You may be tempted to give your baby a multivitamin to be sure he's receiving all the vitamins he needs, but consult your doctor first. Babies can easily overdose on vitamins. Too much vitamin D can slow your baby's growth and cause malformed bones. Too much vitamin A can cause confusion, liver problems, and vomiting. If a multivitamin is necessary, the Canadian Pharmaceutical Association recommends vitamin drops for children under age three because young children cannot properly chew tablets.

Fluoride. Fluoridated water can reduce children's cavities by 40 to 60 per cent. If your community has fluoridated water, your baby does not need a fluoride supplement. Bottled water usually doesn't contain significant amounts of fluoride. Most home water-filter systems do not affect the fluoride, but the reverse-osmosis filter does remove fluoride.

If you're unsure whether your tap water is fluoridated, contact your municipal office to find out your community's fluoride level. The level of fluoride will be identified in parts per million (ppm).

Chewing a bagel may feel good if she's teething.

Six to Twelve Months

The Fluoride Controversy

If your water supply is not fluoridated, you should consider whether or not to give your baby a fluoride supplement. But the Canadian Dental Association and the Canadian Paediatric Society offer opposing viewpoints, which leaves the choice up to you.

The Canadian Dental Association does not recommend fluoride supplements for children under age 3 in communities with no fluoride in the water supply. One concern is that exposure to more fluoride than is required to prevent cavities can cause fluorosis. Fluorosis causes white flecking on the teeth but is not otherwise considered a health problem. Fluorosis, which can weaken tooth enamel, leaving the teeth susceptible to cavities, is a sign that the child's exposure to fluoride should be reduced.

The Canadian Paediatric Society considers that the advantage of preventing cavities outweighs the risk of developing fluorosis. It recommends that you start fluoride supplements when your baby is six months old if the fluoride level of your water supply is less than 0.3 parts per million (ppm). The chart below shows recommended dosages.

Canadian Paediatric Society Fluoride Guide

Concentration of fluoride in municipal drinking water	< 0.3 ppm	0.3-0.6 ppm	>0.6 ppm
Age of baby	Amount of fluoride supplement needed, per day		
6 months to 3 yrs	0.25 mg	0 mg	0 mg
3 to 6 yrs	0.50 mg	0.25 mg	0 mg
6 to 16 yrs	1.0 mg	0.50 mg	0 mg

To avoid fluorosis, the Canadian Paediatric Society also recommends that children limit the amount of toothpaste per brushing to the size of a pea, that they use toothpaste with fluoride no more than two times per day, and that parents supervise brushing to ensure that toothpaste is spit out and not swallowed.

If you give your baby fluoride drops, chewable tablets, or lozenges, store them in a locked cabinet away from children. Accidental swallowing of 230 to 500 mg of fluoride can be fatal in children.

Commercial Baby Food

You can't beat the convenience of commercial purées. When your baby is hungry, all you have to do is open a jar. Strict regulations ensure that commercial baby foods are preservative-free and high quality. Some companies, by using produce grown through organic farming methods, are reducing pesticide use. Some tips:

➤ Check the expiry date and safety seal.

➤ Read the label. You might choose baby foods without added sugar and starches. You don't want to encourage your child's sweet tooth. Puréed fruits and vegetables without starch contain more vitamins and minerals.

➤ Check the order of ingredients. Ingredients are listed in order of quantity, from the most to the least. The list may offer some surprises. In a jar of bananas, you expect mostly bananas. But the ingredient list may read: *water, bananas, sugar, tapioca starch, orange juice, citric acid,* which means that there's more water than bananas.

➤ Think twice about preserved fruit desserts. They may contain little more than sugar and water.

➤ Junior foods offer food that's large enough to chew, but small enough to swallow whole without causing the baby to choke. Between seven and nine months, it's time to switch your baby from puréed to chunkier foods. If you delay introducing this chunkier texture, your baby may not develop proper chewing skills and may resist more textured foods into toddlerhood.

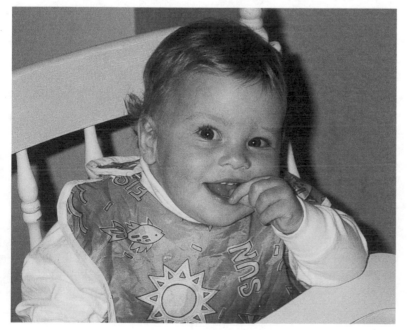

When's lunch?

Premastication

Chewing food in your mouth, then giving it to your baby is a centuries-old tradition practised by some Inuit and Native people. The practice of premasticating food is a convenient and sanitary way to make baby food, according to a brochure by Health Canada and the Tree of Peace Friendship Centre in Yellowknife, N.W.T.

Serving

When you open a new jar of baby food, listen for a pop. If the jar doesn't pop, return it to the store for a refund. Spoon the amount of baby food you need into a serving dish. Recap the jar and refrigerate it. Use refrigerated food within three days. If you know your baby will eat the full contents of one jar, then you can feed directly from the jar. But if you've fed from the jar and there's food remaining, discard it. The baby's saliva, carried on the spoon you use to feed her, will have contaminated the remaining food. Commercial baby food can be served cold, at room temperature, or warmed. To warm baby food, use one of the following heating methods.

A pan of simmering water

1. Bring a small amount of water in a pan to simmering, not boiling.
2. Spoon food into a heat-resistant dish, then place the dish in simmering water until food is warmed.
3. Remove the dish, stir the food, and check its temperature.

A microwave oven

Make the microwave off-limits to occasional baby sitters for heating baby food. They can easily overheat the food and accidentally burn baby's mouth and throat.

1. Not all commercial baby foods are suitable for microwaving. Check the heating instructions on the jar.
2. Do not heat food in the jar. The jar will become burning hot and may shatter. Instead, spoon the food into a microwave-safe dish.
3. Microwave as directed on the jar. Since baby foods can be easily overheated, it's recommended that you remove the dish, stir the food, and check its temperature every five seconds. At Medium, a full jar at room temperature usually takes between 15 and 30 seconds, a half jar from the refrigerator takes between 30 and 45 seconds.

Some baby-food companies offer a 24-hour cross-Canada toll-free service to answer your questions. Check the label on the jar for the appropriate phone number.

Sleeping

Between six and twelve months of age, most babies sleep from 12 to 14 hours within a 24-hour period. By their first birthday, they usually sleep at night for a sustained 10 or 11 hours. All is not completely calm, however, in the Land of Nod; with the onset of separation anxiety around eight months, babies often begin again to waken during the night. The teething process also may disrupt a baby's sleep—and that of her parents. And parents of those babies (about 12 per cent) whose circadian rhythms are not yet stable can expect to hear their baby's crying as often as three or four times a night.

If, as your baby approaches her first birthday, she is still waking for a late evening feeding, you may want to discourage her. She is probably waking more from habit and the expectation of food than from hunger. You can eliminate the feeding by attending to her when she cries, but not picking her up for a feeding. You may also want to feed her more during the day and at bedtime. She will begin to compensate on her own for the loss of her midnight snack by eating more during the day. Expect her to be upset with this change of events for a few nights.

If you prefer to eliminate the feeding more gradually, you might reduce the time she nurses by offering only one breast. If you're bottle-feeding, switch from formula to water. After a few reduced feedings, she may start sleeping through. If she doesn't take the hint and continues to complain, you may have to let her cry until she goes back to sleep. After three or four nights, most babies will sleep through.

> **Avoid a late evening feeding by feeding your baby more during the day.**

Sleep apnea

If your child snores in his sleep, you may want to check with your doctor. Sleep apnea, meaning a temporary stop in breathing, is as common in children as it is in adults, but for different reasons. In children, the apnea is caused by an increase in the size of the lymphoid tissue of the tonsils and adenoids to the point where they obstruct the child's breathing. Children don't generally develop apnea until about the age of three years, but it can happen earlier. Snoring always accompanies this condition, which is treatable by surgery.

The end of the nap

Just before a baby turns one, he's ready to do without one of his regular naps. A few babies give up both naps at about the same time; others still need them for a few months more. Most children give up the morning nap first, keeping the afternoon nap as part of their routine until they are four or five years old. Expect your baby to exhibit some crankiness in the transition period from two naps to one; you may feel a little cranky yourself.

Helping baby sleep

Make bedtime a relaxed and intimate time for you and your baby in order to ease her into sleep. Before you lay her in her crib, spend some wind-down time together. Cuddle up with a picture book or sing some lullabies. Provide some soothing noise, such as a tape recording of lullabies, after you place your baby in her crib. Tuck her in with a familiar blanket or leave a favourite toy with her, then turn out the lights, except the night-light.

"When our first child was born, I used to hold him and walk him around until he fell asleep, and then put him down in his crib. Because this became a habit for him that was difficult to break, we tried a different approach with the next two boys. We placed them in their crib and encouraged them to go to sleep by themselves. Although they yelled a bit for the first couple of nights, they soon realized that they would have to fall asleep by themselves."

COLIN, FATHER OF THREE, SCARBOROUGH, ONT.

Sometimes mom needs a rest as much as her baby does.

Crying

By the age of six months, the majority of babies cry much less often, and when they do it's usually from frustration, helplessness, or anger. Your baby may be unable to pick up the toy that fell from his crib, and he lets you know by crying. Or he can't understand why you stopped him from pulling on a shelf (that happens to be full of canned goods), so he cries.

The best way to deal with his helplessness is to lend a hand before the tears start. Pick up the toy and give it back. To reduce the baby's frustration and anger at being constantly pulled out of dangerous situations, baby-proof your house as much as possible. If you cannot remove the danger in a particular room, move the baby to another room and distract him with something interesting and safe.

At about eight months of age, your son or daughter usually begins to get upset when you go away. This separation anxiety is normal for babies of all cultures. It may even occur at bedtime when your baby bursts into tears when you leave the room.

The best way to deal with baby's helplessness is to lend a hand before the tears start.

The Crying-It-Out Dilemma

Whether or not you respond to the plaintive nighttime cries that break your sleep is up to you. No one can say with authority whether such behaviour spoils a child or encourages an unfortunate habit. You should respond in whatever fashion makes you feel most comfortable. Lots of parents consider the most appropriate approach to be occasional, but strictly controlled, nighttime visits to stroke their child's back, talk comfortingly to her, or sing a song. But they never lift her out of the crib.

If you want a plan for reducing your child's nighttime sleep interruptions, you might try "Ferberizing," named for Dr. Richard Ferber, renowned author of *Solve Your Child's Sleep Problems* and director of the Center for Pediatric Sleep Disorders at the Children's Hospital in Boston. His theory involves a gradual approach to letting the baby settle into sleep on her own.

➤ Decide how long you can tolerate your baby's sustained crying. If it's fifteen minutes, set a first benchmark of five, or even two, minutes.

➤ Put your baby to bed, leave the room, and allow her to cry for the duration of your first benchmark.

> ➤ Return to her briefly and comfort her with words—but don't pick her up.
> ➤ Leave the room while the baby is still awake, whether she's still crying or not.
> ➤ If she continues to cry, return and repeat this reassurance after a longer period of time.
> ➤ Repeat as necessary, always increasing the time you leave her to cry by a couple of minutes. When she reaches your pre-determined crying threshold, leave her to cry until she falls to sleep.
> ➤ If she drifts off to sleep but starts crying an hour or so later, begin again.
> ➤ Your baby should be soothing herself back to sleep with no parental intervention in a few nights.

While it works with many babies, the method is controversial because it means leaving the baby to cry herself to sleep. Some argue that this is damaging to the child, but no one knows for sure. Parents must, of course, consider why the baby may be crying. Perhaps she's teething or she's experiencing separation anxiety. This age is a difficult time for babies, and parents have to be sensitive to these anxieties in assessing whether to respond to the cries. Always listen to the tone of your baby's cry, especially once she's been sleeping through the night on a regular basis. If it sounds urgent or unusually upset, check in on her—there may be good reason for the cry.

Communicating

Baby's first word—that major breakthrough in her progress toward speech—is still weeks or months away. But by six to eight months of age, she learns how to alternate her gaze from your face to an object. This allows her to use unspoken communication to get what she wants. The baby gazes at a toy, then at her mother or father, then back at the toy. The meaning is clear: *I want that.* When the parent responds by handing over the object, there has been an exchange of information. That's real communication.

This is a time when you should be sensitive to your baby's gaze. If the child wants a toy, bring it into the conversation. Describe it. Ask your baby what she thinks about it. At this point your baby is interested in learning more about how language works with objects. Build on words. If a ball catches your infant's eye, you might say, "Look at the ball. It's a blue ball. Look at the big, blue ball." Games and rhymes are ways to expand her listening vocabulary and comprehension of what the words mean.

A baby's understanding of language in the first year is always ahead of her ability to vocalize. As early as six months, an infant is beginning to understand the names of family members. Ask a baby where mommy is, and she will turn and look at her. Your baby's ability to distinguish different types of vocal sounds is also changing.

Research indicates that up to the age of five or six months, infants are good at distinguishing a variety of speech sounds, called *phonemes,* from all languages. But between six and twelve months, they lose the ability to distinguish the phonemes that are not part of their parents' language, the language they hear every day.

> **As early as six months, an infant begins to understand the names of family members.**

During the same period, their vocal ability improves quickly. The next step toward language is a string of cooing sounds, called *babbling.* Some babies start babbling as early as four months, others may not start until eight months or later. Once they discover it, babies appear to play with sounds for the pure joy of sound. When your baby sees you, she will hold "conversations" with you, taking turns babbling and pausing while you respond. She might begin at five months with consonant sounds like *m-m-m* or *b-b-b;* between seven and eight months, she can utter about a dozen different phonemes, mostly simple combinations of consonant and vowel such as *ba* and *ma.*

Babies also begin showing rhythm in their vocalizing between the ninth and twelfth months, and they play with the pitch of a sound, sliding up and down between low and high sounds. Listen to your child when she starts to babble and show her how you enjoy it. You're helping build on your baby's skill at taking turns and this encourages her to try more. The important thing is to provide lots of language stimulation. Studies show that young babies adopted from an institution where they received little stimulation had not developed many language skills. Yet in a new home where they received lots of attention and were exposed to lots of conversation, they made huge advances in a very short time.

About a month after the babbling starts, babies begin experimenting with slightly more complex sounds, using two syllables like *ma-ma, da-da,* and *bye-bye.* Although they may not use them appropriately, the words begin to stand out more from the stream of babbling. By about eight or nine months of age, babies begin to understand the word *No,* a word that will come back to haunt you a few months from now. They understand more complex speech, too, although they cannot yet reproduce it. A nine-month-old can point to the family pet when you ask, "Where's the doggie?" He is also learning to use sound to get his parent's attention. He begins to mix combinations of very different sounds and may use inflection in his voice remarkably like real speech.

Then close to the first birthday, you experience that moment you've been waiting for—the first word. It may not be as clear a sound as you might have expected. It may not sound like the real word, but if he uses it time after time to describe the same thing, it is a word. While your baby may use the word consistently, he may see no point in confining a perfect-ly good word to just one meaning. He could use the same word to describe two or three objects, or apply several names to one object.

Researchers identify the first word as a sound that the child uses consis-tently to refer to a person or object and that he uses in an appropriate way. These early words are almost always "labels" for things around him—people, pets, favourite toys. Within a couple of months either side of his first birth-day, your baby may add two or three more two-syllable words, such as *na-na* for *banana* and *buh-buh* for *baby.* Respond when your baby uses these words and repeat them back—the right way—as part of your conversation. If your baby says *buh-buh,* you might answer, "Yes, look at the *baby*!" This repeated naming of people and objects helps him sort out what the words stand for, even if he can't say them yet.

Talking directly to your child and holding his attention as you speak also helps him develop his imitative abilities and his language skills. This kind of human interactive language is the only effective way of learning language; passive listening to radio or TV does not help a child develop the neural networks that are essential to language development.

While children might utter only a few words, their understanding of words is advancing at a great pace. Take the opportunity to talk about what your baby is looking at and what appears to interest him. As with all aspects of development, don't be alarmed if your child doesn't speak as much or as often as some children—they all progress at their own speed and their language accomplishments may vary by a year or more. But by twelve months, your baby may say eight or ten words, including his own name.

Forget the Flash Cards

A popular theory of some years ago was that a parent could speed up a child's comprehension and encourage other early reading skills by using vocabulary flash cards as soon as the baby could sit up and focus. The idea has since been discounted by most linguists as a waste of time. Babies don't learn language out of context by memorizing words one at a time; they learn language as part of their play and their interactions with others.

Parents help babies learn words and how they work together in sentences and questions by modelling how language works—in their daily conversational exchanges between themselves or with the baby. If parents are sensitive to the baby's needs and surround him with purposeful language just slightly ahead of his ability, they "pull" him along more quickly than any set of vocabulary flash cards.

Basic Care

Your baby's increasing mobility will affect his day-to-day care in several ways. Dress him for maximum freedom of movement and speed, and since your baby will spend much of his time investigating the world at floor level, pay extra attention to the cleanliness of his area of exploration, of the toys that he loves to put in his mouth, and his hands that constantly move toward his mouth

Teething

Each baby's experience of teething, and therefore her parents' experience of it, follows an individual pattern. Some babies sail through teething, others suffer with every eruption. For some babies, gums are red and swollen for weeks before any tooth appears; for others, parents discover their baby has produced a tiny new tooth without any prior fussing. On average, a baby's first teeth appear around his sixth month, but some get their baby teeth as early as three months or as late as twelve months of age. If you or your partner were an early teether, your child may follow the same pattern.

Emergence pattern

Babies are born with a full complement of 20 primary teeth below the SEE PAGE 159 gums, which push through in a fairly predictable pattern. The first teeth to appear are usually the lower central incisors. Next come the upper central incisors, and then the lateral incisors, the teeth that flank the front teeth, on the top and bottom. After that, babies typically skip a spot and move on

If you or your partner
were an early teether,
your child may follow
the same pattern.

to their first molars, upper and lower, between 14 and 18 months. The canines fill in the space a few months later and the second molars finish the set some time between the child's second and third birthdays.

Relieving the pain

Although no one has been able to measure just how painful teething is, it's clear from their behaviour that the discomfort of teething can make some babies really miserable. The two best solutions are counter-pressure and the application of cold. Teethers help; so does your finger for baby to chew on and for rubbing his gums. For cold relief, offer safe sizes of frozen vegetables to chew on, chilled puréed fruit, or a cold wash cloth. A frozen teething ring combines the two kinds of relief. For safety reasons, never tie a teether on a string around a baby's neck.

When nothing else works, try acetaminophen. Avoid over-the-counter numbing gels. They may numb the tongue as well as the gums and interfere with baby's swallowing. Their effect is short-lived, leading to overuse and serious side effects: when the gel is absorbed into the bloodstream, it can cause methemoglobinemia, a change in the oxygen-carrying capacity of the blood.

Can you blame it on the teeth?

Although parents connect a variety of symptoms to the arrival of a tooth, doctors are often reluctant to attribute a rash or loose bowels or irritability to teething for the very good reason that this "diagnosis" could mask other health concerns that might need attention. Many an ear tug that was originally attributed to teething ended up actually being an ear infection. You'll get to know your baby's teething pattern and be a good judge of when a symptom relates to teething or when it needs further investigation by your doctor.

EMERGENCE
PATTERN

Signs of Teething

Drooling from increased saliva production.

Face rash caused by drooling. Pat off the drool—don't rub it. Also, lubricate the irritated area with a mild cream.

Throat-clearing, again from increased saliva.

Chewing. A teething baby will bite down on any hard surface—a table edge, crib rail, books, toys, or teethers— for some relief. A baby may massage his gums with his tongue, fingers, and fist. Occasionally he'll bite down while nursing, which requires a prompt *No*.

Irritability.

Indications of pain, such as sharp crying, rubbing his face.

Diarrhea. Parents often notice looser bowel movements when babies are teething, but doctors are reluctant to assume a connection for fear of missing a more serious diagnosis for which diarrhea is a symptom.

Low-grade fever. Inflammation of the gums can sometimes result in a low-grade fever. Teething rarely causes a fever higher than 38°C (100.4°F).

Reluctance to feed. Suckling puts pressure on swollen gums. If your baby takes to the breast eagerly only to pull away in pain, the onset of teeth may be the cause.

Wakefulness. If your baby is showing signs of teething during the day, expect some disruption in his sleep at night, even if he was previously a steady sleeper.

Ear pulling. The gums share nerve centres with the ears and cheeks— a baby may indicate discomfort in her gums by grabbing at her ear.

Central Incisors
6-8 months

Lateral Incisiors
8-10 months

Canines & First Molars
12-14 months

Keeping Clean

Babies are messy creatures, and the messier your baby is, the more likely she is to be learning and developing. Her constant dribbling is a sign that she's getting her teeth. Her mucky face is testament to her new-found ability to put food into her own mouth. Try to think of mess as your baby's badge of honour: It means she's learning life's lessons. To make life easier on you while she learns, here are some suggestions:

➤ Always have a spare set of clothes and an extra bib with you.

➤ Keep a cloth bib on a teething baby.

Second Molars
24-30 months

> ➤ Buy several large, soft plastic bibs with a lip at the bottom to catch the dribbles.

> ➤ Put newspaper under baby's highchair, then just gather it up and throw it away at the end of the meal.

> ➤ Don't leave baby alone with a bowl full of mush unless you are prepared to clean it up when it is hurled from the highchair.

This age is a good time to begin modelling hand-washing habits. Wash your child's hands after meals and after she has played with any household pets or has crawled around outside. Since babies often explore their genitals at change time, wash your baby's hands when you wash your own hands after a diaper change. Disinfect the changing pad at least once a week.

Some kids need encouragement to enjoy preparations for bathtime.

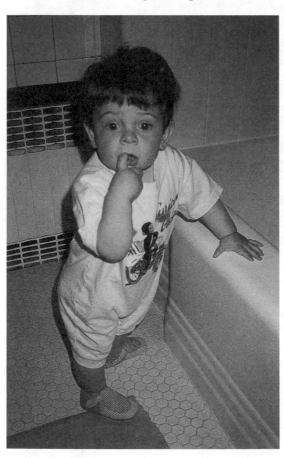

Bathing

Once your baby no longer sits still where you put her, you'll have to establish firm rules around bathtime. Of course, you must continue to supervise her baths, but you should stress that standing and other antics aren't allowed in the bath. Sit her back down and tell her a firm *No!* Then distract her with a toy. She will probably enjoy playing with empty plastic tubs or other fill-and-float toys. If she slips about in the tub as she reaches for her toys, try sitting her on a facecloth or a non-slip mat.

Dressing

Many vigorous crawlers, especially those babies who perform a kind of commando-crawl using their upper bodies, actually wiggle themselves right out of their clothing. Overalls are the best for babies on the move. The shoulder straps keep everything in place, and the reinforced knees hold up well, considering the friction they endure. Shirts with a crotch are also helpful.

"When my children were learning how to walk, they hated wearing shoes. Eventually I gave up the battle, and just let them wear little padded slippers when they were outside or if it was particularly cold. I think they liked being able to feel the floor with their feet."

TERESA, MOTHER OF THREE, B.C.

Your baby does not need to wear shoes at this stage. In fact, she would probably feel most confident in bare feet or wearing non-skid socks. She might wear non-skid socks or soft booties to protect against the cold, or light sneakers for moving around on smooth surfaces. The shoes she wears at this age will not affect the development of her feet.

Visiting the Doctor

In the second six months, your doctor will continue to check whether your baby is growing normally, and that she shows no physical abnormalities. In addition, the doctor will assess whether your child meets certain developmental milestones: reaching, imitating, listening, and laughing. This is also a critical time for identifying any serious problems within the parent-child relationship.

"The first time my little girl had a fever, I was terrified. She was suddenly so listless and she wouldn't nurse. My doctor was very reassuring, and I just gave her some acetaminophen and in a day she was fine again. Now I've learned that when she goes off her food or gets very quiet she is probably getting sick, and I bundle her into bed."

JULIE, MOTHER OF TWO, BOWEN ISLAND, B.C.

During this period, your child may experience her first cold or flu, and you may wonder whether or not it's necessary to visit the doctor. Doctors agree that parents may seek medical attention too soon, and that 95 per cent of symptoms will resolve themselves within a few days. If your child has a temperature of about 38.5ºC (101.3ºF) by rectal thermometer, and if she has been exposed to other children with temperatures, observe her closely for a change in behaviour so you can report her symptoms accurately to your doctor. Has she stopped eating? Is she irritable or sleepy? Does she have trouble breathing, or is she breathing fast? Is she drooling?

Fever is a protective mechanism, so fever and a change in behaviour are SEE PAGE 284 reliable signs of illness. Call your doctor immediately if your child's fever persists and is accompanied by changes in behaviour, if she exhibits tremors, if she becomes extremely lethargic, or if she has a rash.

Taking the temperature

A fever is indicated by one of the following:
- ➤ a rectal temperature equal to or higher than 38.5°C (101.3°F).
- ➤ an oral/tympanic temperature equal to or higher than 38°C (100.4°F).
- ➤ an axillary (in the armpit) temperature equal to or higher than 38°C (100.4°F).

Mobility and Physical Skills

Sitting

Babies learn to control the muscles in the upper half of their bodies well before they learn to control those in the lower half. At about six months of age, your baby will begin learning to control her hips, knees, legs, and feet; she'll begin to sit up without support, but only for a few seconds. Gradually, she will learn to balance herself, and you can help her practise this balancing skill in a variety of ways.

Put her in a sitting position with cushions or pillows around her to provide a little support so she can sit and learn to balance herself for longer periods. When she starts wobbling, she'll fall comfortably into the soft pillows rather than on to a hard floor. When playing with your baby on the floor, sit her facing you between your outstretched legs so she can grab on to them for support. Place toys in front of her so she will reach for them and eventually develop the muscles that help her balance herself without using her hands as props for support.

As your baby learns to sit without support, she will be able to use her hands more freely to gesture and to play with toys on her own. Once she can sit and play alone, she gains some independence. But she will need help to get into a sitting position at first. Soon she will reach to you with her hands, signalling that she wants you to pull her up. Then she'll try to use furniture and other supports as a handle to help her sit up.

Being able to sit up alone is an important stage in a baby's development of physical skills.

Safety is important at this stage, and the safest, most comfortable place for sitting practice is a well-padded floor. If you sit your baby on an armchair, sofa, or bed, you'll have to keep constant watch that she doesn't tumble down to the floor. As your baby becomes strong enough to sit alone, she will begin to lunge forward to reach nearby toys or other objects of interest. Encourage this lunging forward by placing a toy in front of the baby just out of her reach. Lunging forward is a physical skill that leads to crawling on her tummy, then creeping forward on hands and knees.

Crawling

Crawling around on their tummies is a first means of locomotion for many babies. Once they begin to roll over at about six months, they rock back and forth on their tummies in the crawling position, but don't make much progress forward at first. It takes more activity and muscle-building before your baby begins to use his hands, arms, and knees to move forward, and he may have trouble moving in the right direction at first.

Their style is less important than the physical effort they expend and the experience they gain in doing so. Some babies start by crawling backwards or sideways, before moving forward. Some slither on their stomachs, others use their arms, hands, and feet, with their bottoms and knees raised. They begin to scoot about on one knee and drag the other leg behind—which leads to creeping.

Some babies never crawl at all—crawling and creeping are not skills that are predictable stages in every child's development. It's important, however, to encourage your baby and give him ample opportunity to move around and explore the world, using whatever styles of locomotion work for him. You can encourage your baby to crawl by placing toys or other interesting objects just beyond his reach. As he becomes more adept, create obstacle courses for him to crawl through and over, using pillows, sofa cushions, or a foam rubber roll. Hide behind the obstacles and play Peekaboo to pique his interest even more.

Give your baby lots of supervised time on the floor so that he has the opportunity to move and explore. Cover his knees so that his skin won't chafe or get sore, which could be uncomfortable and discourage him from crawling more. Be alert to the danger that your baby might tip or pull over a chair or his carriage. He should wear a safety harness when you put him into a highchair, carriage, stroller, or car seat.

Crawling opens up a new social skill for your baby because he can now come to you. He doesn't have to wait for you to come to him. Crawling means that your baby takes a more active role in exploring the world. He also develops his problem-solving skills by trying various styles of crawling or other methods of locomotion to get where he wants to go or reach the thing that interests him.

After your baby can comfortably crawl forward, he may begin crawling upward too. He will enjoy climbing over pillows, cushions, or furniture, and up stairs under your watchful eye. This can be a nerve-wracking time for parents. You'll need to help him get back down the stairs at first, and teach him to back down step by step rather than to crawl down face forward. He may use another method altogether for getting around or learn to pull himself up and begin standing, then cruising (standing and moving while holding on to items for support), and eventually walking.

Creeping on hands and knees opens up a new social skill. Your baby can now come to you.

Learning to Stand

When you hold your baby in a standing position on your lap, she won't be able to support herself until about seven months. But she will enjoy "stepping" and bending her knees and bouncing up and down while you hold her securely. As she gains strength in her legs and hips from this and other practice, she will soon stand for a few seconds on her own when you pull her up to a standing position. Between nine and twelve months, she will begin to pull herself up by using furniture, rails, the bars of a playpen, or your clothes. Encourage her by putting a toy on a sofa or low table where she will have to stand up to get it.

Teach your baby to use her feet as a firm base of support. If the feet are turned in, gently turn them out so she can plant herself more firmly. If your baby falls easily, support her legs by placing your hands behind her knees. Once your baby can pull herself up to stand, she may hold on to the furniture or another support to stay standing and look around for a while.

Once he gains confidence from standing and holding on, he won't be long in taking that first step.

Although your baby may enjoy pulling herself up, standing and looking around, she won't know at first how to sit down and will take quite a few falls. Or she might cry for you to come and rescue her. You can help her learn how to sit down by lowering her body gradually to the floor. She will eventually learn to let go of the furniture and use her hands to help her sit down. Take care that she doesn't lose confidence or hurt herself.

As your baby learns to stand holding on to your leg, you will gradually feel less of the baby's weight as she provides more of her own support. Once she is comfortable pulling herself up, standing and looking, she'll inevitably want to begin moving around. She'll begin cruising by inching her way along a sofa or another piece of furniture, holding on for support. At first, she may cruise in a sideways, tentative fashion, moving both hands together, clinging for support. But with practice, she will gain confidence and cruise along faster, moving hand over hand. She'll soon discover that her legs can bear her whole weight, and she'll rely less and less on her hands for support. At some point in her cruising adventures, your baby will let go for a few moments, stand freely, and take those first unsupported steps. These are tremendously exciting developments and a cause for great family celebration.

It's easiest for your baby to balance herself using her bare feet. Shoes can be awkward and socks can make hard floors slippery and treacherous. Once a baby can stand and cruise, she'll be eager to stand and play. Put some of her favourite toys just out of reach to encourage this. But remember that a cruising baby is likely to reach and grab for any object en route. Be sure to babyproof your rooms—remove light, flimsy furniture that won't support her or could topple over on her; cover the sharp corners on furniture you can't remove. Put out of reach any breakable objects and the electric cords for table lamps, telephones, and similar items.

As your baby makes progress toward walking, you'll be excited and want to encourage her. Just remember to allow her to progress at her own pace. About half of babies walk by the time they are one year old, but there is great variation in the age range. Some babies start as early as nine months, others may not walk until they are nineteen months old.

How quickly a baby moves through the sequence of standing, cruising, and walking without support depends on many factors: the baby's self-confidence, motivation, muscle strength and physical coordination, opportunity, and genes. Hurrying a baby on to the next milestone can damage his self-confidence and slow his development. Of course, once your baby is walking, your initial excitement may be tempered by the necessity of keeping up with a fully mobile toddler.

Be Wary of Walkers

Concern about incidents with walkers led Health Canada to introduce a voluntary standard in 1989. Since no walkers with wheels met the standards, distributors took them off the market. Today, stores sell activity bouncers or rockers with no wheels that allow babies to stand and hold on and, thus, exercise their legs but stay in one place.

However, parents can still buy walkers with wheels in the U.S. and at yard sales, so injuries still occur. The most common and the most serious injuries in wheeled walkers involve the baby toppling down a flight of stairs. A baby in a wheeled walker may pick up enough speed to crash through a safety gate. He can easily trip over toys, loose rugs, and other objects in the way.

For developmental reasons, walkers have some drawbacks. Research shows that the babies who spend a lot of time in walkers show delays in learning how to walk correctly. A baby needs to develop muscles in the legs and hips through her own efforts, and practise the many body movements and skills, like balancing and falling, that are needed for walking. Crawling and cruising prepare your baby for her first unsupported steps and walking. Too much time in a walker limits this kind of exploration.

Playing and Learning

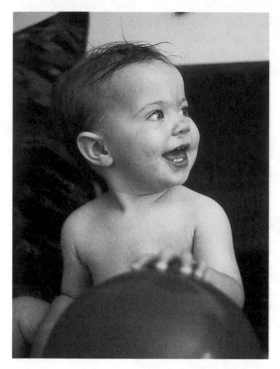

By the age of six months, your baby also begins to use his arms, hands, and fingers to grab, feel, and manipulate objects in ways other than by putting them in his mouth. He sometimes uses his hands to feel the texture of a carpet, blanket, highchair, or even your hair. He will begin to differentiate his arms, hands, and fingers, and then learn to use his fingers and thumbs separately. Give your baby lots of opportunity to handle many different types of objects. This type of play will be tremendously stimulating and help him to learn many different hand skills over the next six months.

At first, your baby will pick up objects by using his whole hand as a scoop. But by seven to eight months, he will begin to use his fingers and thumbs to pick up and hold on to objects very tightly. He still has to learn to relax his fingers to release the objects. Once he does learn, he'll love to practise his new accomplishment by relaxing his fingers to drop objects off his highchair or out of his crib. Of course, then he'll need to have the object back. You may feel as if you are the pet dog in a prolonged game of Fetch.

A safe open place with simple toys encourages play.

SEE PAGE 181

When he begins to use his thumb and index finger in a pincer grip to pick up small objects, usually about eleven to twelve months, you will know he has reached a key milestone. Another major advance he makes during this period is to begin using his index finger rather than his hand and arm to point at things. As soon as your baby is ready to begin moving around on his own, set up a safe and open space for him to play with toys and other items that give him opportunities to develop fine motor skills with fingers, thumbs, and hands.

Games

Once your baby can crawl, she will enjoy balls and toys with wheels, which she can push, handle, and crawl after. Once she learns to let go of objects, she'll be able to throw balls and other toys too. Soft foam or cloth balls are best so your baby can get a good grip on them.

Playing with blocks is great for developing hand skills and for learning all about different sizes and shapes. As your baby learns to transfer blocks and other toys from hand to hand, this shuffling back and forth becomes part of play and extends the length of her playtime. Give her an object, hold out your hand, and then ask for it back. Once she catches on, she'll want to keep doing this time and again.

Toy telephones are very popular with this age group. She will enjoy removing and replacing the receiver, and pulling the phone around by the cord. She will have fun pushing buttons and hearing the noises that her actions produce.

Thinking and Knowing

When you encourage your baby to explore the world through body movement and touch, you stimulate his mind, too. He learns the properties of various objects, how his body works, and how his actions have an impact on his immediate environment.

During this period, your baby begins to form mental pictures, associations, and memories. As you point to and label familiar objects in his life—pets, furniture, people, and toys—he'll start to recognize the words and make connections. He'll also associate certain cue words like *Go!* with actions like crawling forward. This evidence that he is developing listening skills and connecting words with objects and actions represents the major advances in his mental development.

He also begins to develop the concept of object permanence. Previously, when you hid a toy, he would forget all about it. Now you can interest him in playing a game to find the missing toy. Hide a toy under a blanket, and watch him delight in pulling off the blanket and finding the toy. Play Hide-and-seek by bobbing your head behind a piece of furniture or a blanket. Peekaboo is the classic game for teaching object permanence.

Finger games like This Little Piggy and The Itsy Bitsy Spider will continue to entertain your baby and teach her how to connect words and actions. Pop-up toys delight babies at this stage. By simply pressing her finger, she can make exciting things happen. Musical toys, like a music box, a drum to bang, or maracas to shake, are great fun and show her how she can make things start and stop. Toys on strings are entertaining and she will learn how to make toys come to her. Toys that make noise or move when she pushes or pulls, give your child a sense of her own power over objects and show her that her actions have an impact.

> **Pop-up toys delight babies. By simply pressing her finger, she makes exciting things happen.**

Your baby may be able to start colouring with a fat crayon by the end of her first year. Take a crayon yourself and draw on paper, then give your baby a crayon so she can colour, too, by imitating you.

Parent as Playmate

In these six months, your baby develops some physical independence, but with it comes a growing emotional attachment and dependence. As she plays and learns many new skills, she needs your constant encouragement and support. Her ability to communicate with you grows, too, as she begins using language, making meaningful gestures, understanding and responding to some of what you're saying.

Your baby may tell you when she wants to play by her body language. She may smile, wave her arms or open them wide, and turn toward you

as a signal that she's ready to play. Help your baby to increase her vocabulary of words that she understands, even if she's not able to say them for months. Talk to her while you're playing together, pointing to and naming items and actions, and explaining what you're doing. Play talking games with her, too. Sit across from one another and point to your nose, her nose, daddy's nose, eyes, hands, feet, and other body parts. Your baby will also love to copy simple gestures, like clapping or waving, and eventually simple words like *Bye-bye*.

Sometimes play can be very serious business.

Your baby will enjoy reading books with you at this stage. Talk about the pictures, adding details to the story, and she'll begin to associate them with the objects they represent. She'll enjoy opening up books herself and turning pages, or playing with glossy magazines when you've finished them—or before.

You may discover that, once your baby starts to exhibit separation anxiety, she'll cry whenever you leave the room or move out of her sight, no matter how intently she had been playing. Even if you aren't actually playing with her, your presence is essential for her to enjoy playing and exploring independently. As long as she is in a secure emotional environment, playing helps her become more independent and show more initiative over time.

When your baby can see you while she is crawling and playing, she will explore more confidently, comfortably, and freely. As you move around the room, she'll crawl after you. When you go into another room, take her with you so she can continue to play and not miss you. If you have to move out of her sight, speak to her so that she can still hear you.

What Goes in Must Come out

Emptying things out of cupboards, containers, and drawers is a big hit with most babies at this age. He'll love taking things out of waste baskets, toy boxes, or your pockets. Set aside an open box or cupboard with items he can safely empty out and explore. Babies usually enjoy examining, shaking, and feeling each object, banging it on the floor or against another object, discarding it, and then moving on to the next plaything. You might put items in an old purse, a box, or a paper bag. Keep his interest up by changing the items and storage places regularly.

Kids of this age love pouring water into and out of cups, plastic jugs, or toy teapots—try it in the bathtub first. As their hand skills improve, they might enjoy a set of stacking cups to learn how to fit the cups on top and inside of each other.

"I've been reading to Georgia since she was six months old. She'll sit and turn pages. If she sees the book's upside down, she'll look and turn the book over so that it's right side up."

SUSAN, MOTHER OF THREE, TORONTO, ONT.

Keeping Your Baby Safe

As your baby begins to grope, pull, and wiggle her way through the house, you need to stay a couple of moves ahead of her, anticipating danger and moving offending objects out of the way. To make your job of supervision easier, eliminate anything that she might pull down on herself or pop into her mouth.

The first thing to do is to get down on your hands and knees or lie on your back and look at the world from your baby's perspective to see what might attract her interest. You'll be surprised at how many dangling cords you'll see—from lamps, irons, kettles, and telephones. If you study the floor or the carpet up close the way your baby will, you'll notice tiny items—a straight pin, a lost button, a pen cap—that the vacuum cleaner missed. Start now to childproof your home to protect your baby and to give her as much freedom of movement as possible.

SEE PAGE 190

Protect the Crawling Baby

➤ Push table lamps or table-top telephones to the back of the table. Twirl the lamp cord around the table leg and plug it into the socket.

➤ Cover all electric outlets with outlet covers made of strong plastic. Be aware that the prongs on inexpensive or old covers can break and become a choking hazard. Let baby know not to touch outlets, even when covered. Not every place he visits will have covered outlets.

➤ Tie up cords of window coverings. Buy a commercial shortener or wind the cord around hooks attached high on the window frame.

➤ Put away the long tablecloths that can be pulled down along with whatever is on the table. Use place mats instead.

➤ Avoid using corner guards on coffee tables or other low furniture; some don't adhere well and can become a choking hazard. Choose elasticized corner pads or remove the offending furniture.

➤ Install safety latches on cupboards and drawers.

➤ Put an out-of-reach latch on the outside of bathroom doors.

➤ Use safety gates, but don't rely on them alone, in case they are left open at some point. Use safety gates that can be bolted into place at the top of stairs; the pressure-mounted ones are also popular and convenient, but neither type should have toe holds that a child could use to climb over.

➤ As soon as your baby can go up the stairs, teach him to turn around and go down stairs feet first. Take him to the top of the stairs, physically lift him and turn him around on the top step. As you back down, pull one of his legs down, then the other until he gets the pattern. When he's ready to learn to go down frontward, stand behind him to steady him as he holds on and goes down the steps on his own. Practise this over and over.

➤ Never lift a child by pulling on his arms. You might dislocate his elbow or shoulder.

➤ Choose only toys recommended for a child the age of yours; keep them in an open toy box without a lid.

➤ Teach older siblings not to share the toys that are too small for baby and could cause him to choke.

➤ Choose a playpen that meets current safety regulations as a safe haven for your baby when you're called away. Look for one that's portable and has a thick floor pad and rigid side rails.

➤ Make sure all windows are lockable, and don't rely on window screens to prevent a child from falling out.

➤ Cover balcony railings with netting so that your baby can't wedge his head between the bars.

"What do you do with a five-year-old who leaves the gate open? We tried bribery, praise, rewards—you name it. Finally we realized that the only way to keep her seven-month-old sister safe was to teach her to turn around at the top of the stairs. It worked."

HEIDI, MOTHER OF THREE, WATERDOWN, ONT.

A playpen can be a safe haven from which to view the world.

Thriving As a Family

Around their child's sixth month, new parents usually take a deep breath and reflect upon who they were before the baby exploded into their lives and who they've become since. The most difficult period of adjustment is over.

For many parents, this is the time they remember why they fell in love with their partner in the first place. They turn again to some of the interests they used to share. They try a nighttime baby sitter. If your baby's sleeping through the night, she won't even notice that you're gone. It's important for parents to re-connect. New moms and dads who have become too focused on their baby risk losing touch with each other altogether—which is not beneficial to any family relationship. You've grown and changed from the people you were before you became parents. If you don't reintroduce yourselves, you may become strangers who just happen to share a bathroom.

> **After six months, the most difficult period of adjustment for new parents is over.**

It's ironic that the most important thing you can do for your child is to maintain a strong relationship. Although it's harder to find time, it's as important to carve out time for yourselves as a couple as it is to devote time to your child. Parents who exhibit their love for each other, who talk through issues, who pull together in hard times, and who role-model the importance of individual relationships within a group relationship provide a strong family framework for their children.

Finding Time for Each Other

Once you acknowledge that your marriage is a priority, you'll find it easier to justify planning time together. Some suggestions:

- ➤ Schedule a regular date night, even if it's just an hour for a walk and a cup of coffee.
- ➤ Build up a roster of reliable baby sitters, or join a baby-sitting co-op.
- ➤ Plan a weekend away once a year or even once every six months. If money is tight, arrange a house exchange with another couple. They come and stay at your place with the kids. You stay at their place, kid-free.

"When our daughter was eight months old and her cousin was about fourteen months, my sister gave us a weekend to ourselves. She and her husband came and stayed at our place with both kids, and my husband and I stayed at their house. They had put all the toys away and left us a nice bottle of wine. It was great—especially since we weren't in our own place where we might have been tempted to do chores instead of focus on each other. Our families ended up doing these exchanges for years."

CHRISTINE, MOTHER OF TWO, TORONTO, ONT.

Now is the time to reintroduce your-selves. Otherwise you risk becoming strangers who happen to share a bathroom.

A Baby's Point of View

Exploration is my mission now. With your loving attention and encouragement, I will touch, smell, mouth, crawl around, and eventually walk across my world.

My Body

- My back is getting stronger. Between six and nine months, I start to sit unsupported for brief periods.

- I might try rocking while I sit, and I'll probably fall over. I'm testing my balance.

- When awake and on my tummy, I start to "airplane"—I fling out my arms and legs and try to move.

- Sometime between seven and twelve months, I start to crawl on my belly, then creep. Since my upper body is stronger than my legs, I might push off and find myself going backward.

- I might scoot around on hands and knees, or on two hands, a knee, and a foot, or by bouncing along on my bottom. Or I might skip the creeping stage altogether and go straight to standing and cruising or walking.

- Using the furniture, I pull myself to my feet. I might cruise from chair to couch, holding on most of the time. If I can't sit down easily, I'll either collapse or stand there and cry till you help me.

- Once I've learned to stand, I'm better in bare feet or nonslip socks than in shoes. I need to feel the floor with my feet in order to balance.

- Even before I'm walking, you have to watch me all the time. I can still risk a bad fall by crawling upstairs, trying to crawl downstairs, or climbing onto a coffee table.

- I might be walking by myself at nine months or wait until I'm closer to sixteen months.

- I use my index finger to point. Watch me, because I might try to stick it in an electric outlet.

- I can drink from a two-handled cup with a lid, using both hands.

- I may have only two baby teeth or as many as eight. Just because I have teeth doesn't mean I should stop breast-feeding—I learn quickly not to bite.

- I'm eating a variety of solid foods, but breastmilk (or formula) is still the main part of my diet.

- I use my mouth to explore the world. By feeling things with my sensitive lips and tongue, I learn about shapes, textures, and sizes.

- I can bring my hands together. I might clap my hands or bang two blocks.

- I throw things like food, utensils, and toys to practise the art of uncurling my fingers and letting go with my hand. I work on this skill by continually dropping things on purpose out of my highchair or stroller.

- I like to hold an object in my hand, or maybe one in each hand. I don't want to let them go even when I'm crawling.

- My thumb now works separately from my fingers, so I can pick up tiny objects like a crumb. Make sure there's nothing dangerous like a staple or pin on the floor, because I'll put it in my mouth.

- I might pull off my socks or hat, just to show you I can do it.

- By twelve months, I've tripled my birth weight and grown to one and a half times my birth length.

My Feelings

- My new mobility excites me but also scares me. I'm fearful of my growing independence, since it means I can move away from you.

- I need you near me all the time. I might panic when you're out of sight, even if you're just in the next room.

- Now that I'm developing depth perception, I may begin to fear heights. Even if I've climbed up on a chair dozens of times, I may suddenly find myself frozen on it, too frightened to move.

- Starting around eight months, I become fearful of strangers. I'm very choosy about who picks me up.

- I'm becoming more sensitive to other children. If they cry, I might cry, too.

- I express many emotions through my moods. You'll know when I'm happy, sad, hurt, or angry.

- I'm also learning to recognize your emotions. I can tell the difference between friendly talking and angry talking.

- Sometimes I get so excited that I squeal with anticipation and pleasure.

- As a result of my new fears, I may have trouble sleeping, even if I've been a good sleeper in the past. To ease my tensions and help me relax, I may have to rock on my hands and knees (I might do it vigorously enough to move my crib across the room), bang my head (it won't do any permanent damage), or fondle my genitals.

- If I don't want a particular toy or food, I'll show my displeasure by pushing it away or spitting it out.

- I develop strong taste preferences. I know what I like.

- I get very excited by the various sounds I can make with my voice.

- Things that didn't bother me before may frighten me now: the bath, the vacuum cleaner, the sound of the toilet flushing.

My Feelings, continued

- I become angry if you take away a toy.

- I'm affectionate with you and other people I know well. I demand that you stay close.

- If you put me in a playpen or baby seat when I'd rather be on the move, I'll loudly protest my frustration at being confined.

- I might show jealousy if you pick up another child. I need constant reassurance that you'll always be there for me.

- More and more, I enjoy seeing myself in the mirror. I smile delightedly and pat my reflection, and might try to kiss it. I'm thrilled by my growing awareness of myself.

- I'm happy when I get your approval and unhappy when I sense your disapproval. Toward the end of my first year, I start to feel the new emotion of guilt over something I've done that displeases you.

- Because of my anxieties about my rapid progress in becoming mobile, I might regress to an earlier stage. If I've been walking, I might suddenly go back to crawling until I get my confidence back.

My Mind

- I know my name. When you call me, I look up or turn around.

- My memory is improving by leaps and bounds, especially around eight months. I recognize familiar songs and rhymes.

- I understand that even when things are out of my sight they still exist. So if you take the pencil out of my hand and hide it, then I'll protest because I know it hasn't vanished altogether but is somewhere else.

- I understand simple questions. If you say, "Where's the kitty?" I'll turn around to try to find him, even if he's out of the room.

- I'm starting to pick up cues. When you put on your coat, I'll burst into tears because I know that means you're going out and leaving me. When you put my coat on me, I'm happy because I know that means we're going out together.

- I concentrate so hard when I'm learning a new skill that I might temporarily forget an old one. While I'm busy learning how to throw things off my highchair tray, I might forget how to use a cup.

- I can imitate simple games like Peekaboo. I know now that when I cover my eyes and I can't see you, you're not really gone.

My Mind, continued

- I like to sit in your lap and look at simple books with clear, colourful pictures while you tell me about them. I'll try turning the pages, but I usually can't turn just one at a time.

- When it's time for you to wash me up after meals, I anticipate the action by holding my hands out for you. I usually hate having my face washed, though.

- By eight or nine months, I imitate your speech sounds. I pay closer attention to your conversations with other adults.

- Between eight and twelve months, I may start to say up to ten words with meaning, like *ma-ma* or *cookie*. Or I may not have any real words yet. Still, I enjoy stringing together sounds like *lo-lo-dee-ma-da*.

- I listen closely to songs you sing to me, and I'm an active participant in finger games. I concentrate intently on certain toys, as if I'm trying to figure out how the wheels turn or the pieces fit together.

- As my concentration improves, I'm harder and harder to distract. By nine or ten months, I can be quite persistent.

- As my eyesight gets better and better, I stare at things I'm otherwise familiar with, like your face.

- If I'm fussy and you don't know why, it might be because whatever you're doing is something I'd like to try myself. I might cry when you feed me even though I'm hungry, because I want to try using the spoon myself.

- I tend to favour one hand over the other.

- I'm starting to understand the concepts of *in, out, up,* and *down*. I love putting objects in a container one by one, such as blocks in a cup, then dumping them out.

- By the end of my first year, I can build a tower of two blocks after you show me how, and stack and nest a few beakers with your help.

- I understand far more than I can express. If you ask me, "Where's the airplane?" I'll look up. If you ask, "What does the doggie say?" I'll attempt to bark. I understand *No!*

My World

- You're so important to me that I don't like to share you with anyone.

- When I start to crawl, I gradually become aware that I'm moving away from you. I turn around and check often to make sure you're near.

- Instead of always crying when I want you to notice me, I try to grab your attention by shouting or coughing.

- I try to be sociable using shrieks and grunts, and I mimic your facial expressions.

- I use more and more inflection and expression in my sounds. I might say, "Ah-me-ba?" as though I'm really asking you a question. Talk to me as though we're having a real conversation.

- I begin to experience separation anxiety. Don't hurry me into new situations.

- I'm afraid of strangers. I might accept them in a casual way as long as they don't get too close to me and you're right there every second.

- I'm eager to share with you every new skill I learn. I want you to be as excited for me as I am for myself.

- I'm most comfortable around people I know well. I like to perform for my special home audience and hear your approval. I probably won't want to show off my latest skills away from home.

- I become familiar with social rituals. By ten months I may say, "Bye-bye" or at least give a little wave.

- I want to be included in any social gatherings, even if I just sit on your lap and watch. I need to observe, even if I'm not quite ready to join in.

- When I'm in a room with another baby, I may watch, smile, try to touch or grab, and make talking sounds. Or I may just ignore him.

- As close as I am to you, I'm determined to be independent. More and more, I want to do things myself, but with you right beside me.

- My sense of humour begins to show. I might laugh at a funny word you say. Or if you laugh at something I've done, I'll repeat it to keep you laughing, and I'll join in.

- I'm developing a sense of myself as distinct from you and from every other person and object.

- Toward the end of this year, I'm starting to develop an attachment to a stuffed animal or doll. Even though I haul it around by the leg, I might be surprisingly tender with it.

- For my first birthday, I don't need a big party. In fact, a large, noisy gathering full of people I don't know well would be confusing and over-whelming. I'd prefer a small, quiet, family celebration at home.

he toddler phase can be a confusing time. Your child is no longer a baby. He's beginning to get around on his own two feet, albeit in a somewhat wobbly fashion. He's starting to express himself with words. He's developing his own likes and dislikes. Yet he is not a child either. He's still afraid of venturing too far into the world on his own. Even though his language skills are growing rapidly, he still cries when he's frustrated or disappointed or just feeling low.

At this stage, your role as parents is to help him be independent in all the ways he can be, but at the same time to be there for him, to be the people on whom he can depend. He needs someone he can trust completely to protect him and reassure him. Providing that security when he needs it is one of the most important things you can do, especially when your baby is sick or hurt or upset. Research suggests that responding in a positive way and providing a feeling of security are even more important than the way you play with your child. If he knows he can count on you, he will develop confidence in himself and learn how to relate in a loving way to other people. If your toddler comes to you in the playground with a scratched knee, give him a cuddle. What he needs at that moment is to know that you care about how he feels before you send him back to play.

Some parents think that a toddler will learn to handle the little knocks of life more quickly if they tell him it's not so bad and insist he get over it without a cuddle. But children who don't get a loving response when they feel hurt or upset work even harder for attention and often become whiny. Children who learn they can count on their parents for love and attention are more likely to learn how to calm themselves down and how to care about other people.

Feeding and Nutrition

At around age one, baby experiences a surge of independence, which extends to her experiences with food. She is open to new tastes, and she wants to feed herself. Your baby is developing her pincer reflex—the thumb-and-forefinger manoeuvre that allows her to capture small bits of food—and feeds herself slowly, but with ever-increasing confidence. Now you can push her chair up to the family table and include her in mealtimes.

She is highly imitative and will quickly absorb the family attitudes toward good food and good manners. At the age of one, your baby can enjoy most of the foods the rest of the family eats, as long as they are served in a safe form. Children remain susceptible to choking on food until about three years of age. Grate most hard vegetables and fruits rather than cutting them in adult bite-size; avoid wieners cut in rounds, popcorn, peanuts and most other nuts, grapes, and hard candies.

Nutritional requirements

Toddlers from one to two years require approximately one-quarter to one-third of the adult portions recommended in Canada's Food Guide to Healthy Eating. Each of the four food groups provides its own set of nutrients, which include fat, protein, carbohydrates, vitamins, and minerals. But no food group offers sufficient nutrition on its own; only a balanced diet offers complete nutrition.

Your toddler will want small servings, frequently offered. Along with three meals a day, offer her a mid-morning, mid-afternoon, and perhaps a before-bedtime snack. Offer at least four servings of breads and cereals—as little as a quarter of a muffin constitutes a serving. Serve two to three portions of meat or alternatives—a tablespoon of peanut butter equals a serving. Offer four or more servings of fruit and vegetables—fruit juice is fine for two of those servings, but don't allow your child to fill up on juice.

"When my daughter was a year old, she had as many rolls as the Michelin Man. I was really worried that she was too fat. A year later she weighed the same, but she was a lot taller and, therefore, much thinner."

JULIE, MOTHER OF TWO, BOWEN ISLAND, B.C.

Give up to three servings of dairy products—try a few spoonfuls of yoghurt or quark or grated cheese. Offer whole milk from age one to age two—toddlers need more fat than adults to promote growth and development, especially of brain cells and nervous tissue.

North American pediatricians disagree about how quickly fats should be reduced in the diet once a child reaches the age of two. The Canadian Paediatric Society recommends a gradual decline in fat intake from age two through late adolescence. When growth is complete, fat should comprise no more than 30 per cent of a healthy diet. The American Academy of Pediatricians favours an immediate reduction in fat intake at age two.

Pincer Grip

Vegetarian Diets

Children can thrive on vegetarian diets, whether they are ovo-vegetarian (non-animal, but including eggs) or lacto-ovo-vegetarian (no meat, but including dairy products and eggs). In fact, vegetarians may reduce their risk of developing conditions like obesity. Parents of vegetarian children may still refer to Canada's Food Guide. Select foods from all the food groups, but choose protein-rich alternatives to meat such as tofu, legumes (beans, lentils, chickpeas), nuts, and eggs.

There is clinical evidence, however, that children on a highly restricted vegan diet of non-animal foods grow more slowly and have less body fat than children with more varied diets. Also, because vegan children do not eat dairy products or eggs, they risk not getting sufficient energy, protein, iron, calcium, vitamin D, vitamin B_{12}, and riboflavin. If you have questions about your child's vegetarian diet, contact your public health unit. A dietitian can confirm whether your child is receiving the necessary nutrients, and answer any other questions you may have.

Foods are as much fun to examine as they are to eat.

Canada's Food Guide to Healthy Eating

Enjoy a variety of foods from each group every day. Choose lower-fat foods more often.

	Daily Servings	
Grain Products	5 - 12	Choose whole grain and enriched products.
Vegetables & Fruit	5 - 10	Choose dark green and orange vegetables and orange fruit.
Milk Products	2 - 3	Choose lower-fat milk products.
Meat & Alternatives	2 - 3	Choose leaner meats, poultry, and fish, dried peas, beans, and lentils.

Note: Taste and enjoyment can also come from "Other Foods" and beverages that are not part of the four food groups. This category includes high-fat, high-calorie foods like soft drinks and chocolate bars that add little more than energy to a diet, so use these foods in moderation.

Different Preschoolers Need Different Amounts of Food

The amount of food preschoolers need depends on their age, body size, activity level, growth rate, and appetite. A child-size serving is anywhere from one-half to the full size for each food group. Generally the size of portion increases with age. For example, a two-year-old may eat a half slice of bread, and a four-year-old a whole slice.

Examples of one child-serving:

Grain Products
½ to 1 slice of bread
cold cereal*

   *Approximate volumes for one serving:
   flaked cereal 125 to 250 mL
   (½ to 1 cup)
   puffed cereal 250 to 500 mL
   (1 to 2 cups)
   granola or dense-type cereal 30 to 75 mL
   (2 tbsp to ⅓ cup)
75 to 175 mL (⅓ to ¾ cup) hot cereal
¼ to ½ bagel, pita, or bun
½ to 1 muffin
50 to 125 mL (¼ to ½ cup) pasta or rice
4 to 8 soda crackers

Vegetables and Fruit
½ to 1 medium-size vegetable or fruit
50 to 125 mL (¼ to ½ cup) fresh,
   frozen, or canned vegetables or fruit
125 to 250 mL (½ to 1 cup) salad
50 to 125 mL (¼ to ½ cup) juice

Meat and Alternatives
25 to 50 g (1-2 oz.) meat, fish or poultry
1 egg
50 to 125 mL (¼ to ½ cup) beans
50 to 100 g (¼ to ⅓ cup) tofu
15 to 30 mL (1 to 2 tbsp) peanut butter

Milk Products
25 to 50 g (1-2 oz.) cheese
75 to 175 g (⅓ to ¾ cup) yogurt
Preschoolers should consume a total of
   500 mL (2 cups) of milk every day.

Are Supplements Necessary?

If your child is eating according to the Food Guide, is growing well, and is healthy, she doesn't require vitamin, mineral, or fibre supplements. Indeed, supplements in cute shapes may do more harm than good because they are a temptation for children. If your child eats an overdose of these vitamins, seek medical attention immediately.

North American children are most likely to be deficient in iron and calcium. Iron, which enhances cognitive functions and learning, is found in meat, poultry, fish, seafood, dark green leafy vegetables such as spinach and broccoli, dried fruits such as prunes and apricots, and iron-fortified breads, cereals, and pastas. Encourage your child to also eat foods containing vitamin C, which improves the absorption of iron in the diet.

Growing children also require calcium to develop strong bones and teeth. If your child rejects plain milk, try it over cereal. Or try home-made banana, peach, or strawberry milkshakes—milk is the preferred source of calcium because it is fortified with vitamin D, which is essential to the absorption of calcium. Other dairy products such as cheese, yoghurt, quark, and cottage cheese also contain calcium, but lack vitamin D. A child who cannot drink milk because of a cow's milk allergy or who is not exposed to sufficient sunshine will likely require a Vitamin D supplement.

Although fibre is essential to a healthy diet, too much fibre can interfere with your child's ability to absorb essential nutrients, cause diarrhea, and discourage appetite. Feed your child a balanced diet, avoid low-fibre fast foods, and do not offer fibre supplements.

Breast-Feeding and Bottle-Feeding

Breast-feeding after twelve months offers emotional nourishment for mother and child, but there is no nutritional advantage to nursing children beyond the first year. If you choose to wean during this period, you can be confident you are not compromising your child's health or nutritional requirements. Bottle-fed babies no longer require iron-enriched formula, and they can safely make the transition to cow's milk. Whether you are breast- or bottle-feeding, ensure that your toddler does not fill up on milk or other liquids before mealtimes.

Eating Like a Toddler

It's true that toddlers have great interest in new foods and flavours. That does not mean, however, that they have the same interest in eating the bounty laid before them. Their growth pattern changes in the second year, and a child may gain considerably more in height than in weight. As long as you continue to offer your child regular, nutritious meals, don't be alarmed by an inconsistent appetite. Remember it's growth that fuels the child's appetite, not the reverse. Parents who want to avoid problems feeding their independent-minded toddlers should memorize "The Golden Rules of Feeding."

The Golden Rules of Feeding

Parents and caregivers are responsible for serving a variety of nutritious foods at an appropriate time and place.

- → You schedule regular meals and snacks: usually three meals and three snacks each day.
- → You shop for and prepare meals using a variety of foods from Canada's Food Guide.
- → You provide a pleasant, engaging environment for those meals. You do not, for example, serve dinner in the back seat of the family van three nights a week.
- → You present the food in a form that is manageable for your child. A toddler needs food that is cubed, diced, mashed, or puréed.
- → You give your child the utensils she needs to eat independently. A toddler needs a highchair or booster seat, a child-size spoon or fork, and a lidded cup with spout, a "teacher beaker."
- → You establish and enforce appropriate table manners; "cleaning the plate" does not constitute good manners.

Children are responsible for how much and even whether they eat.

- → I can choose to eat or not to eat the meal that is served to me.
- → I can eat as much or as little as I like of the meal that is served to me.

And for a toddler, the Golden Rule additionally means:

- → I can eat my food in any order or combination.
- → I can feed myself by any method.

Snacks and Treats

Your toddler is the best judge of her own appetite. She will stop eating when she's no longer hungry, and she won't starve herself. However, she will expect—and in fact, she needs—frequent small snacks to round out her daily diet. Learn to recognize your child's hunger signs, and try to offer her a snack before the grumpiness, fatigue, requests for breast or bottle, or temper tantrums erupt.

Mealtime Strategies

Tips to reduce mealtime stress for you and your child:

➤ Offer the same food the rest of the family is eating, but in an easy-to-eat form. Tear a chicken breast into pieces. Serve a little pile of sweet spaghetti squash or rice. Mash a baked potato.

➤ Choking is a serious hazard for children under three. Avoid serving your toddler whole nuts, large beans, popcorn, whole grapes, wieners cut in circles, or large berries. Always supervise your toddler's meals.

➤ If your child wants to eat only jam sandwiches at lunch time for a week, let her. Keep offering a variety of foods, and eventually the food fad will pass.

➤ Children eat food that is familiar to them, so if your family enjoys spicy curries or pickled fish, don't hesitate to serve a small helping to your toddler. She may not eat it immediately but, with enough exposure and with your example, she will eventually enjoy it. Introduce new foods one at a time.

➤ Don't rush the child through her meal. Food is just one more thing for her to explore. If her dawdling gets in the way of family routines, serve her meal a bit ahead of the rest of the family.

➤ If your toddler joins you at the table, you can ease the need for cleanup by putting a vinyl place mat under her plate. She will likely still need a bib. Serve only small portions at a time; let her ask for seconds. That way, she won't be tempted to hurl the leftovers onto the floor.

➤ Begin the process of teaching manners, but don't turn the table into a battleground. What are your minimum standards at the table? Maybe you expect everyone in the family to contribute to mealtime conversation. Maybe you want to discourage open-mouth chewing. Maybe you would like every family member to participate in saying grace. Make sure you are not expecting more from your easily distracted and increasingly wilful toddler than she is able to give, or mealtimes will become a power struggle.

Typically, snacks are served mid-morning and mid-afternoon, and sometimes before bed. Ideally, you offer foods that fall within the Food Guide's four essential categories. Avoid frequent servings of "other foods" such as chocolate bars and colas, whose high-fat and high-calorie content contribute only energy to your child's overall nutrition. By all means, allow your children to enjoy such foods in moderation—even an ice-cream cone is a suitable snack choice.

Many Canadian parents were raised to think of food in terms of "good" food and "bad" food. By extension, many people have learned to think of themselves as good or bad depending on the food they eat. You can help your children to have a more constructive attitude toward the food they eat by dividing it into different categories—"everyday" foods and "sometimes" foods. The foods with high nutrient content—the ones that make up the four food groups—can be enjoyed frequently. "Sometimes" foods are usually the ones advertised most heavily during Saturday morning cartoons; they won't harm your child as long as they're add-ons to an already well-balanced diet.

"When my daughter was just learning to feed herself, she developed a fondness for frozen diced vegetables. She called it "pea candy." I would put a handful of frozen peas on her highchair tray while I was preparing the meal, and she would happily munch away. She particularly liked pea candy when she was teething."

ROSALYN, MOTHER OF TWO, B.C.

It is true that children will select a well-balanced diet on their own when they are offered only healthy choices. Children naturally prefer a varied diet. But once junk foods are added to the menu, you can't rely on your child to make the right decisions. You will have to be vigilant, steering your child toward a healthy diet through a constant barrage of marketing hype.

Child-size dishes and utensils encourage independent feeding.

Age One to Two-and-a-Half

Feeding Concerns

Food allergies

Parents with a personal history of allergies may have children who are prone to allergies. Some of the most common food allergens are cow's milk and other dairy products, wheat, egg whites, citrus fruits, nuts and nut butters, fish, seafood, chocolate, and soy products. Sometimes safe food items that come in contact with these food allergens can also cause difficulties.

A child may eat a certain food many times before the allergy is recognized. Food allergies may cause an immediate immune system reaction that can be fatal. This severe reaction, which can kill a child in minutes, is called *anaphylactic shock* or *anaphylaxis*. An allergic child may also develop swelling, wheezing, hives, vomiting, or diarrhea. If your child experiences breathing difficulties or swelling of the lips or tongue, seek immediate emergency medical help. For other allergic reactions, consult your doctor.

Some children may outgrow early allergies; other children, like those allergic to nuts and fish, seldom outgrow the allergy; indeed, it often gets worse. If your child is diagnosed with a serious allergy, ensure that everyone in your family knows where to find and how to use an EpiPen, an easy-to-administer spring-loaded syringe containing adrenaline, which could save your child's life. In most provinces, you need a prescription for EpiPen. You may also want to keep liquid antihistamines in the house to treat less severe allergic reactions. A child with a family history of allergy should avoid allergenic foods until age three. Families can contact the Allergy/Asthma Information Association (AAIA) 1-800-611-7011.

Food intolerances

Food intolerances are different from food allergies. They do not involve the immune system, and often there is no explanation for the intolerance. A child who is intolerant of a particular food may have brief but uncomfortable episodes of bloating, diarrhea, gas, or other symptoms after ingesting a specific food. In some cases, the child may lack certain enzymes such as lactase, which breaks down lactose (the white crystalline sugar found in milk) into digestible glucose and galactose and which is normally present in the intestinal wall. A child who is deficient in lactase may react to foods containing lactose. You may offer your lactose-intolerant child a milk-free substitute or milk that has the lactose removed, or give her enzymes that help break down the lactose. Consult your doctor or a dietitian.

Overweight

A chubby child will not necessarily be obese as an adult. Children may grow first either in girth or in height; many plump toddlers may grow to be beanpole-thin preschoolers. The reverse is also true: A thin toddler may suddenly gain weight by the time she reaches school age. If you think that your child's weight gain isn't right for her height, consult your doctor who can refer to the standard growth charts. Don't put your child on a diet. Instead, review your own and your child's lifestyle, the foods you eat and your meal patterns. Perhaps your child's diet is too high in calories. Maybe you're offering too many between-meal snacks. Or if she still has a bottle, she may be consuming too much milk.

"I let my child play with the vegetables while I was preparing the meal. He was so curious about everything anyway, so I would give him the colourful red and yellow peppers, or the nobby potatoes, and he would sniff them and examine them, and when I finally served them to him, he seemed more willing to eat them because they were sort of familiar."

BRAD, FATHER OF TWO, BOWEN ISLAND, B.C.

Ensure that your child engages in lots of vigorous exercise every day. One reason more Canadian children become overweight is that they aren't physically active. Your child will learn good health routines by example. Do simple activities together; pack a healthy snack and go for a walk to a local park. Good eating and exercise habits are the recipe for health and fitness that your child will carry into adulthood.

A timely snack keeps a toddler's spirits up.

Age One to Two-and-a-Half

Keeping Your Toddler Safe

As your toddler expands his skills and his horizons, protecting him from danger is a major part of your parenting job. Most parents set aside some time to childproof their home all at once. Although childproofing will make your job easier, it won't eliminate the need for supervision. Children this age need to be watched most of their waking moments. And although there will always be that moment when you're not watching or the time when your child is visiting a home that isn't childproofed, it's important to let your child know what your safety rules are: Don't go near the stove; don't touch an electrical outlet; never run in a driveway or into the road; if you find matches, bring them to mommy or daddy. To reinforce these cautions, you might reward your child, in whatever way you think appropriate, for coming to you with pills, matches, or sharp objects he has found. The following lists provide a starting point for you in childproofing the different areas around your home.

Although childproofing makes your job of supervisor easier, children this age need to be watched most of their waking moments.

Kitchen

- ➤ You may prefer to keep treats away from your toddler but, if she knows where you keep them, she may try to get at the hidden stash when your back is turned and hurt herself. Choose a cupboard that's far from the stove and that doesn't require climbing to reach.
- ➤ Whenever possible, use the back burners of the stove for your cooking and turn pot handles inward so that a toddler can't reach them.
- ➤ If you have a chest freezer, keep it locked and hang the key out of sight. Children, attempting to reach into a deep freezer to retrieve a Popsicle, may fall in head first.
- ➤ Keep small appliances away from the sink. A child, leaning over a sink to wash his hands, may inadvertently knock the appliance into the water and get a shock.
- ➤ Keep your toddler's highchair away from sources of heat, curtain cords, tables, plants, counter tops, and people traffic.
- ➤ Keep knives and food processor implements in a separate latch-locked drawer away from other utensils.
- ➤ Keep all cleaning products locked away and in the original containers with the information about their contents.
- ➤ Don't keep foods in the same location as any poisonous substances.
- ➤ Put a lid on the garbage can. Lock the trash compactor.

"I usually unplug the frying-pan cord from the electrical outlet first. But one time I unplugged the electrical cord from the frying pan first. My two-year old reached up and put it in his mouth. He received serious burns to his mouth and face."

TRIKA, MOTHER OF FOUR, BRAMPTON, ONT.

- ➤ Tie dry-cleaning bags in a knot before discarding them; if recycling empty plastic grocery bags, store them out of your child's reach.
- ➤ If you purchase a new dishwasher, choose one with an interior lock, which will prevent a toddler from opening it mid-cycle. Keep the detergent locked up with the other kitchen cleaners.
- ➤ Keep flammable items such as paper towels on a holder, and store pot holders or dish cloths away from a heat source.
- ➤ Install sturdy safety latches on all cupboards and drawers.
- ➤ Place a fire extinguisher on the wall in the kitchen away from the stove.

Bathroom

> Most household water heaters are set between 50 and 55ºC (122 to 131ºF). Lower the water heater's temperature to 48ºC (118ºF), hot enough to kill bacteria, but not so hot that it can burn tender skin.
> A child this age still lacks the reflex to hold his breath when his face is under water. Although you may no longer need to keep one hand on him in the bath, don't leave him alone.

"I was packing. As I turned my back to add something to the suitcase, my three-year-old reached into my make-up bag and guzzled facial toner."

MICHELLE, MOTHER OF ONE, ONTARIO

> Don't fill the bathtub more than a few centimetres; a child can drown in as little as 4 cm (1.5 in.) of water.
> Even leaving a child alone while the water is draining is dangerous because a facecloth or toy can plug the drain and leave enough water for the child to drown in.
> Make sure rubber drain plugs are secured to the bathtub drain and are not small enough to cause a choking hazard.
> Place a non-skid mat in the bathtub.
> Keep the toilet lid closed. Children have drowned in toilets or received bumps and concussions from the toilet seat lid.
> Install safety latches on all cupboards and drawers.
> Lock away all poisonous substances, including medications, cosmetics, perfumes, and mouth washes.
> Ensure all medications have child-resistant caps.
> Place a hook-and-eye latch on the outside of the bathroom door to keep a crawling baby out.
> Make very sure your child cannot lock the bathroom door from the inside, or ensure that you can unlock it from the outside.
> Use non-breakable cups, soap containers, and toothbrush holders.
> Place a cover over the tub spout to avoid dripping hot water.
> Ensure you have locks on cupboards, drawers, and medicine cabinet.
> With a clear shower curtain, you can still see baby, but her splashes are contained.
> Keep bath toys in plastic baskets with drainage holes.
> Keep a bench or chair near the tub for the supervising parent.

Bedrooms

➤ Put safety latches on night-table drawers or any other drawers that contain items that might harm your toddler.

➤ Secure bookshelves to the wall with special hardware; ensure dressers can't be tipped over.

➤ Don't allow your child to play under his crib where he might unhook the mattress; current safety standards for cribs prevent that possibility.

➤ Don't use an electric blanket for a child.

➤ Locate night-lights away from the bed and bedding. Don't use night-lights that resemble toys.

➤ Put a smoke alarm in any bedroom whose door will be shut at night or where children are sleeping in bunk beds, because smoke rises.

➤ Check toys regularly for missing or broken bits.

Living Room

➤ Lock up alcoholic beverages.

➤ Put decorative matches out of reach and out of sight. Keep all matches and lighters out of reach.

➤ Cover electrical outlets.

➤ Free-standing lamps should be put in storage or placed behind heavy furniture.

➤ Cover the fireplace with a tight-fitting screen.

➤ Remove unsteady furniture, glass coffee tables, and any ornaments that could shatter when knocked over.

Home Office

➤ Lock away any poisonous substances—ink for the printer, for example.

➤ Store sharp items or small items that could cause choking in drawers equipped with safety latches.

➤ Tie up electrical cords and wires, and tuck them behind the desk.

➤ Place a safety latch out of a child's reach on the outside of the office door.

Basement and Garage

➤ If you have an extra fridge in the shed or basement, use a fridge lock—they're sold in baby stores.

➤ Lock away all poisonous substances and power tools.

➤ Store laundry products on a high shelf.

➤ Keep doors to the garage and basement locked.

➤ If your laundry facilities are in the basement, add a spring door-closer to the basement door. That way, when you're carrying a load of laundry, the door will close automatically behind you.

Visiting

When you are visiting other homes with your child, remember that the home may not be childproofed.

> Before putting your toddler down for a nap at someone else's house, check bedside tables and the nearby bathroom for small objects or potentially poisonous substances.

> Check the toys that your host offers to your child for missing or broken bits.

> Be alert for purses or briefcases left where your toddler can reach them. They may contain medications.

> Be alert to unsteady furniture, glass coffee tables, and any ornaments that could shatter.

> Ask to move dangerous items out of the way or to move to another part of the house for the visit.

> Check for doors that open onto a pool or into a basement.

> Never leave a toddler unsupervised near water, whether it's a tub, a pool, a river, a lake, or the sea.

Foiled Again!

Toddlers love to race from room to room slamming the doors behind them. To prevent hurt fingers, toss a towel over the top of a door so it will no longer bang shut. A sock over a door handle and held in place by an elastic band will make a door difficult for a toddler to open.

Poison Proofing

The most common household emergency involving young children is poisoning. A toddler under two and a half is at prime risk, although any child under five years of age must be considered at risk.

You can prevent poisoning by knowing where and when and how a child may poison himself. Most poisonings take place during hectic family times, typically between 11 o'clock and noon or during preparations for the evening meal. Childhood poisonings usually occur in the place where the product is stored. Poisoning by pesticide, for example, is likely to occur in the basement or shed; by medicines, in the bathroom; and so on.

Put all poisons out of your children's reach and sight in a locked cabinet. If a child can see it, he may make every effort to get to it, no matter what the obstacles. Children discover pills in purses, pockets, glove compartments, bedside tables, and once in awhile in bathroom medicine cabinets. Babies and young children gobble house guest's pills, chug down mouthwash left beside the sink, and rub their eyes or lick their fingers after dipping them in detergent. They gulp cleaning liquids straight from the store shelf, chew on art supplies, eat plants, and drink cleaning products left in washrooms.

A child who swallows one of the following products will require immediate attention: hard liquor; alcohol-based adult cough syrup, iron pills and vitamins; shampoo, nose sprays, mouthwash and denture cleaners; perfume (which may contain up to 90 per cent ethyl alcohol) and suntan lotion; spot remover and shoe polish; some herbs and herbal medicines; home and oven cleaners; pesticides, bug sprays, and mouse or rat poison; and some household plants.

Children who have been poisoned once are at risk of poisoning themselves again. Why? A child may not connect the liquid he drank at three o'clock with the awful result he experienced later. Curiosity may get the better of him. He may have forgotten the hurt, but remembered the attention. One bad experience with round, red pills may deter a child from ever touching that kind again—but long, green pills are a different matter. The child's parents are more likely to think that the child learned the lesson from the first poisoning and that continued efforts at poison-proofing are, therefore, unnecessary. As a result, they may not be as conscientious about putting away the poisonous substances they previously put way out of the child's reach.

Let a toddler satisfy his curiosity about the fish, but keep an eye on him.

Age One to Two-and-a-Half

Safety Tips

→ The dining room table doesn't care if woody pine or lemon delight is used to buff it. Boycott furniture cleaners that a child could confuse with food.

→ Do not leave opened containers of cleaning products out while you run to answer the phone or door.

→ Keep all products in their original containers, so the details of ingredients and antidotes are readily available.

→ Do not buy children's vitamins that are shaped like animals or cartoon characters. They are too tempting.

→ Do not leave medication by a child's bedside or on a shelf in the bathroom. Keep it locked in a medicine chest. Children may decide to help themselves in the middle of the night.

→ Never leave pills in pockets or purses.

→ Avoid taking pills in front of children.

→ Clear unnecessary medicines out of your medicine cabinet frequently. Keep it locked.

→ Buy over-the-counter medication in containers with child-resistant caps. Note that "child-resistant" caps are not necessarily "child-proof." With or without this cap, keep medication locked up.

→ Never medicate yourself or other children with another's medication.

→ Keep ipecac syrup on hand to induce a child to vomit—except when the child has swallowed corrosive products or petroleum products.

→ Keep the telephone number of the Poison Control Centre next to your phone.

Camphor Oil

Many people use camphor oil—a volatile, potentially lethal compound—as a cure-all. It's a preparation that, when applied topically, produces heat. Not only can one easily confuse camphor oil with olive oil or castor oil, but the only warning on the box is **Harmful if swallowed.** The U.S. has banned camphor oil in concentrations of over 11 per cent because of its high toxicity. In Canada it's still possible to buy camphor oil over the counter in concentrations of up to 20 per cent. A small child who ingests as little as 5 mL (1 tsp.) of camphor oil may die. In other words, get it out of the house.

Basic Care

For the parent with endless time and patience, a toddler's firm resolve to do things for himself is a source of delight and pride. It's a little less charming to the beleaguered parent who is trying to catch a bus, to get to work by nine, or to make dinner for other family members. During this age, everything from feeding to dressing to bathing to sleeping becomes a potential battleground. For parents, the rule is: Don't engage.

As much as possible, let your child have the time he needs to try things for himself; be there to assist, but not to control. Turn routine tasks into games, or invite your child's help. Play Peekaboo while dressing, or ask him if he can find the red shirt in his drawer. When time starts to run out, give gentle warnings that soon you're going to have to take over. Respect the fact that your toddler is beginning to take charge of his own little body.

Learning to Use the Toilet

What parent isn't keen for a toddler to start using a potty and eventually the toilet? It's a welcome relief to eliminate the work, the mess, and the expense of diapers. But you can't rush a child who isn't ready. So how do you know when he's ready?

Soon after your baby turns a year old, he might become aware that the wet feeling in his diapers or the puddle on the floor is coming from him, although he has no control yet over his bladder or his bowel movements. In a few months he may be able to tell you when he feels the sensation, but *I have to go* often means *I'm going.* There's no time to rush over to the potty or toilet, let alone get his pants down.

But by the age of two or two-and-a-half, he has the necessary physical control *and* the communication skill to tell you when he needs to use the potty. Rushing a child before he's ready only ends up frustrating both you and him. Take it slow, take it easy. Encouragement is important. Tell him, "Good job," even if he misses after giving it a try. Don't punish, shame, or blame a child for mistakes. Accidents are common until about five years of age.

> **If your child won't use the toilet or shows signs of worry, postpone the learning process.**

The key to success is to stay calm. If your child won't use the toilet or shows signs of worry, postpone the learning process. If your child spends part of the day with another adult, make sure you discuss how your child is learning to use the toilet. Have other caregivers use the same words and follow the same routines.

Signs of Readiness

→ Stays dry for long periods.

→ Can walk to the potty or toilet and sit on it.

→ Can pull loose pants down.

→ Can tell you when he needs to go.

Toileting Tips

→ The best time of year to start placing a child on the potty is during the spring and summer when children need fewer layers of clothes.

→ Empty her dirty diapers into the toilet or potty. This may help her understand what she is supposed to do.

→ Start by saying it's time for her to use the toilet like mom or dad. Let her watch you use the toilet.

→ Explain in simple terms what happens when she goes to the bathroom. Tell her what happens to her urine or bowel movement when it goes in the toilet.

→ Teach the child the words *pee* and *poo* that everyone understands.

→ This is a good time to replace overalls with pull-down pants.

→ Take her to the toilet when she tells you she has to go. Keep your child company.

→ Never force a child to use the toilet. You're only setting up a power struggle that can lead to more problems.

→ Stay patient. Don't get angry if she misses.

→ Give it up if it isn't working, and try again a few weeks later.

Hygiene

➤ Trim nails short with small, blunt-tipped scissors or clippers.

➤ Give your child a step-stool in the bathroom so he can learn to wash his own hands after using the toilet.

➤ Teach him how to lather and rinse.

➤ Give him a facecloth and let him wash himself in the bathtub.

Hair Washing

Hair washing can become a problem at this age. Some children are frightened by having their heads in, or even near, water. You don't want to force the issue and risk starting a lifelong fear of water, but you do have to wash the week's muck out of your child's hair. You'll have to experiment to find a satisfactory solution. Try some of the following suggestions:

➤ Once she's had her first haircut, you could try playing hairdresser or barber in the bath, pretending to cut and style each other's hair.

➤ Let her wash your hair first. Let her apply and lather the shampoo in your hair before she does her own hair.

➤ Don't lay her back in the tub. No matter how firmly you hold her, she doesn't feel safe for whatever reason. Keep her sitting up.

➤ Consider alternatives to the bathtub: standing her on a stool to wash her hair under the kitchen sink, or standing in the shower.

➤ Don't try to get her used to the feeling of water on her face by splashing at her. You'll just make things worse.

➤ Always use a no-tear shampoo.

➤ Keep the lather and the water out of her eyes and face.

➤ Offer, but don't force, a facecloth to protect her nose and eyes while you're washing and rinsing. After you've lathered her hair, she can hold the folded facecloth over her eyes while you slowly pour warm water over the top and back of her head to rinse.

➤ Let her rinse herself using a hand shower.

➤ Even children who don't mind having their hair washed object to the after-wash comb-out. A spray-on detangler will reduce anxiety.

Playing hairdresser in the bath can result in a great new "do."

Dressing

➤ When buying clothes, keep in mind that your child will soon want to choose his own clothes when he gets dressed for the day. If it will bother you to have him looking uncoordinated, choose colours that can be mixed and matched.

➤ If he wants to wear one blue sock and one red sock, let him. Save your energy for the big battles, or buy only blue socks.

➤ Your child may quickly display an aversion to certain kinds of fabrics. Respect his taste.

"My daughter doesn't like to wear what she refers to as 'crunchy' clothes—clothes that are made of stiff cotton or man-made fibres like acrylic. People would give her the wrong kind of clothes at Christmas, and she'd refuse to wear them. We'd get into these battles until I finally decided to accept that she only likes to wear cotton knits."

JULIE, MOTHER OF TWO, BOWEN ISLAND, B.C.

➤ If your child is learning to use a potty, dress him in clothes that he can easily remove by himself. Choose trousers with elastic waists instead of fly-fronts.

➤ Besides a good waterproof coat and boots, invest in waterproof pants that can be worn over his regular clothes.

➤ You don't have to have his first shoes specially fitted, but you will want to make sure that his toes are not squashed, and that there is no painful rubbing anywhere. Check the fit of his shoes every few months; it's not unusual for young children to grow through three shoe sizes in one year.

➤ When your child goes out to play in the sun, make sure he wears a wide-brimmed hat and an SPF 30 sunscreen. In the sunny months, make the application of sunscreen the last stage of getting dressed. But you still need to reapply the sunscreen every two hours or after each swim.

➤ Children might start wearing sunglasses with a UV filter by age one, if they will keep them on. If they won't or can't, stick with the wide-brimmed hat and keep them out of the sun until they're old enough to wear the protective sunglasses.

Dental Health

Once your child has all his baby teeth—sometime between his second and third year—arrange a first visit to the dentist. If your own dentist isn't comfortable treating small children, ask your friends and neighbours to refer you to a suitable dentist. Some dentists only treat children under eighteen; their offices can be as much fun as an amusement park!

The first visit should serve simply to put your child at ease in the dentist's office, so don't wait for an emergency. If you yourself are uncomfortable about visiting the dentist, don't pass your anxieties on to your child. Don't say, "The dentist won't hurt you," or "It won't be too bad." Treat a trip to the dentist matter-of-factly, no different from a trip to the grocery store. The dentist could give your child a "ride" in the big chair, count his teeth, give him a new toothbrush and a sticker or toy treat. He may also demonstrate proper brushing and flossing techniques, but leave any problems to the next visit. Caring for your child's teeth means that you:

➤ Make sure he gets enough calcium and vitamin D in his diet.
➤ Continue daily brushing and fluoride supplements, if required.
➤ Floss his teeth regularly.
➤ Let your child see you brushing and flossing your teeth.
➤ Let him choose his own toothbrush.
➤ If your child isn't fond of toothpaste, offer a children's brand with fluoride, to be used no more than twice a day until he is six.
➤ Make sure your child rinses after brushing and doesn't swallow the toothpaste.

"Brushing teeth was a big problem until we invented the sugar bug game. We pretended to see sugar bugs in our kids' mouths, and we'd pretend to chase after them with the toothbrush. We'd say, 'Aha! Thought you'd get away, did you? Oh, there's another one.' The kids thought it was hilarious and they'd let us brush for as long as we wanted."

BRAD, FATHER OF TWO, BOWEN ISLAND, B.C.

Visiting the Doctor

Continue with regular visits to your family physician for vaccinations and booster shots, for review of any parental worries and guidance on what to expect. Also your doctor will document growth and weight and assess physical, mental, and emotional development. Familiarize your child with what to expect during these visits by "playing doctor" first. Use a toy doctor's bag to show the child how the doctor will examine his eyes and ears; let him listen to your heartbeat. Also, since a toddler will easily become bored while waiting in a crowded doctor's office, bring toys or books as distractions.

Sleeping

Sometime between her first and second birthday, your child will gradually reduce her daily sleep time to a total of twelve or thirteen hours. The afternoon nap, the last remnant of daytime sleep, may disappear at about two years of age. That's the usual age at which one out of four kids no longer requires an afternoon nap. But most children still need a daytime nap until they reach age four or five. Each child's sleep pattern is unique—there isn't any average sleep behaviour.

Getting to sleep

For many toddlers, the main sleep difficulty isn't waking during the night but settling down in the first place. At this stage, a child's brain is developing very, very quickly. All day he has been absorbing new knowledge and experiences through all his senses, and information is whirring about in his head. It's difficult for him to slow down to a relaxed state for sleep.

Somewhere between the ages of one and four, about 25 per cent of kids are awake for more than half an hour from when they're put to bed before they drop off to sleep. Don't put your child into bed until you're reasonably sure he will go to sleep in less than half an hour. Many parents find that a long session of comforting and cajoling a toddler into bed is a real source of end-of-day frustration.

> **Don't put your child to bed until you're reasonably sure he will go to sleep in less than half an hour.**

Develop very predictable bedtime activities. Roll out a nightly ritual of baths and bear hugs and bedtime stories, always in the same progressive order. Give yourself and your baby a half hour each night to go through all the steps. Start at 7:30 p.m. and aim for an 8 p.m. bedtime. By the time your child is about one year old, he should be making it to about 8 o'clock before the long nighttime sleep. The only acceptable bedtime beverage, other than water, is milk. Avoid cocoa, juice, and any soft drinks before bed.

Help your child to comfort himself while getting to sleep or when he wakens in the night by encouraging him to have a transition object, which might be a teddy bear or a favourite blanket. The attraction for a transition object happens around one year of age and that object can be tremendously comforting for a toddler. A small, dim night-light in the room, and perhaps a low-level sound—like a fan or air conditioner—can help.

Once you've established your bedtime routine, don't give in to whining and whimpering. Experts advise that your routine is more important than ever during this stage. If you capitulate to your fussing child and pull him out of bed to watch a television show together, you'll make bedtime even tougher for both of you the next night. He needs his sleep.

Crib to bed

Around your child's second birthday, it's time to help her make the momentous move from her crib to a child's bed. To help her get ready for the change, engage in lots of discussions and big-bed stories. Let her help pick out her new bed or the bedding that will cover it. And then play it safe by keeping her crib in the same room for a time, so that your child has the extra time she needs to ease the transition. Put the mattress on the floor for a few nights and let your child sleep on it to help her learn to "centre" herself.

"Ashmir has never been much of a sleeper. For the first year and then some, she shared our room and also our bed. She woke up through the night well into her second year. I always listened to other mothers tell their stories of how they finally got their babies to sleep through, hoping I'd find the answer there. We finally put her in her own room, but I could never bear to hear her cry. My husband always had to hold me back."

KYLA, MOTHER OF ONE, TORONTO, ONT.

Nightmares

No one can say for sure what causes children's nightmares. For many children, they begin after the age of two when the child becomes more verbal, although they can certainly begin earlier than that. A nightmare occurs during the dream cycle, usually in the latter half of a night's sleep. It is typically brief in length, and awakens the child. We don't know why kids have more nightmares than adults. It may be that the world contains more new things for children than for adults and novelty tends to be more frightening. You won't know many details of your child's nightmares or bad dreams until he can describe them to you. When your child wakens from a bad dream, comfort him and help him go back to sleep.

- → Sit in the dark with your child for a bit, and talk quietly about happy subjects.
- → Tuck in his stuffed animal or doll.
- → Pat his back.
- → Offer a glass of milk or water.

If nightmares increase and become a problem, review and restrict your child's daytime television-viewing habits. Some kids have such vivid imaginations that they can't distinguish between reality and fiction. For persistent or severe nightmares, consider taking your child for professional counselling.

Night terrors

A night terror is a bad set of emotional experiences, usually without dream content, that brings on feelings of absolute fear. A night terror occurs at the soundest point of sleep, generally between one and four hours after a child goes to bed. It's an emotional response, accompanied very often by thrashing limbs, bulging eyes, or a contorted face. A child experiencing a night terror usually wakens in a state of sweaty panic, with a very rapid heartbeat, and a look of genuine confusion and fright.

Your child may call out for you and then push you away. Or he may cling to you desperately. But it's not unusual for him to appear unaware of your presence. On average, night terrors last between ten and thirty minutes and are forgotten by morning. If your child wakens from the night terror, comfort him. He may, however, fall back into a calm sleep without waking first. Let him sleep.

Although a night terror will not harm a child, it can be as frightening for a parent to watch as it is for a child to experience. The prevailing explanation for night terrors is that a child's brain simply doesn't have the kind of control over all aspects of the body during sleep that it will later acquire. By the time of puberty, his night terrors will be all but gone, and his nightmares will be much fewer.

Communicating

Within six months after their first birthday, children have about a dozen words in their speaking vocabulary. Almost all of them name the people or things that interest them—parents, pets, and their own body parts. They rarely name things that don't move or that aren't used in a game. The number of their spoken words increases slowly up to about eighteen months. At that age, a toddler might still have only twenty words, but he has begun to include some one-word sentences like *Go, Eat, Bad, Up,* and the all-purpose command, *This.* But the favourite one-word exclamations are *Mine!* and *No!,* the most powerful of all. Toddlers seem to enjoy the power of saying *No!* and delight in trying it out on long-suffering parents.

> **Babies rarely name things that don't move or that aren't used in games.**

At this point, children experiment with language, trying out new names or sounds. They might invent their own words for things—*Boo* might be a favourite teddy bear. They might repeat words but apply them to the wrong objects, just as a tourist might pick a word out of a travel dictionary and use it in the hope that it suits the situation.

The clarity of their words starts to improve, but don't expect too much of your child's pronunciation. Some sounds like *bah* and *da* are easy to make, but others require a considerable amount of skill. To make the sound of *l*, for example, you have to put the tip of your tongue on the roof of your mouth, just behind the teeth. For young toddlers, that's still too difficult. They use other sounds instead, typically *w, m,* or *y,* so *lunch* could come out as *yunch.* Toddlers have similar problems with the sound of *r* They cannot make hard consonants like *t* and *g* at the beginnings of words, so they simply substitute other ones that are easier to make—*too* comes out as *doo* and *goose* as *doose.*

> **Shape your responses to show you understand your child and to model the right pronunciation.**

Some consonant combinations, like *thr* or *str,* are tough, too, especially at the beginning of words, so toddlers use a different one altogether—and *stream* comes out as *deem.* Consonants also give trouble at the ends of words, so young speakers simply leave them off, as in *bai* for *bike* or *muh* for more.

Trying to correct a child's pronunciation, however, can discourage him from trying, if he learns that his cheerful chatter always meets with a language lesson. The best approach at this age, and through a child's first years, is to model the correct way. If your toddler wants an apple and says *appo,* respond by saying, "You want an apple? Let's go get an apple." This tells your child you understood her, but also models the right way to say it. Don't hold back the apple and make the child say it "the right way." Your child may just withdraw and be less keen to speak the next time.

It's in your child's second year that you will see a difference in how boys and girls learn and use language. Don't be worried if your son doesn't chatter away as much as your daughter did at eighteen months. All babies are different but, on average, girls acquire language much more quickly until about two years of age, when the boys begin to catch up.

A child adds words slowly to his speaking vocabulary in the first eighteen months, about 20 words, but that grows to between 100 and 200 words by his second birthday. Meanwhile, the child's understanding of words races well ahead of his ability to say them. At eighteen months, toddlers understand as many as 50 words. Amazingly, that increases more than twenty times to about 1,200 at two years of age. In these six months, the child also begins to grasp more complex syntax. He can follow a two-step command like "Go get your coat, then open the door." He may no longer need you to point to the coat in order to understand. If you say, "Show me the dog" while reading a picture book, he can point to it. He also begins to understand the idea of putting things in categories. He begins to realize that the word *dog* applies to the picture in the book, to the family pet, and to the animal across the street.

As the child's vocabulary of words grows, two styles of learning begin to emerge. Some children concentrate on building up their bank of names for things, up to 50 words; others quickly pick up words that express emotions or desires, such as *Up* for *Pick me up* and *Want* for *I want it.* It's an individual preference, as far as researchers can tell, and not an indicator of a child's intelligence or language ability.

By the second birthday, a child can usually compose two-word questions like *What's that?* or sentences like *All gone* or demands like *Me cookie* and *Go car.* Between two and two-and-a-half, children start using modifier words like possessives and adjectives. They refer to the *big car* or *my bear.*

The age of your child is a rough guide to the length of sentences he's capable of uttering. At the age of one, children use one-word sentences, at two years of age, two-word sentences, and so on up to the age of five or six. It's true that children pick up language at their own speed, but if your child isn't using 5 to 10 words by the age of two, or if he isn't making two-word sentences by the age of three, it's worth discussing your concerns with your doctor. Hearing problems are the most common reason for language difficulties. Or the child may simply be having a problem pronouncing words clearly enough for you to recognize. Whatever the trouble, it is always better to find out early enough to help.

When children start using two-word sentences, they've begun to learn syntax, that part of grammar that applies to arranging words in meaningful sentences. The amazing thing is that they get it right. When they put *more* and *juice* together, they say *more juice*, not *juice more*. Researchers say your child is not just copying you, but he has figured out the pattern for himself. He changes the order of words only if he wants to change the meaning. If he's angry at the cat, he might say *Bad cat*. But if he wants to tell you that the cat is misbehaving, he says *Cat bad*. It represents a sophisticated understanding of the patterns of language, an understanding that sometimes leads to the misapplication of a "rule." We usually make plurals by adding the letter *s*, so it makes sense to the toddler to say *mans* for *men* or to call one leg of a pair of pantyhose a *pantyho*. We indicate an action took place in the past by adding *-ed* to the end of the word, so why not say *I goed up*? It takes some years to understand that language has almost as many exceptions as it has rules.

> **Hearing problems are the most common reason for language difficulties.**

You can help your child figure out the rules the same way you help her learn how to pronounce words. Find a natural way to repeat her message back to her as part of the conversation and provide a model of the right way. When she tells you, "I goed up," reply by saying, "Oh! you went up! Aren't you a big girl!" Don't constantly point out the mistakes. Children learn very early to be self-conscious if they are corrected too often, and they may stop trying.

The children who use their language well come from homes where language is an important part of family times, such as supper together, and social times. Talk about what you're doing as you do it together. If you open a box say, "See how this opens," as you demonstrate the action. When you lift your toddler into his highchair say, "Up we go!" Describe actions and objects as you are using them: "Let's put the red block on top of the blue block and move the green ones to the back."

Remember that, even if your child can understand you, it's not always easy for him to understand strangers, and vice versa. Don't hesitate to repeat another person's words to help your toddler sort out what she's saying. You may also have to interpret your child's words to the stranger.

Reading is one of the best ways to involve your child in language. Start reading to him as early as possible. Choose picture books that interest him and read him the story. If the pictures stimulate his interest, talk about the details or ask him to tell you about what he sees—the pictures are usually created to convey much more than the words alone.

Toddling, Walking, Running

Most babies can move forward on their own two feet by their first birthday. Some are only at the stage where they pull themselves up to stand by grabbing on to furniture and then they cruise along slowly with support. Others will cruise along more smoothly and confidently, moving hand over hand.

Bare feet are sometimes the safest "footwear" for learning to stand up.

Others may cruise and periodically let go, toddling for a few unsupported steps. Some will walk without any support at all.

Keep in mind that early, impulsive walkers are sometimes more awkward and injury-prone than later walkers, who may walk more assuredly once they finally begin walking. The age of walking doesn't predict your baby's intellectual or athletic ability. At this stage, he's learning to talk, and he's beginning to acquire fine motor skills, so some of his energy and attention may be focused in these areas. Give him lots of chances to practise his techniques. He won't want to be confined to a stroller, high chair, or playpen for long.

Once your baby is cruising confidently, you can encourage him to cross small gaps between one piece of furniture and the next. Gradually widen the gaps so that eventually he will be motivated to toddle a few steps across the open spaces. He may be ready to try walking, supported by your hands. You might encourage him to take steps on his own by positioning

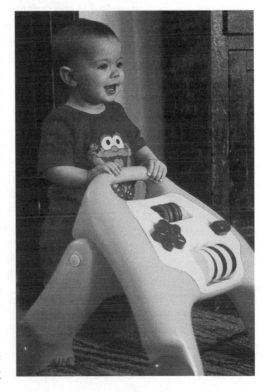

Once your toddler can walk comfortably without needing his hands for support, he'll begin to use his hands to explore more of the world.

yourself a few steps away and saying, "Walk to daddy," so that he is motivated to toddle into your inviting, supporting arms.

At first, your toddler's walking style will be awkward and unsteady. He'll weave, wobble, and waddle, lurching forward and falling time and again. With practice, his walk will progress from a wide, stiff-legged gait to a more rhythmic, knee-bending gait, with the feet closer together. In time, he'll begin to stride forward briskly, with an authoritative marching gait. To help him gain control over his walking, take him out to a big, open space like a park where he can move around and fall freely. He will love it.

In the first stages of walking, your toddler won't use her hands for any purpose other than balance or support. Once she becomes more comfortable with the process of walking, she'll begin to use her hands to carry, play with, or pick up toys. As she learns to stoop over and pick up toys, her balance will improve.

She'll love toys that she can pull or push along while walking, like a wagon, pushcart, or toy animal on a leash. If you put toys on a shelf close to the floor, she might toddle over to get her own toys or put them back. Of course, sometimes she'll just sweep her hand across the shelf and knock the toys onto the floor.

Toddlers still like walking with a parent, holding on with one or both hands. Once your toddler can walk around, it's great to explore the world outdoors in parks, playgrounds, or quiet neighbourhood streets. As her walking becomes more proficient, she'll start to concentrate on what she sees while you're walking or listen while you talk about what you both encounter.

You may notice that your toddler will comfortably toddle off on her own while you stay still or sit down. She knows you're there as a secure base, so she feels free to move around and explore. Researchers note, however, that if the child is left alone or with a caregiver she doesn't know, she moves around and explores a lot less and plays less freely.

Then you may find that she won't follow you when you start moving away to take her home. If you try to take her hand, she may refuse it or stop and start many times. When you move, she may feel that you're going away from her when she wants to be close to you. You'll need to carry her or put her in a stroller if you want to move more quickly.

Just like adults, toddlers have very individual walking styles. Some toddlers start out walking with their feet turned out, but later they turn their toes in. During their second year, it's very common for their toes to turn in because of a natural change in the angle of the upper leg as it meets with the pelvis. Also, because babies don't develop much of an arch in their foot until later, they often compensate while walking by turning their feet inward. The condition of intoeing does evolve over time and very rarely needs surgical intervention. However, if the pigeon toes interfere with walking or don't straighten out over the next year or two, or if your toddler walks in some other unusual way, consult your doctor.

On the run

A child's advance from walking to running is an exciting, but challenging, new development. Your toddler suddenly has a new-found power and ability, and can dart away from you at any time. At first, she may often trip and fall until she learns to bend her knees more and lift her feet higher.

Try to set aside times each day when she can go outside to run and play. It's safer and more fun than bumping into furniture and walls in the confined spaces of home. Take her into the open space of your yard, a park, or a playground and watch her run, climb, kick, and jump freely. Give her lots of opportunity to play in wide open spaces so that she can improve her abilities at running, climbing, and jumping. In doing so, she will learn to control, coordinate, and manage her body. She may enjoy playing with a ball as you show her how to roll it and run after it. Once she can run, she'll love to play games where she runs away from you and you try to catch her.

Playing in wide open spaces will help her learn coordination.

Climbing

In the latter part of the second year, your child's urge to climb anywhere and everywhere increases, and he'll try to climb up steps, or onto chairs, sofas, and tables. A climbing toddler may climb out of his crib and let you know it's time to move him into his own bed. Be vigilant, but provide opportunities for him to climb safely.

A toddler loves to climb up stairs, but you'll need to help him come down safely. You might get, or make, a set of three or four steps with a small platform at the top on which he can play and practise climbing. Toddlers also take great pleasure in climbing up, over, and down daddy or mommy. Climbing up and sliding down is also good training and great fun—whether at the park or at home. Cheer him on as he develops each new skill; recognizing his accomplishment spurs him on to the next achievement.

Well-equipped playgrounds offer children opportunities for new challenges.

Jumping for joy

Once your toddler can run, she will soon be jumping. Give her the encouragement and the space, and she'll be jumping up and down for the sheer exhilaration of experiencing this new gymnastic manoeuvre. Put on some catchy music. Your toddler will feel the rhythm, invent her own steps, jump to the music, and do her own little dance. You'll both love dancing to the beat of each other's steps.

Cushioning a Fall

Toddlers learning to walk will inevitably take quite a few falls. Since you can't prevent your child from falling, it's much safer to let him walk on carpeted surfaces than on hard, slippery floors. It's also much better for his confidence if he doesn't hurt himself or give himself a fright. Bare feet are best for walking at first, because the child can feel the floor and use his toes for balance. Socks alone on a hard, slippery floor can be treacherous, unless you choose nonslip socks. Shoes, if used, should be light and flexible, but have nonslip soles.

Playing and Learning

Your toddler's physical skills progress by leaps and bounds as he learns to walk, run, kick, jump, climb, and ride. Physical games like hand-slapping high fives and low fives are lively and develop hand co-ordination. His hands become much more adept as he learns how to use objects as tools for particular purposes. But your toddler will still be proud to be lifted up to ride high on daddy's shoulders.

Outdoor play in a yard, park, or playground gives him an opportunity to enjoy and practise walking, running, climbing, and jumping freely. Small slides, swings, and seesaws are challenges that he'll want to try: Watch carefully and hold on to him when needed.

Most children find it fascinating to feed ducks in a pond or birds in a birdhouse and watch insects at work—these activities give them a sense of the natural world. A paddling pool or lawn sprinkler and hose are great ways to play with water on a warm summer day. Your toddler can also start to play with sand, but teach him not to throw or eat it. Let him pour water on sand, so he can see the change that takes place and feel the difference between dry sand and the wet sand that can be moulded into shapes.

Moving furniture around and building hideouts with sofa cushions is another physical activity that your toddler may really enjoy. And don't forget other popular games, such as Duck, Duck, Goose; Ring-around-the-Rosy; and Pop Goes the Weasel. Your toddler might also try throwing or kicking a ball, and you can show her how to get better at doing it.

Push-along and ride-on toys, like cars or animals on wheels, are very popular with toddlers. These help improve her balance, build confidence, and offer a thrilling new experience. Between two and two-and-a-half years of age, a toddler may be ready for a tricycle.

Playing and Thinking

In her second year, a toddler has the mobility, dexterity, language skills, and curiosity to explore just about everything in her world. Expand her world by taking her to new places—a different park, your neighbour's rec room—where she can see and touch and experiment with new objects. At this age, she experiments in order to figure out how the world works. She drops things and watches them fall down. She pushes a ball and it rolls; she pushes a block and it doesn't—and she learns. She learns the different properties of various objects, shapes, and materials. She learns how to group similar objects together, like blocks of different sizes and shapes, or similar animate beings, like pets—which behave quite differently from toys.

As her hand control improves, she enjoys playing and learning with toys that she can build, stack, fill, fit together, or sort. She'll enjoy stacking blocks on top of one another and then knocking them down. You can show her how to build a tall tower or a wall, and she may begin to build simple structures in which she might put a toy.

Stacking cups of different sizes can be fun, and she'll soon learn how to stack them in the right order. She will become more aware of differences in size and shape, and learn how to coordinate her hand movements. Toddlers love learning how different objects fit together. They are fascinated by putting pegs in holes or keys in locks, by opening and shutting boxes, and by unscrewing jar tops. As your toddler handles and stacks objects, you might teach her concepts of size, colour, and shape by describing objects— large, small, round, or square; red, blue or white.

Sorting games help her learn how to group together objects that are alike. You can put a bunch of different toy animals together in a pile and then show her how to sort cows, pigs, and sheep into different groups. With even simple jigsaw puzzles, you may have to help her learn how to try out and fit the pieces together.

Quiet play is just as important as active, physical play. By looking at books while you read to him, your toddler learns to associate pictures in books with familiar objects, animals, people, and scenes. Books with bold, clear illustrations are great and, as he gets a little older, illustrations with more detail will interest him.

Toddlers love to learn how different objects fit together. In this case, one kid and several bears do fit into a basket.

Artist at Work! Minimal Mess!

Your toddler will love these creative activities and they don't require major cleanup time.

- ➤ Give him a pail of water and a large exterior paintbrush. Let him "paint" the walls or the sidewalk outside.

- ➤ Make up a finger-paint palette with small amounts of a few edible "paints"—chocolate pudding, strawberry yoghurt. Let him paint his plate or other flat surface.

Reading to him helps to increase his vocabulary and understanding. Once he decides he likes a story, expect that he'll want to hear it over and over. Books of nursery rhymes and songs are entertaining and develop your child's memory and sense of sequence as he learns the right moment to chime in on the chorus or repetitive parts. Books that have pop-up art or fold-up pages let your child become directly involved with a book, even when he can't yet read.

Your toddler may like it when you draw pictures for her and make up stories about your drawings. If you give her the crayons, she'll begin scribbling, which marks the first step toward writing and drawing. Finger paints are also great for this age; she will enjoy seeing what happens when she mixes different colours together. Soon you'll be able to display a gallery of her artwork on the refrigerator door, which will give her a great sense of pride in her accomplishment.

Social and Emotional Development

Your toddler wants you to be near him when he plays, and sometimes he wants you to help him, but he also wants to do things in his own way. He's both exploring and experimenting. Make suggestions, give him good ideas, show him things, but don't dominate. Let him be the leader. You can help him to play and concentrate for longer periods of time by stepping in when he gets stuck, giving him encouragement, and helping him to complete challenging tasks.

At this age, your toddler is much more aware of what you say and do. He'll want to help you and imitate what he has seen you do. Imitative toys like a tea set, a play house, or a toy telephone give your child a chance to play games where she imitates you in real life. This is great for encouraging speech as she invents conversations on the phone or with a doll.

Your toddler may become attached to a transition object, like a toy animal or blanket, as a comforting presence to take everywhere she goes. Although toddlers enjoy being with other children, they tend at first to play *alongside* rather than to *interact with* the other toddlers. Nonetheless, as

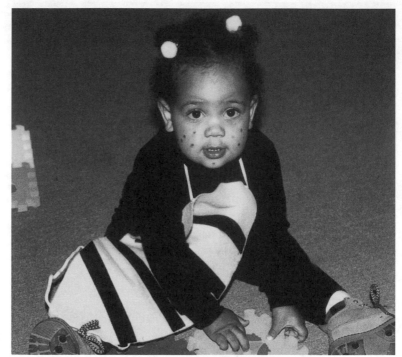

A few face paints and just the suggestion of a costume bring fantasies to life.

Imagination: Let's Play Pretend

In pretend play, your toddler may begin to use one object to represent another. She might drink from a seashell, for example, or pretend a box is a stove to cook on. This symbolization is an important milestone in her emotional and cognitive development.

There are many good reasons to encourage your toddler's imaginative play. Toddlers who learn to use their imaginations are better able to entertain themselves and less likely to become bored. Imaginative play promotes their verbal and social skills because they use words to advance the plots for their characters and interact with stuffed animals, dolls, and other toys. Your toddler may enjoy dressing up in hats, vests, and other clothing for costumes and finding props to put on a performance.

In pretend play toddlers develop problem-solving skills because they try to predict "what happens next" and to use objects creatively as props to move their stories forward. Toddlers might also reveal their fears and worries in their fantasy play, which might release their concerns or give them a sense of control over them. Be attentive to these nuances, because their play is a way of communicating when they don't have the vocabulary to describe their thoughts and feelings.

they become more aware of each other, social interaction will begin and you may need to supervise—or intervene if and when they get into conflict with one other. Over time, you can help your toddler learn how to play cooperative games with siblings and other toddlers. Make it easy for toddlers to share. When they're playing with others, offer toys with lots of pieces or material to go around, such as modelling clay or interlocking blocks or crayons.

As your toddler gets closer to age two, he'll begin to use his imagination to animate objects, toy animals, dolls, and other toy people. He may use these "animated" creatures to act out scenes from everyday life and show his feelings. This adds an exciting new dimension to his play. Make-believe play increases his language skills in social interaction, provides a wonderful way to express and release feelings and individual or imitative creativity.

Puppets are wonderful toys to encourage this kind of imaginative play. You might help make puppets from old socks or mittens by sewing on buttons or beads for eyes and nose and using string for the hair. Paper-bag puppets offer children the fun of painting faces.

Put TV in Its Place

How much television or videotapes their children should watch is an issue that all parents discuss. There's evidence that viewing violence on television, even the violence in cartoons, increases children's aggressive play because children imitate the behaviours they see. But the broader issue is whether excessive TV viewing deprives your toddler of the tremendous benefits to be gained through a wide range of play activities. If your child is watching TV, he's not running around, playing with other children, drawing, reading stories, building castles, or otherwise exercising his body and stimulating his imagination, mind, and feelings.

Playing should involve active doing and learning, not just passive watching. Look at TV as one small part of your toddler's overall play activities, and establish, then monitor, the types of program that your toddler views. Choose programs that are appropriate to his age and that reflect your family values. Make TV time interactive by discussing the programs you watch with your toddler.

Enforcing limits on TV watching will be easier and more effective if you have play activities planned for when his TV programs are over. Set a positive example by using TV in the way that you want your child to use it—for information as much as for entertainment. With forethought, your selection of programs turns TV viewing into more of a learning experience and less of a baby sitter.

Behaving Appropriately

What's appropriate behaviour for a toddler is often very strange behaviour for a parent to understand. When you're in a battle of wills with a tiny person who is determined, for example, to not put on his snowsuit despite the zero-degree weather, it's easy to question why your child is compelled to exhibit some of these behaviours at this stage in his development. But the opposition of children in this age group is all about self-identity, something that your ornery toddler is working very hard to establish.

At this age, your child begins to see himself as a distinct and separate person. For all his short life, he has been completely dependent on you and other caregivers—a baby is not aware of himself as an individual separate from his mother or primary caregiver. But this awareness develops in the second year of life as he becomes more self-sufficient and independent.

He can feed himself, he can walk, he can speak. He wants to know more about himself and see what else he can do. Can he make the VCR work? Can he flush the toilet? Your child wants to try everything and will complain loudly when you stop him. Around eighteen months, he may begin to say *No!* to almost every request, not because his personality has suddenly changed, but because he wants to show you that he's becoming his own person, with a separate identity and individual needs and wants.

As your toddler begins her second year, she gradually discovers that she really isn't the centre of the universe, and that's a frightening and frustrating revelation. Your child wants to be in control and have things done her way. She is annoyed at having to follow rules, and she's frustrated that she can't make her body do all the things that she wants to do.

By this point, she has had a bit of practice at being her own person and she might dislike being told not to do what she feels like doing, or not to eat what she feels like eating. As you put more demands on your toddler to follow rules and routines, you will often find yourself in face-offs over everything—from getting dressed in the morning to not playing with the telephone. You need to allow her to do as much for herself as she can and go at her own pace, at least some of the time. But you also need to set clear limits and gently remind her when you must take charge. Tell her, "You can't go outside without your snowsuit, but you can pick which pair of mitts you want to wear."

In spite of their opposition to everything and their need for control, toddlers are very teachable. Your child will imitate your activities around the house as well as your mannerisms and your spoken expressions—so watch what you say! You may gain unflattering insights into your own speech and behaviour through this little mimic. Children's language skills increase rapidly in this period, and their unique personalities start to blossom. Your toddler absorbs knowledge and experiences so fast that she will constantly amaze and entertain you with her newfound skills and abilities to communicate.

A Toddler's Mental Development

As your toddler's separate identity becomes more pronounced, he alternates between wanting to operate independently from you and wanting to keep you close to be assured of your constant love and support. He continues to want you there all the time, even as he explores his independence. So he plays by himself for a short while, then comes running back to you to make sure you're just where you were when he left you. He may protest when you go out or when you leave him with another caregiver.

Toddlers have a very short memory and an even shorter attention span, which means they can be distracted during a tantrum or if something is frustrating them. As their memory improves, however, your efforts to distract them become less and less effective.

Being still focused on self, toddlers are rather poor at socializing and they're naturally aggressive. Your toddler won't hesitate to snatch a toy from another toddler because he's not yet able to recognize that others have the same feelings that he has. He may also roughly push a child out of the way to get at the toy he wants. Sometimes he might hit another child for no apparent reason. This aggression is part of his drive for independence and identity. Aggressiveness also makes him feel more important. Sometimes there's an element of curiosity in it: Let me pinch this baby and see what happens. When the other baby starts wailing, he may do it again just to see if he gets the same reaction.

Typical Toddler Behaviours

Here are some typical toddler behaviours, with tips on how you might respond.

Running away from you. He catches your eye, gives you that achingly cute smile, then suddenly turns and tears off across the room. After a few steps, he turns again and comes back to you, giggling. Then he darts off once more. This is a game toddlers love to play. Running off is one way they practise being separated from their parents. But they don't want to be too separate, so they come back. This is a wonderful game to play with your toddler in a safe place, but it can be very dangerous if he tries it in places that are not so safe.

➤ Play the game often at home to give him lots of opportunities to practise and enjoy his separateness.

➤ Let him know where he is not allowed to play the running-away game, but don't count on his remembering.

> In areas or at times that you judge to be unsafe, always carry him or hold on to him.

> Some parents use a harness on children who love to run. If you're comfortable with the concept, get one that fits over your toddler's chest, but still allows him freedom to move within your reach.

Temper tantrums. He throws himself on the floor, kicks his heels in the air as if riding a bicycle, and screams at the top of his lungs. Or he holds his breath until his face turns blue. The sheer force of his anger can stun you. Remember, however, that he's not behaving this way as a personal attack on you or in reaction to your request that he not poke the cat. Tantrums are a natural part of toddlerhood, and sometimes the only expression of a child's frustration—a feeling he can't express any other way.

> When your child erupts in a tantrum, you must remain calm and allow the tantrum to wind itself down. He needs to know that you're in control when he's feeling so completely out of control.

> Don't try to reason with him, but talk to him calmly and, once he begins to settle down, try to distract him. "I know you're upset that we can't find your teddy. We'll find it soon. Let's see if it's in your bed. Maybe your doll is in your bed."

> If your child has several tantrums in a day, look at his sleep schedule to make sure he's getting enough rest.

> Offer meals and snacks before he becomes cranky with hunger.

> Try to eliminate unnecessary frustrations—for instance, put latches on the doors of rooms he shouldn't enter.

> Without being rigid, keep up a regular routine with him every day.

Refusing to share possessions. Before two-and-a-half, your toddler is too young to understand sharing. Don't force him to share, and don't shame him if he won't. If he's the aggressor and grabs another child's toy, quietly tell your child *No!* and give the toy back. If the two children can't play without interfering with each other, then it's time to pack up and move on.

Playing with genitals. It may make you uncomfortable that the minute you take off his diaper, his hand dives between his legs. But it's a very common action at this age, and the best thing to do is to ignore it. As he gets older and better understands what you say, you might place limits on this behaviour and let him know that playing with his genitals is not something to do in public.

A Toddler's Fears and Stress

"Mommy, I'm scared." Many fears are normal at this age, and one fear once overcome is soon replaced by another. Separation anxiety is the most common fear of toddlers, and almost all experience it. Also common at this age are fear of the dark and fear of falling asleep. Some toddlers are terrified of dogs; others won't go near a toilet because they think they might fall in and disappear; still others are frightened of sudden loud noises and run toward you if someone switches on the vacuum cleaner.

You may also find, to your surprise, that your toddler is afraid of costumed characters like Santa Claus and clowns. If you've planned an outing that includes one of these characters and your toddler dissolves in tears of fright, it can be upsetting for both of you. Don't push her to go closer or try to reason with her. Just reassure her and remove her far enough away that she feels secure. She might be willing to peek from a safe distance at the object of her terror.

Why do these fears appear at this age? A toddler is still adjusting to the larger world outside of home, and most of what he experiences is new. Like most people, toddlers are frightened by the new and different—new people or different places or unusual experiences. Also a toddler is moving from feeling secure at the centre of her world to a dawning realization of how small and powerless she is in the larger world. From that perspective, many new people or experiences can seem gigantic and overwhelming. A toddler is also developing a rich imagination and her memory is improving. So she will remember that a dog once scared her by barking fiercely, and her imagination allows her to embellish the memory and see other more frightening possibilities.

With lots of reassurance, parents can help turn their child's cries of fear into shouts of joy.

There are several ways you can help a toddler gain control of his fears. Gradual desensitization may work for some; for example, if the child is afraid of the noise of a particular appliance, give him opportunities to touch it when it's turned off. Then he might be willing to watch from his mom's arms while dad turns it on. Finally, he might agree to sit in the same room while you run the machine. Ask him what you can do to help, but above all, don't belittle him or push him to do something he's afraid of. He will build confidence as he overcomes his fears.

You might also create stories to help your daughter deal with her fears. If she is frightened of monsters, you can weave a story about the magical power of her teddy to watch out for monsters as she sleeps and turn them into snowflakes. When you do this, you aren't lying to your child or confusing her with fantasy, but rather you're entering her own world of imagination.

While toddlers have their own fears, they also pick up on their parents' fears, so your behaviour as a role model is important. If you're squeamish about the sight of a drop of blood or panicked by a spider, try to keep your reactions to yourself.

Television is a potential source of fears. Most parents shield their toddlers from television programs that are frightening—including some cartoons and programming for children. But sometimes, a character or an image in a commercial or a cartoon that an older child or an adult would find amusing will frighten a toddler, who still lives in a world where the line between fantasy and reality is fuzzy.

Signs of Stress

Sometimes a child's fears go beyond what you expect for his stage of development; try to ascertain whether they are signs of real stress. For instance, if your toddler is suddenly afraid to go outside and cries if either parent leaves the house, he may be showing stress. Toddlers cannot verbalize their stress, so look closely for the following:

- stomach aches or rashes that have no other apparent cause
- less interest in food
- changes in behaviour during toilet learning
- more temper tantrums than usual
- an increase in nightmares or night terrors or sleep interruptions

If you feel that your child is exhibiting one or more of these signs of stress, try to figure out what may have changed in his day-to-day routine that might cause him to react. It may be something obvious, like a recent move or a change of caregiver, or it may not be one particular event but an accumulation of changes. Maybe there's another two-year-old now at his baby sitter's and, at the same time, his dad was away last week on a business trip. Or it may be that he's starting to use the toilet, but he's resisting the change.

Give your child time to become familiar with new environments while you are nearby to reassure and help in the adjustment.

Once you've identified the cause, you can either eliminate it or give him lots of reassurance and time to adjust to whatever changes are happening in your lives. If life has become too busy, he may need more quiet time with mom or dad every day; or you may need to eliminate some activities from a hectic routine; or you may postpone helping him learn to use the toilet for a month. If he's reacting to a change of caregiver, you should spend time with him and his caregiver together, perhaps a few minutes every morning, both to monitor their relationship and to let your child know that you understand that this is new for him and he needs time to adjust. Most childhood fears disappear on their own in a few months. But if the fear lasts longer than six months, if the child's sleep is continually interrupted, if he loses weight or if his play is affected, then it's wise to consult your doctor.

Accepting a New Sibling

The birth of a new sibling can be very threatening to a toddler. The event, which is so joyful for his parents, may be frightening to a child if he's the firstborn and hasn't had to share his parents' love before. Children are very possessive of parental love and attention.

Children also have a natural drive for power which shows itself in that competition for the love and attention of parents that we know as sibling rivalry. Sibling rivalry is perfectly normal, and sibling jealousy is both inevitable and an important and valuable part of the growth of a child. These competitive battles are the way in which the child gropes toward becoming an individual.

It has been accepted knowledge that, the closer in age the two children are, the stronger will be the older child's feelings of jealousy and rivalry. However, Nina Howe, a developmental psychologist and professor of education at Concordia University in Montreal, thinks that children who have had their parents all to themselves for a longer time may feel the most resentment. Whichever it is, and it will be different for each child, the resentment is greatest when the age gap between the children is one-and-a-half to three years and the sibling is the same sex. If the older sibling is six years or more older, then he becomes a mentor and teacher to the new one whether he wants to or not.

Older children love to "help" their younger siblings, whether it's appreciated or not.

Telling your toddler

Some experts say to tell the older child in a matter-of-fact way as soon as the pregnancy begins to show. She won't fully understand, but she'll have lots of time to get used to the idea, and the fact that a baby is coming will become part of her reality. Others advise telling the child later so that she doesn't have too much time to worry about the impending arrival.

Either way, let her know close to the birth that you will be away in the hospital for a day or two and that grandma will be coming to stay or whatever your planned arrangements are. Prepare for her sibling's arrival by:

➤ helping her make a gift for the baby. It could be a picture for the nursery or a welcome card.

➤ taking her to a prenatal visit to the doctor.

➤ giving her opportunities to spend time with an infant so that she can learn how one behaves.

Don't raise her expectations of soon having a playmate, because a new baby will mostly sleep, eat, and cry for the first few months.

If you plan to move your toddler into a new room or into her own bed from her crib, do it several weeks before the new baby arrives to separate the event in her mind from the baby's arrival. She's moving into a big bed because she's a big girl, not because the new baby needs her crib. If your toddler is still comfortable in her crib and it's possible to leave her in it, then do so. She may be happier with the new baby if she is in familiar surroundings when her new sibling arrives.

When baby arrives

With the baby's arrival, you walk a fine line to get the balance of attention just right. You don't want to make such a fuss over your new child's arrival that your toddler feels left out; at the same time you don't want to play down the arrival so much that your older child is given a false impression of the importance of the birth. The new child in your arms also has needs that you want to meet, including the need to be welcomed into his new family. Trust that you will strike the right balance. Just as the adjustment to the firstborn had moments that were both smooth and awkward, so will the process of adjusting to the newborn sibling.

Here are ways to help your toddler understand his new role as the elder sibling in the family circle.

➤ Have a stash of presents for big sister. When gifts arrive for the new baby, pull out a big-sister present for your toddler.

➤ When talking about the new baby to a visitor or on the phone, let your toddler hear you describe how she's helping you care for her new sibling.

➤ Now is the time for dad and toddler to create their own comforting routines. When mom is nursing the new baby in the morning, dad and toddler might have breakfast together that includes your toddler's favourite toast fingers.

Dealing with typical behaviours of the older child

Expect some changes in your toddler's behaviour when the new baby arrives. Some toddlers regress to an earlier stage. If he's been using the toilet, he may start having accidents again. He may have bad dreams or begin to cling to one of his parents. He may want to be carried like a baby, to nurse at your breast, or to drink from a bottle. This can be a tough time for a parent— you're so busy with the new baby that the regressive behaviour of your toddler can cause a lot of extra work.

Your toddler might act out and try to hurt the new baby. Remember that this hostility is really directed at you for bringing home a "replacement" child. But since your child can't attack you, her source of security, she takes out her feelings on her new sibling. You might buy a baby doll with which the older child can safely act out feelings of anger. Don't try to reason or explain, just give your toddler firm limits on her behaviour and supervise her when she's with the baby.

Thriving As a Family

The three of you are just about to head out the door to a family gathering when your twenty-month-old refuses to put on his winter boots. You can feel the tension building. You're all getting angry. A temper tantrum is in the offing and you're not sure who is going to blow first. Sometimes you wonder who is the parent and who is the child.

The first lesson of managing negative emotions in a family is that children learn by example. The second lesson? No parent is perfect; everybody loses it from time to time. When your child reaches this age, you, as a couple, need to spend time talking together about what your expectations are, what you each mean by discipline, and by putting limits on behaviour. Parents need information about child development at every stage of a child's life, but they particularly need it when their child first displays anger or refuses to cooperate.

For some parents, their child's natural inclinations to be obstinate can seem like a personal attack. You may find yourself reacting in ways you always told yourself you wouldn't—shouting angrily at your child or swatting him on the bottom. You will both very likely be on the receiving end of your child's angry outbursts. Toddlers are simply not yet capable of restraining their emotions. Your reasonable response should be to ignore the outburst, try to distract your child, and hold him while he flails. Tantrums are most likely to occur during periods of hunger, fatigue, or stress, so try to solve those problems and head off any tantrums before they start.

You may also find yourself in major disagreement with your partner about how to handle particular behaviour. Keep the lines of communication open by sharing your frustrations. Talk about your own experiences as a child, about how your families operated. Every parent's expectations are strongly influenced by their memories of what they experienced growing up, and those memories and expectations may differ in many ways.

Most often, you'll be able to stand back and understand your child's behaviour for what it is. But parenting a toddler is an extremely stressful task that will occasionally send even the best of parents over the edge. If you get to the edge, forgive yourself. Next, apologize to your child. Explain that what you did—yelled, slapped, said something hurtful—was wrong. Explain that sometimes mommies and daddies have bad days, too. Always let him know that you still love him.

The same rules apply if you and your partner have a fight in front of your child. It may be frightening for him to watch his parents when they are very angry. Explain that mommy and daddy still love each other. Let him see you make up when you do. Don't forget the power of humour to diffuse tense situations between parent and child and between mother and father. Kids at this age can be very funny and an unending source of amusement to their parents. Choose to focus on the silly side.

A Toddler's Point of View

As you talk to me, I begin to learn the language to describe my world and to express my feelings. Don't be surprised if soon I want to tell you No!

Age One to One-and-a-Half

My Body

- I'm always on the move. I scoot upstairs, crawl downstairs backward, clamber up furniture, charge through rooms.

- I'm impulsive. I grab at anything—a plant, a vase, the dog's tail. I might dash out into the street.

- When I throw a ball, I push with my whole arm. To kick a ball, I run right into it. I take corners wide.

- If you try to snuggle with me on your lap when I'd rather be on the move, I stiffen up and slide down. But when I need a cuddle, I put my arms up and say *Up, up* or maybe just *Eh-eh*.

- Some days I eat as if I'm starving, shoving the food in with my hands. Other days I may have no appetite at all. I gain weight more slowly now, but I develop a rounded tummy.

- I might balk at having a bath. I hate having my hair washed.

- I need to be protected from exploring big, messy, potentially dangerous things—makeup drawers, garbage cans, litter boxes.

My Feelings

- I start out my second year fairly happy, but I become more serious and intense over the next six months.

- I'm very self-centred right now. I tolerate hugs and kisses, but I may not return them without prompting.

- I'm fearful of many things—thunder, big dogs, the dark.

- Once I can walk, I feel out of control when I'm placed on my back. I squirm when you change my diaper. I'll be less impatient if you change me beside a mirror or while I'm standing.

- Whatever you're holding, I want it.

- I enjoy dancing or bouncing rhythmically to music.

- I understand *No!* I may even be saying it myself. But if you say *No!* to me after I touch the glass bowl, I have an irresistible desire to touch it again. I'm not purposely defying you—I just can't help it.

My Mind

- I use a single word to express a complete sentence. *Ball?* may mean *Can we go outside and kick the ball around the way we did yesterday?*

- I use trial and error, mostly error, to solve problems, such as jamming the wrong piece into a toy.

- I'm starting to realize that the world is big and complex and I'm small and severely limited. It's frustrating.

- My memory is still pretty short. Just because you tell me something once doesn't mean I'll remember it forever. My attention span is the shortest it will be in my whole life.

- I'm more interested in real things—the phone, the TV, your camera—than in colourful, plastic imitations. I haven't developed enough of an imagination to play make-believe.

- I'm exploring opposites. Ask me to bring my shoes, and I might throw them into the other room.

- If you tell me that handling my toy roughly may break it, it won't stop me. I have to see it break in order to learn that lesson myself.

My World

- I become more dependent and independent at the same time. I may act like a dauntless explorer, but cry when you leave the room.

- To keep you connected to me as I wander farther afield, I keep coming back to you to dump things that I've found into your lap.

- I love playing simple games with you, as long as I never lose.

- I don't share. I don't have the remotest understanding of the concept. The more I'm pressured to share, the tighter my grip.

- I relate to other children only when I feel like it. I'll ignore another child until she takes one of my toys. Then, I'll grab it back.

- A structured day, with definite times for meals and naps, helps me understand sequence and makes me feel secure.

- I love an audience. If there's enough applause, I'll gladly give repeat performances.

- I'm learning about my place in the family.

Age One to Two-and-a-Half

Age One-and-a-Half to Two

My Body

- I barge around like a wind-up toy, head forward, arms out, not stopping till I crash into something.

- I experiment with movement. I run, climb, walk backward, ride on a riding toy, throw everything in sight, and twirl till I get dizzy and fall down.

- I can undress myself—and often do, so that I can run around naked. To stop me doing it in public, put my overalls on backward.

- If I haven't found my genitals yet, I will now.

- My diaper stays dry for longer periods, but I'm probably not ready to use the toilet.

- My dexterity is improving. I can turn one page at a time, turn doorknobs, undo latches.

- I'm gradually showing that I'm either right- or left-handed. Please don't try to change my natural inclination.

- Although I have more teeth, up to sixteen, I'm eating less. Instead of eating my peas, I might shove one up my nose.

My Feelings

- I get frustrated and angry that my body won't do what I want it to. I try to drink, and I spill. I try to jump, and I fall.

- I use my whole body to show my emotions. I yell, stamp my feet, make faces, throw toys, hit, bite, and scratch.

- When I'm having a full-blown tantrum, it means that all systems are out of control. That's why I need you to stay calm and in control till the tantrum spins itself out.

- If I tell you *I hate you*, I don't mean it. It's just the strongest word I know to show you the intensity of my feelings.

- I'm confused by my change in status. I used to be the centre of the universe, with you and other people doing my bidding. Now I feel that I'm no longer in charge. I'm experiencing the frustration of limits, the limits of my body and the limits imposed by your rules.

- When you ask me to do something, I say *No!* But I'll be surprised and upset if you always take me seriously.

- I may appear indifferent to the people I used to like.

- I want my own way in everything, and I want everything right now.

My Mind

- Instead of always using trial and error, I try to figure things out in my head first. I might turn the puzzle piece first instead of trying to jam it in wrong.

- I may use sentences of two or three words, such as *More juice* or *Me go now*. I have a vocabulary that ranges between two words and more than a hundred.

- I realize that there are different names for everything. I often ask, "What's that?"

- Although I may be able to recite numbers, I can't really count. But I do know the difference between one cookie and more than one.

- I can point to parts of my body as you name them, and to objects in a picture book.

- I'm beginning to understand time. I can't figure out *in an hour*, but I'll understand *after dinner*.

- I can't reason. I won't understand if you tell me, "Stop hitting her because hitting hurts, and if she hits you back, that will hurt you." Just say *No!* and remove me.

- I imitate you sweeping or making tea or talking on the phone. I'm developing an interest in games of make-believe.

My World

- I flip-flop between wanting to be close to you and wanting to be separate.

- I need room indoors and outdoors to explore, but no matter how well you've childproofed, I'll get into things you've never thought of. I need supervision most of my waking hours.

- I'm fascinated by the telephone, but I don't keep up my end of the conversation. I might just listen or smile or nod my head. I hate it when you talk on the phone and ignore me.

- Oral communication is not my strong point. If I want something and I don't know how to say it or I'm too tired to think, I'll grab your hand and lead you to it, pointing.

- I love helping with housework. Give me short, easy jobs, like putting away a few groceries on a low shelf.

- I can play for short periods by myself if you're nearby.

- I'm not ready for cooperative play. I'm so possessive with my things that I might hide them from other children.

- I like being the centre of attention at home.

Age Two to Two-and-a-Half

My Body

- I'm in better control of my body. I can go on tiptoes, run easily, jump, and walk up and down stairs, either alternating feet or going two feet to a step.

- I may eat only one good meal a day, and it won't necessarily be dinner.

- On a walk, I might push my empty stroller half the way, then get in it myself to be pushed home.

- My diaper may be dry all day. If I show an interest in using the toilet, gently help me learn. If I'm clearly not interested, I may not be ready for another few months.

- I can do more and more things myself—feed myself consistently, wash myself in the bath. I may also like to clean my highchair tray and polish the bathtub faucets.

- I can hold a cup with one hand, but I still do a lot of knocking over and spilling.

- I revel in the feel of sand, modelling clay, water, and mud. I need to get dirty.

- My hands don't always work independently of each other. If you ask to see my new toy watch, I'll hold out both arms.

My Feelings

- I'm more relaxed and happier than I was a few months ago. My emotions are not as dramatic as they used to be, or as they will be again.

- I'm affectionate. I might spontaneously give you a kiss.

- I enjoy the process more than the result. On a trip to the store, I care less about getting to the store than about walking along the curb, stopping to look at a worm, or just dawdling for its own sake.

- I may not say *No!* as often as I did before, but I use other ways to say *No!* to a situation I don't like. I might run around the room, refuse to sit, or cling to you.

- I can be demanding at bedtime. I stall for time, climb out of bed, ask for endless drinks of water.

- I may have a strong fear of people in costumes—clowns, trick-or-treaters, or Santa Claus. Don't tell me not to be afraid. Just hold me close.

- I may still need my night-light on.

My Mind

- I talk in short sentences of three or four words like *Cookie all gone now*. I babble away to myself, getting extra practice in language.

- I might ask *Why?* but I probably won't understand the answer. I just know that it keeps you talking to me, which is what I want.

- When I speak, you can usually understand what I say, although strangers might not.

- I like things to be whole and unbroken, so don't give me two halves of a broken cracker. Give me a whole cracker—better yet, one for each hand.

- My drawings may be starting to look like something. But don't ask, "What is it?" It might not be anything but an experiment with colour or line or with the feel of a paintbrush in my hand.

- I'm beginning to remember people, places, and events.

- I make up stories to avoid responsibility. If I break a glass, I might say the dog did it. It's not lying; it's wishful thinking.

My World

- In a group, I'm more likely to talk to adults than to children.

- If somebody says *Hello!* to me or asks a direct question, I may or may not answer.

- When I'm with other children, I play beside them, not with them. Just because we don't play together doesn't mean we're not enjoying ourselves.

- If another child shovels stones into her pail, I'll copy her. If a few kids move from the sandbox to the swings, I'll drift over with them.

- I'm as possessive as ever. I often say, "That's mine!"

- I still grab, hit, and push to get what I want.

- I like repetition. I still need a regular routine to help me understand the sequence of the day's events.

- I love doing little errands for you, like fetching your shoes.

Age Two-and-a-Half to Five

uring your child's first three years, you have gradually relaxed the fierce protectiveness of your love by giving her opportunities to explore her world, by encouraging her, and by reassuring and comforting her when she encounters difficulties. As your child becomes more independent, more of a separate individual, she continues to need your encouragement, your reassurance, and comfort. But she needs more from you—she needs your firm guidance and loving discipline.

Some parents think that *discipline* means *punishment,* but the word has its root in the Latin *disciplina* from *discere,* meaning *to learn.* In setting standards for your child's behaviour, you provide the foundation for her to learn, to learn guidelines for making choices, to absorb models for decision making and problem solving, to develop self-discipline.

"I think my child lives on love and air."

ROSALYN, MOTHER OF TWO, WHITE ROCK, B.C.

Your child's expanding world still presents an almost limitless choice of activities to undertake, of objects to touch and play with, of people to deal with in situations where you, her parents, cannot always be nearby. If you don't set limits and establish guidelines for your child, she may feel at a loss or even abandoned, not knowing how to make choices or how to find her way when everything is still so new to her.

Failing to provide guidance results not in a spoiled child, but in a child full of anxiety. She is swimming in a sea of wants; she needs your help to plan her route. Anxious children are more likely to show their stress by having temper tantrums and will have more trouble relating to other children their age.

Children respond better and feel better about themselves when approached positively. Instead of saying, "Don't throw your coat on the floor," try saying, "Please hang up your coat." Same message, but a more positive approach. Catch your child being thoughtful. Praise her for it. When you're having a good time playing quietly together, tell her how much fun you're having. Children, like people of all ages, respond better to the positive.

Feeding and Nutrition

By the age of two-going-on-three, your child is comfortable at the family table and has absorbed the rules and routines of mealtimes. In his growing quest for independence, however, he's likely to challenge those routines. Suddenly he is skeptical about every new food on his plate. He ignores his favourite food. He only eats one kind of sandwich. He demands snacks at all hours and then stubbornly refuses dinner. How you deal with this stage will be important in helping your child develop a healthy attitude toward food as he grows.

What Does My Child Need Now?

Your child continues to need meals and snacks made up from the four essential food groups—grain products, milk products, fruits and vegetables, and meat or protein-rich meat alternatives. You may need to increase the quantities as she grows. Canada's Food Guide takes into account the smaller appetites of two- to five-year-olds and specifies appropriate portions, ranging from a half to a full serving. SEE PAGE 183

Depending upon your child's age and activity level, she should be eating between 5 and 12 child size servings of grain products each day; 2 to 3 servings of milk products; 5 to 10 servings of vegetables and fruit; and 2 to 3 servings of meat or protein-rich meat alternatives. If you can't believe that your little person could eat so much food, keep in mind that half a slice of bread equals one child-size serving of grain products; a juice box equals two servings of vegetables or fruit; and a mere tablespoon of peanut butter equals one child-size serving of a meat alternative. Take time to record your child's diet for one or two weeks, and you'll probably find that he's consuming the minimum daily requirements.

Your child may already have a breakfast routine. Don't let anything get in the way of that good habit. A nutritious breakfast kick-starts your child's brain functions and enhances his ability to learn. Eating breakfast also positively affects a child's mood and behaviour.

Strategies for Picky Eaters

The major complaints from parents of preschool-age children are that they will not eat and that they will only eat junk foods. Remember The Golden SEE PAGE 185 Rules of Feeding: *You decide what to serve and when and where to serve it; it's up to the child to decide whether or how much to eat.* When well-intentioned parents try to cross that line and wheedle, cajole, or threaten their preschooler into clearing his plate, they set up a power struggle that can make mealtimes miserable for the entire family. If you can accept that food is one of the first things your child can say *No!* to and have control over, it will help you disengage from the battle.

Set clear boundaries around food and eating. If your child chooses not to eat at a particular mealtime, don't scold or lecture. And don't become a

short-order cook who jumps up from the table to prepare a separate meal for your finicky eater. First make sure your child isn't ill: Nausea could put a child off his food, or an ear infection could make it difficult for him to swallow. If there isn't a medical problem, then let your child leave the table without a fuss, just reminding him that the kitchen doesn't open again until snack time. Then keep your word. You will probably have to live with some short-term fussing, but don't weaken. Your child will be genuinely hungry the next time he arrives at the table.

Some other strategies to interest your preschooler in the food you serve:

➤ Eat the way you want your child to eat.

➤ Eat together as a family at least once a day. Talk with your child about the most interesting, or worst, or best things that happened to each of you that day. Encourage conversation and discussion.

➤ Take your child shopping. Let her help select the produce and other foods that will be served during the week.

➤ Let your child help in the kitchen. He's more likely to eat dinner when he's seen what's gone into it, and he'll be proud of his contribution.

➤ Grow some of your own food—even if it's just a potful of parsley. One little girl who despised green beans claimed them to be her favourite food after she grew some in her dad's vegetable garden.

➤ Give unfamiliar foods silly or exotic names. Who could resist Toad-in-the-Hole?

➤ Serve food cut into interesting shapes. Use a metal cookie cutter to cut shapes out of sandwiches.

➤ Choose healthy fast foods. Pick up barbecued chicken from the supermarket; boil up some perogie; microwave a burrito; add some cheese and vegetables to a plain pizza crust.

➤ Serve vegetables raw.

➤ Let your child dip his vegetables—in yogurt, preferably, but in ketchup or salad dressing, if you're desperate.

➤ Offer plenty of water—which prevents dehydration and constipation and won't dull your child's appetite.

➤ Don't keep junk foods around the house, so that neither you nor your child will be tempted by them.

➤ Peer pressure can work magic. Your child may be more willing to try new foods at preschool or when he has a friend to dinner.

Preventing Long-Term Eating Disorders

If your child has problems with food and eating, think carefully about whether your own attitudes may be influencing him. The primary purpose of food is to nourish the body. It should not be used as a reward or as a punishment.

Don't soothe a disappointed child with a cookie, or discipline a mischievous act by withholding dessert. Reward the child's success with an extra bedtime story instead of candy. When food becomes entangled with feelings of self-worth, eating disorders such as anorexia, bulimia, and chronic dieting can result in later years. Your positive, non-judgmental approach will help your child have a healthy attitude toward food and eating throughout his life.

"My husband makes a great minestrone soup, but my daughter thought it was revolting. Then one day he was inspired to serve it as 'Princess of Arabia Broth'. My daughter devoured it, and now asks for it all the time."

JULIE, MOTHER OF TWO, BOWEN ISLAND, B.C.

Sleeping

At two and a half, your child probably sleeps eight or nine hours a night and, possibly, another hour in an afternoon nap. Most children have dropped the last nap, but one-third of kids still enjoy an afternoon siesta up to age four or five.

If your child is still waking in the night, it's possible that her circadian rhythm hasn't been completely established. But it's more likely that some noise has disturbed her. Your child may wake when she hears you come home from your night class or because the dog barks. As much as possible, try to control the light and sound levels around your child's room.

If your child is no longer restrained in a crib, he may let you know when he's awake by suddenly appearing in the TV room. All you can do is gently take him back to bed. If your child tends to be a night wanderer, consider what dangers he might encounter unsupervised in another part of the house. Take whatever precautions are necessary to keep your child safe. SEE PAGE 190

Perhaps your child begins to sleepwalk, which can be alarming. No one knows why people sleepwalk. But if your child does, erect a few barriers to keep him safe. Put up a baby gate across the stairs or close his door—the idea is to present an obstacle that would require his wide-awake skills to manipulate. It's a myth that you should never wake a sleepwalker, so if you happen to waken your child, don't make a big fuss. Just reassure him, tell him that he had been asleep, and return him to bed. Sometimes a little milk will help him doze off again.

Basic Care

A preschooler seems born to help. He has developed many of the necessary motor skills to help you and himself and to perform a variety of everyday tasks. He'll help you unload the groceries, fold the laundry, pay the bus fare. He'll put on his own clothes and shoes, brush his own hair, wash his own hands. He may not do any of it to your standards or schedule, but he'll work with great pride of purpose whenever you let him try. Celebrate that independence, and help your preschooler to help himself.

Dental Care

SEE PAGE 147

Your preschooler still needs your help with brushing his teeth. Once a week, you might like to have your child brush his teeth and then chew a disclosing tablet that will colour the plaque and tartar that he missed. It's an entertaining way to teach him proper brushing technique. You should ensure that your child brushes no more than two times a day with fluoridated toothpaste, and use water only or non-fluoridated toothpaste the other times.

Some children begin losing their baby teeth as early as their fourth year, others not until their sixth year. Your child may be quite alarmed by the fact that his teeth have begun to fall out—it can be a little painful to lose a tooth, and there is sometimes a small amount of blood. For a child who hasn't yet developed a concept of money, the promise of the tooth fairy's visit makes no difference whatsoever. As soon as you notice your child's wiggly tooth, explain that the tooth will soon fall out but it will be replaced with a grown-up tooth that's already in his mouth.

Learning to Use the Toilet

Now is the time to put away those daytime diapers. Diapers and disposable training pants keep the child feeling dry so it's more difficult for him to relate his bodily functions to the wet result. During the day, put your child in cotton underwear. Let him know that it's OK if he has an accident and that there are fresh clothes that he can put on. Show him where to find clean underwear, pants, and socks. Avoid training pants because they can be difficult to pull on and off.

By this age, most children stay dry during the day, but still have problems making it through the night, even at the age of four. Let him wear diapers or disposable training pants at night until he's dry most nights.

When your child won't use the toilet

Try to view the toilet from your child's perspective. First, he has to climb up on this huge hole into which he then lowers a very vulnerable part of his body; when he's finished his business, he has to push a lever which causes a loud, sucking noise, and whatever was in the toilet completely disappears! Children may fear being flushed down the toilet or having a monster sneak up through the toilet and grab them. They also may feel sad at letting something of themselves get flushed away. To a child, feces or urine may not be unpleasant; they are something he produced, something that's part of him; giving them up isn't always easy.

When a child is struggling to stay in control, she may refuse to have a bowel movement. This retention of feces will cause her considerable discomfort and even infection if extended to the extreme. Sometimes, explaining the bodily needs of nutrition and elimination, of how her body uses food and eliminates what it doesn't need in *poo* and *pee,* can help a child understand why she should excrete urine and feces.

> **Children may fear having a monster sneak up through the toilet and grab them.**

Even when your child uses the toilet at home, she may not be willing to use a public toilet. The unfamiliarity of a public washroom can be frightening. The toilets themselves are big and they make loud echoing noises when they're flushed. One three-year-old frustrated his parents by wanting to stuff a public toilet with toilet paper each time he used one. After some questioning, he explained that the toilet paper would block out the monsters. With his parents' explanation of how toilets work and with some reassurance, he gradually accepted that there couldn't be any monsters living in the toilets.

Hygiene

> Teach your child, especially a daughter, how to use toilet paper appropriately and to wipe her bottom from front to back.
> Model appropriate hand-washing after wiping oneself and flushing the toilet. Assist the child in handwashing, if necessary.
> Keep up the daily bathtime—most active children need a thorough clean-up at least once a day.
> Make a bedtime story part of the nighttime routine. The promise of a story after the bath will get the most reluctant bather into the water, and the most committed water-baby out.

Bedwetting

For the majority of children, bedwetting is a temporary problem that will correct itself. Some parents try to control bedwetting by restricting the number of drinks a child has in the evening. Although reasonable restriction of bedtime drinks is helpful, refusing drinks before bedtime has no effect on bedwetting, and the refusal may just cause tension between you and your child.

Bedwetting doesn't stop until a child wakes himself up in time to make it to the bathroom. No child purposely sleeps through the urge to urinate in order to wet the bed. Some just develop reflex control later than others.

Some child-care experts suggest that parents not take a sleepy child to the bathroom. If the child isn't fully awake when you carry her to the toilet, you may encourage the very thing you want to avoid—urinating in her sleep.

Bedwetting Facts

Up to the age of five, approximately 15 per cent of children wet their bed during the night.

➤ Many more boys than girls wet their beds.

➤ Bedwetting may run in families.

➤ Bedwetting can be caused or made worse by stress. Events such as a move, changes in childcare, or the arrival of a new baby can trigger it. If it seems excessive, discuss the situation with your family physician.

Grooming: The First Haircut

Sometime before they begin school, most children have their first haircut. Even if you have trimmed your child's hair at home without too much fuss, you may be in for a bit of a battle once you get to the barbershop or the hair salon. Prepare your child in advance. Tell him that he will use a special chair, that his hair will be sprayed with water, that he will have to sit still for several minutes. Offer him a reward for his cooperation. It's probably best not to have his hair washed the first time at the salon and to keep him in the chair as brief a time as possible. If it will help, sit in the chair yourself with him on your lap. Some children refuse to wear the protective cape, so bits of cut hair end up on their clothes and down their necks. Bring him a change of clothing, just in case.

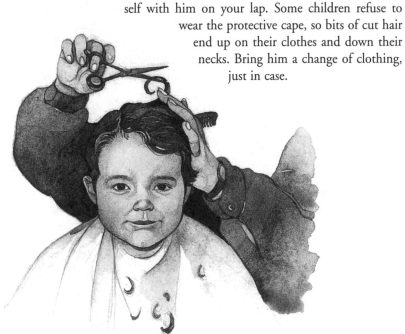

Dressing

➤ Choose clothing that's easy for your child to manage: shoes that slip on or that have Velcro closures instead of laces; pants and skirts with elastic waists.

➤ Store her clothes so she can easily find them: one drawer for socks and underwear, one for T-shirts, one for trousers.

➤ If you want your child to pick up after herself, make it easy: Put coat hooks where she can reach them; put a shoe tree in her closet; place a laundry hamper in her room.

➤ Respect your child's colour and fabric preferences.

➤ On those occasions when you don't want to rely on your child's fashion sense, offer a choice of clothing: "Would you like to wear the green T-shirt or the yellow T-shirt with your grey pants?" Offer your child freedom of choice, but within a controlled set of choices. This technique works well in a variety of situations.

Visiting the Doctor

In preschool, daycare, and playgrounds, a preschooler comes into contact with many more children. It's not unusual for them to get back-to-back colds during this stage. If you're anxious about your child's health but you're not sure that a trip to the doctor is necessary, call your child's doctor to discuss the symptoms. Sorting the problem out by phone may avoid an unnecessary visit to the doctor. Depending on the symptoms, the doctor may want to see the child—once she has consulted with you on the phone, she bears some responsibility for the outcome of any suggested treatment. SEE PAGE 283

Have your child's vision tested before he begins kindergarten. About 15 per cent of preschool-age children have a vision problem. The earlier such problems are detected, the greater the chance they can be corrected and sometimes even reversed. Routine hearing tests, on the other hand, are not recommended for preschoolers unless you have a particular concern.

Medical conditions like asthma or allergies usually emerge by the time a child is five years old. If your doctor diagnoses these problems, she may refer you to a specialist. Similarly she may refer your child for assessments if she sees indications of speech, language, and learning disorders. Regular check-ups with your family physician are still important for assessment of your child's growth, for booster vaccinations, complete physical exams, review of nutrition, and guidance about changes to expect.

Talking

Toddlers go through a language spurt in their third year. In the first six months of the year, they may double the number of words they can use in speech. At thirty months of age, they may have as many as 2,400 words in their vocabulary. Around this time, it's not uncommon for children to add 10 to 20 new words a week. Researchers think the sudden explosion in vocabulary use reflects the fact that children better understand how to categorize words, particularly the names for things and animate beings. If they can fit a new word into a familiar category, it's easier to remember. Interestingly, bilingual children seem to become aware of categories earlier than children whose families speak one language at home.

While he's increasing his vocabulary, your toddler may still have trouble making some sounds at this stage, especially consonant sounds like *s, r, l,* and *th.* He is likely to master the *h* sound first, but the other consonant sounds may continue to cause difficulties until he is four or five.

A toddler is also trying to understand how and when pronouns change in form. His identity is linked to *I* and *me,* but when his parents talk to him he becomes *you.* How can that be, when his parents are *you* as well? It doesn't make sense. Since he's beginning to apply logic to his language, he devises a clever solution to the problem. He calls everyone—even himself—by his proper name and avoids pronouns altogether, as in *Joey go home.*

As with other language mysteries, with enough exposure to language, children eventually separate words into those that follow logical patterns and those that don't. With a language that uses *-ough* for the different sounds of *cough, through, although,* and *enough,* we have to admit that English does not always follow rules—of spelling, pronunication, or grammar. In fact, it's a marvel that children learn as quickly as they do. Don't always try to "correct" them, so that you don't stifle their interest in experimenting with language. Make opportunities to model the language correctly for them, and they will eventually fit it into their perception of how language works. Their more fluent use of language will come as their desire increases to make themselves understood clearly, to achieve what they want, or to satisfy their needs.

With better language skills comes a better ability to ask questions, a skill every toddler delights in practising. Toddlers ask a lot of questions for a very good reason—they want to know the answers. Someone has to tell them the names of things and what those things are used for. Don't forget that everything from the telephone to the bird at the feeder is a new discovery. Answer the questions as best you can. You don't need to give full details. When a toddler asks about the telephone, she doesn't expect a lecture on telecommunications. A simple answer will keep her happy.

As any parent will tell you, the single most popular question is *Why?* Sometimes the *Why?* questions are easy to answer. Sometimes, there is no answer at all, as in the following exchange:

TODDLER: Who that man?

MOTHER: That's Mr. Johnson.

TODDLER: Why?

If there is no answer to a *Why?* question, find a way of diverting the conversation. Ask if she wants to know what job Mr. Johnson does.

If the question is a good one and you don't know the answer, don't be afraid to say so. You cannot know everything, and children's questions could require surprisingly sophisticated answers. If you think the child is really interested, take the opportunity for you both to find the answer, whether in the natural world, in a book, or in other resources at home or at a library. It gives the toddler the message that building up knowledge is fun and worthwhile.

As your child's language skills improve, he may use them in ways that might bother you. Preschoolers like to boast, especially when they are with other children their own age, everything from *My dad is bigger than your dad* to *My mom is older than your mom.* Don't take it too seriously. Just be prepared to intervene if things come to blows.

To some parents, the bigger problem is the use of "dirty" or rude language. Children learn language just by being exposed to it. Don't be upset by it—sometimes they say inappropriate words because they find them funny or just to test your reaction. In either case, the best reaction is to not overreact. Recognize that you have to teach your social guidelines for talking, and calmly tell the toddler, "We don't say that in our house." Keep in mind that your guidelines depend on where you are and who is with you. Words that might not bother you at home can be embarrassing if uttered in front of grandma. Again, tell the child the rules simply and calmly: "We don't say that when we are with grandma." Teach your child what is appropriate to say and when, in the same way that you teach all your other family values.

Slow or Unclear Speech

The concerns that most parents have are that their children don't speak as well as other children their age, that their vocabulary is not large enough, or that they don't speak clearly enough for most people to understand them. Doctors usually advise parents to wait until the child is about three before arranging tests for speech problems. But with the recent advances in knowledge about language acquisition, speech pathologists suggest they should see children as young as two years old, if parents are concerned. The earlier a speech therapist starts to treat the problem, the more effective the resolution. Keep in mind that a child "talks his age" from about age one to age five. A three-year-old should be able to construct understandable three-word sentences. If you're in doubt, discuss it with your doctor and ask for a referral to a speech pathologist.

> A child "talks his age."
> A three-year-old should be using three-word sentences.

Stuttering

Theories about stuttering have changed over the years, but current researchers believe that there may be a genetic predisposition, since it's not uncommon for stuttering and dyslexia to run in families. But even a child with a predisposition is unlikely to stutter without the additional factor of stress. A child's feeling that he always has to compete for attention, for example, might create enough stress to bring on the stuttering. A third possibility is that there is a problem with the development of the child's fine motor ability to coordinate breathing and shape mouth, tongue, and teeth to create particular sounds.

Do not immediately assume there is a problem if you hear your child repeating words or sounds. Almost all children go through a phase of mild stuttering as they try to work out sounds and words for themselves. It should only become a concern if the child starts repeating a whole sound or syllable and seems to come to a halt after each repetition. For example, if a child tries to say *mom* and it comes out as *muh, muh, muh, mom,* there could be a problem. However, a faster repetition of the consonant *m* as in *m-m-m-mom* should not cause concern.

If you suspect there's a problem, don't delay getting help. Speech thera-pists say it is relatively easy to treat children as young as two or three years of age, but much more difficult by the time the child reaches the teen years.

Your Role in Language Development

Throughout your child's fourth and fifth years, his language skills race ahead. By five years of age, most children use up to 2,200 words and under-stand up to 9,600. But it isn't just the number of words that increases. The child also begins to use language in new and creative ways. Ask your daugh-ter to clear up her crayons, and she might tell you she'll do it as soon as she has finished what she's building with her blocks. Such an answer shows she is using language to make an argument and to plan the next few minutes. It also shows that language is enabling her to develop her concept of time. But you might want to ask her to pick up her crayons anyway!

You've probably been reading to your child since he could sit still and lis-ten. Keep it up. Reading aloud to children helps them develop the listening side of oral language as well as a love of words. His speaking skills also develop out of his awareness of the sounds or phonemes that go together to make words and parts of words. Developing a child's appreciation of words and his awareness of story provides some of the motivation for him to read for himself.

In all your conversations with your child, be aware of his age and com-prehension, but don't artificially limit the range of your vocabulary and sen-tences. As the figures attest, children understand far more than they are yet capable of articulating. Respond with full sentences to his chatter, not just occasional one-word interjections such as *mm-hmm*.

When you play with your child, continue to describe what you are doing to expose her to new words and new ideas. Ask questions about what she is doing and help her flesh out the answers by supplying more details of your own. If you ask what she's doing with her blocks and she answers, "Making a house," you might say, "That house is almost big enough for me to fit in." Your response has introduced the idea of size and the concept of fitting one thing inside another—not to men-tion providing a model for the use of the pronoun *me*.

> **By age five, most children use up to 2,200 words and understand up to 9,600.**

Parents are the first models for their children's speech. The more expo-sure children have to language and the more language is part of their fam-ily's everyday life, the more capable the children become of comprehending and using listening and speaking skills. These skills are essential to first learning and then refining the more complex skills of communication—reading what others write or writing what you want others to read.

Playing and Learning

Your preschooler no longer needs to focus on how to stand or walk or run. Now his movements are more agile and natural. Physical games are new ways for him to develop his coordination and strength, to release his high energy, and to have fun with other kids.

He's ready now for more challenging activities, with your supervision. Now you can't pass a playground or a park jungle gym without giving him the thrill of practising his gymnastic skills. He may want to ride a tricycle although he may start by using his feet to push himself. He will eventually learn to pedal and then progress to a small bicycle with training wheels.

Your child may enjoy kicking a soccer ball, and this will prepare her for team sports later. You can also practise throwing and catching together, although at first there will be a lot more misses than catches. For learning how to throw and catch, a small bean bag may be easier than a ball because it's easier to grip.

Your child will become more interested in having physical adventures. Going for a hike in the woods or along a river fits the bill. As your preschooler scrambles over logs, runs on rough terrain, and keeps his eyes peeled for garter snakes, he's working on his balance and coordination and building his observational skills.

At about age four, you can introduce your preschooler to favourite family sports like skiing, skating, or swimming through classes and your own instruction. If your child is keen, get her involved in some of the sports that you personally enjoy. She will pick up on your pleasure and learn by imitating you. As she grows older, you'll be able to enjoy doing these things together as a family, and someday she may beat you down the hill or across the pool.

Social and Emotional Development

Your preschool child becomes much more sociable; by the age of four, she is learning to share, take turns, and play with other children through cooperative games. In make-believe play, children can be doctor and patient, mom and dad, or king and queen. Pretend play stimulates the child's emotional, social, and cognitive development and provides a satisfying outlet, which may reduce acting out of aggressive feelings. Researchers have found that, when both parents are involved and interested in pretend play, their children play for longer periods of time and show advanced intellectual capacity.

Preschool children express their imaginations and solve problems by building elaborate structures with their hands. Your child may spend time assembling train sets, making airplane models, building complex structures—towers, houses, and towns—with wooden or interlocking plastic blocks. He may add toy people to bring the buildings and settings he creates to life.

The First Set of Wheels

At Age Three

Your child is ready for his first tricycle. Look for one that is low enough that he can straddle it with both feet flat on the ground, that has a wide seat, and that's stable when turning corners. To help little feet get a grip, stick bathtub decals on the foot pedals.

At Age Five

A child this age can learn to ride a bicycle, although she should only ride in a park or yard away from the street and the traffic. Take your child with you when you choose a bike so that you get the right fit. She should be able to sit on the seat, with balls of both feet on the ground and hands on the handlebars.

Snap on the Helmet

As soon as your child has wheels, he needs a helmet. It should meet standards set by the Canadian Standards Association (CSA) or the American National Standards Institute (ANSI); check the label. Ensure that the helmet fits snugly, but comfortably.

An older sibling can be a good coach in activities that expand physical skills.

Naming Feelings

Your child at this age is starting to identify with you and to internalize your ideas and guidelines about right and wrong. He wants your approval and may be prepared to put some effort into earning it. He has begun to appreciate you and others as separate people, but also to realize that you and other people have feelings as he does. When he's playing, whether with you or with other children, help him understand your feelings and the probable feelings of other people by naming those feelings. It's as important to help him name and understand feelings as it is to help him name body parts or household items.

Once your child has playmates he likes to be with, try to encourage these relationships. Give him opportunities to invite his friends to come over to play, and take him to the homes of his friends. He'll be influenced by his friends and take pride in showing them his possessions. The art of friendship is an important new milestone in his emotional and social development.

Thinking and Knowing

The preschool child is able to use language to communicate her thoughts as well as to describe actions. She can remember more and observe and plan more than she used to, and she has some experiences to draw upon when making choices and decisions. Her vocabulary is growing by leaps and bounds. Playing can help your child learn to express herself and will expand her vocabulary if you encourage her to talk about what she's doing.

Questions and answers are a big part of what makes playing at this stage such a rich learning experience. Your child will ask lots questions—*What's that?* and *Why?* questions—to learn new words to be able to describe what she sees and to understand how the world works. Whenever you go on outings to a museum, a zoo, an airport, or a nearby construction site, these new environments and experiences will naturally stimulate lots of questions, the answers to which will fascinate a curious child hungry for knowledge. Then you'll notice how she incorporates her experiences into her imaginative play.

Preschoolers are also great helpers and want to be involved when parents are making things. Your child will want to help when you cook or clean, so give him lots of opportunities. If a parent does woodworking, a child can learn to sand and nail or screw pieces of wood together, with close supervision. Your child may enjoy rolling and kneading materials such as modelling clay or Plasticine. He'll start out making simple shapes, but might eventually create more complex shapes—animals, people, cars, or spaceships.

Puzzles and games also help your child understand patterns, to see how things are organized and grouped. Start off with simple jigsaws that have just a few pieces. You may need to fit together the first couple of pieces and then let your child have the satisfaction of finishing the puzzle by fitting in the last piece or two.

Give your child opportunities to play with different materials like leaves, flowers, feathers, fabrics, and egg shells. She might want to create collages of treasures she has found on outings. Together you could draw an animal and then use materials to represent certain features like feathers for a bird, straws for a porcupine, or aluminum foil for the scales of a fish.

Children love making cards for birthdays, Mother's Day, or other special occasions. As your child's memory improves, she'll be ready for a scrapbook to collect mementos and create something special that gives her an opportunity to reflect on her experiences.

Your child's ability to draw and paint will improve as he progresses from scribbling to representing people and objects. Let him try both freehand drawing and controlled drawing using stencils. You may be fascinated to see the feelings and experiences your child expresses through his art.

Board games provide an opportunity to play with your child and to help her recognize numbers and count. She will want to be able to read the number of dots on dice to help her figure out how many squares her piece has to move on the board at each roll of the dice.

Books and stories are a wonderful, entertaining way to develop a child's language skills and understanding. As she gets older, she'll be interested not only in the pictures but the story. Fairy tales, adventure stories, and nursery rhymes may all capture your child's interest. Some books help children prepare for big changes or events in their lives. These might deal with events like going to school, visiting a hospital, or the arrival of a new baby.

It's more important that your preschool child learn to appreciate books as a source of pleasure and enjoyment than that he be pressured into learning how to read before he's ready. Nonetheless, there are books, board games, and television programs that may help your child become familiar with the letters of the alphabet and learn to associate the shapes of letters with certain sounds. But puzzles like alphabet jigsaws or projects like making an alphabet scrapbook can make learning the letters much more fun. For the preschool child, playing is the best form of learning.

Your efforts to cultivate a love of learning in your child will pay more immediate and lasting dividends than drilling her on letters, numbers, or words. Encourage her natural curiosity and tendency to actively explore on her own. Making your child's "educational" experiences entertaining is the surest way to guarantee that she will be a successful learner. Take the play out of learning and you risk dulling your child's natural enthusiasm for learning. Keep the vital connection between playing and learning alive, and you won't have to worry about her willingness or ability to learn in the future.

Age Two-and-a-Half to Five

Behaving Appropriately

As your child moves through her third year, she has better verbal skills to say what she wants and express how she feels, which should reduce her frustration so that she doesn't resort to tantrums to communicate. But the improved verbal skills may seem like a mixed blessing to a parent on the receiving end of the communication. A preschooler with a better memory and stronger verbal skills is persistent about what she wants, whether it's a snack right after lunch, a treat at the grocery-store checkout, or a visit with her new friend down the street even if it's 6:30 in the morning.

Distracting her won't work as well now and, although you've told her *No,* you may find her quite adept at arguing her point of view over and over, in an annoying high-pitched voice. When she starts to whine or wheedle this way, tell her that you won't listen until you hear her "big girl" voice, then tune her out. When she talks to you in a normal voice again, give her lots of attention. If you find that she often whines, consider whether she is getting enough sleep—when children are tired, they're often more whiny.

"I went through a stage with my son where everything came down to a choice. Do you want to eat this cereal or shall I feed you? Do you want to put this sock on or shall I put it on? Do you want to walk up to bed or shall I carry you? It was exhausting, but it kept the fights to a minimum. I knew it was getting out of control when I started giving my husband choices!"

NANCY, MOTHER OF TWO, B.C.

Because your child's imagination is such a powerful force within him, he will sometimes mix fantasy with reality and tell wild stories. You might become concerned that your child is "lying," but a preschooler can't yet understand what "truth" is. That will come between his sixth and eighth birthdays. Don't punish your child or try to make him feel guilty for telling stories. But do explain the difference between his version and reality. Let him know that sometimes telling stories hurts people and that it is always better to tell the truth.

By the time your preschooler is four, he'll begin to be interested in pleasing you—which will no doubt please you! This is the beginning of a developing conscience. Your child will start to understand how his behaviour affects what others feel about him. He learns about being a friend and about what happens when he does something that makes another person feel happy or feel hurt. And if you displease *him,* you might hear, "I'm not your friend anymore!" You may also become more conscious of being a role model for your child. As he grapples with how to treat his new friends, how to decide what is the truth, or how he should behave when he's angry, he'll watch you closely for pointers.

As your child becomes more interested in what you think, your praise becomes a stronger tool for moulding her behaviour. But you still need to set limits and enforce rules with consistency. The mechanics of how you discipline your child will evolve as she grows—the rules will change and the consequences of breaking them will change. But the goal of your discipline won't change: You want to teach your child your values and morals.

It's good to remember what you're trying to achieve when you discipline your child. You're not trying to teach him to follow orders, to do whatever he's told as soon as he's told. Instead, you're teaching your child to take responsibility for his behaviour, to care for and respect others, to manage his anger, to develop self-discipline, to embrace life and all its opportunities. That kind of teaching is going to take a long time—about another ten or fifteen years on average.

Setting Limits

Some parents find it difficult to discipline their children. They don't want their kids to be angry with them or to be unhappy. If they believe that their children need every opportunity for self-expression, the parents may not want to limit their behaviour in any way. In some families, both parents are so busy that discipline, which takes time and consistency to be effective, gets lost in the rush.

But for their healthy development, kids need their mother and father to embrace this responsibility, to set rules, boundaries, and standards of conduct. If you treat your children like your peers, granting them the same freedoms and choices you have as adults, not only will they feel insecure in the face of so many choices, but they may also eventually lose respect for you. Firm and consistent parental guidance is important to children, and kids welcome it, although they may not always acknowledge it. Even though your children appear to resent your refusal to let them do particular things, they will be more anxious if you don't set limits.

Redirection and consequences

With their improved memory and ability to make links, preschoolers benefit from the consistent application of clear consequences to forbidden actions. If your preschooler draws on the wall with her coloured crayons, you may first redirect her by giving her a sheet of paper on which she can draw. Then you give her an explanation. You tell her that, in your family, you don't draw pictures on walls; you draw pictures on paper and then put the paper pictures on the walls. If she does it again, don't nag or lecture. Just give her the explanation again and take away the crayons.

It's so tempting to nag: "I told you not to do that. Look at the mess. Now how are we going to get that off? Why would you do that anyway." But first of all, you're wasting your breath because she's not ready to understand what you say—What mess? It's my work! Why would you want to remove it?—and second, you may actually make the situation worse. Some experts consider that lecturing a three-year-old is counterproductive.

Praise and approval

Your most powerful motivator for good behaviour is approval. Instead of catching your child doing something wrong, catch her doing something right. Let her know you approve of something she did. It will increase her self-esteem. If, the day after Amy has drawn on the wall with crayons, she gets out a sheet of paper to draw another picture, be unstinting with your praise: "That's really wonderful, Amy. I really like that you drew your picture on paper. It's really grown-up of you to know that you should use your crayons on paper. Where should we hang this picture so everyone can see it?"

Time-outs

The practice of taking time out is one way of removing your child from the scene of inappropriate behaviour. It lets her calm down and think about what has just happened. The Canadian Paediatric Society suggests that the best way to make time-outs effective includes:

➤ Picking the right place. There should be no built-in rewards, like toys or a television, in the time-out place.

➤ Keeping the time-out short. It should be three minutes for a three-year-old, four minutes for a four-year-old and five-minutes for a five-year-old. Time-outs should last no more than five minutes. Use your kitchen timer.

➤ Explaining the connection between the behaviour and the time-out.

➤ Not using the time-out to preach or lecture.

Here's how it works. Your four-year-old slaps his just-crawling baby brother for grabbing at his truck. First you comfort the baby (the victim should always get your positive attention first). Then you tell your four-year-old that, in your family, hitting is wrong and, if you do hit someone, you need to calm down in a time-out and think of other things to do in the situation. Then you set the kitchen timer and you send him off to sit in a chair (or wherever you've chosen as the time-out place). When the timer rings, he's free. Don't demand that he give you a list of other things he should have done. Let the situation go, and move on.

Concordia University developmental psychologist Nina Howe suggests a different way, so that the adult is the one who takes the time-out. "Sometimes when they are just driving me nuts and I think I'm going to lose it, I've said to my kids, 'I'm taking a time-out. It's a time for me to go and quieten down and back off a little bit.' That usually puts them into shock. They think, 'Oh, oh. This must be serious.' I go away, and then I can come back and talk about what's happened with them."

To Spank or Not to Spank

In Canada, the issue of spanking is controversial and divides parents and parenting experts alike. Some believe that it's wrong, ineffective, and harmful to the child, and that it should be banned by law. Others think that spanking may be useful, either as a last disciplinary resort or as part of other methods of teaching appropriate behaviour and discipline.

Disciplinary spanking, as some call it, is defined by the Canadian Paediatric Society (CPS) as an open-handed, non-injurious smack on the (clothed or diapered) bottom of the child, applied in order to modify behaviour. Slapping in the face, punching, kicking, pinching, ear-pulling, jabbing, shoving, choking, beating, strapping with a belt, and repeated demoralizing blows are not within the definition of spanking—they constitute child abuse.

Developmental pediatrician Wendy Roberts, Director of the Child Development Centre at The Hospital for Sick Children in Toronto, completely rejects the spanking of children. "One big problem is that it can induce fear," she says. "I hear kids day after day telling me how angry and mixed-up they feel because the daddy that they love so much and have so much fun with can become this evil monster who is angry and mean, and who scares them when he hits them. That's just incredibly confusing for a child. But the biggest reason not to do it is that it teaches children to use the same techniques in peer situations."

Dr. Marie Hay of Prince George, B.C., argues in *Paediatric Child Health*, the CPS magazine, that "if hitting people is wrong, then hitting children is wrong because children are people, too. When bigger children hit smaller ones to take their candy, they are called bullies.... Is it any different when parents hit their children to make them obey?"

But Calgary pediatrician, Dr. Peter Nieman, who helped draft the CPS statement on effective discipline for children, says that, while people have every kind of philosophical opinion on spanking, there really isn't enough current scientific data to support the claim that appropriate disciplinary spanking is harmful mentally or physically. That's what the CPS found after a comprehensive review of the research on spanking. "The emphasis here is on appropriate disciplinary spanking," he says, "where the child is spanked two or three times on the bottom."

Like the majority of childcare experts, however, Nieman discourages spanking and insists that, in the majority of discipline situations, there are more effective methods such as reasoning, time-outs, or setting rules and applying consequences. Spanking should be only a last resort when the child continues to defy the parent. On that rare occasion, the parent needs to re-establish authority, and spanking—done in private, with a loving hug and an explanation at the end—may be appropriate.

Dealing with Fears

Like toddlers, preschoolers are preoccupied by fears, although the fears are likely to be different and more frequent because the preschooler has a richer imagination. While your preschooler no longer feels an intense separation anxiety, or might even have overcome his fear of loud noises, he can now imagine something bad happening to him. Unlike a toddler who may not worry until the thing he fears is about to happen, a preschooler can become afraid even when there is no possibility of it happening. He can conjure up frightening creatures he has never seen. Your preschooler has now begun to ask *What if?* questions. "What if a bad guy comes into the house while I am sleeping, and takes me away?" "What if that monster I saw on TV yesterday suddenly jumps out of the television and turns me into a frog?" While the greater imagination creates all kinds of fears that you may find puzzling, bear in mind that it is an important element of his developing ability to learn.

"I remember talking to Kevin about the afterlife. He wrapped himself in some old towels and pretended he was a mummy. They're using their minds to create new things. That's what my kids like to do."

SUSAN, MOTHER OF THREE, TORONTO, ONT.

Because your preschooler is now spending more hours outside the home, he is exposed to all kinds of situations that can feed his rich imagination and cause him to worry. He worries about the people and events he sees on television and hears other people talk about, like wars, robberies, or children getting kidnapped. He may get very anxious when his parents argue in front of him, even if they are arguing constructively. This is the period when he may have nightmares frequently and may find it difficult to distinguish between them and reality.

How do you deal with these fears? Some of the things you did to handle fears when he was a toddler will be useful—avoiding scary books, movies, and videos, especially at times like Hallowe'en. You may also want to try to figure out what caused the fear in the first place, though sometimes a preschooler's fears have no cause that can be discerned. However, because a preschooler is more verbal and has greater understanding of speech than a toddler, talking about the fears and explaining them is much easier and workable. You should help the child understand that we all have our different fears, and that he is not alone; it may give him some relief to know that. It may also help to tell your preschooler stories of the kinds of fears you had when you were a kid, and if you can do it with humour, so much the better.

It may help to find ways to give him control over his fears. For example, you can tell him that dreams are like television, if you don't like one channel because the program is scary, you can change to another by using your imagination to switch. You can get him to suggest ways in which he thinks he can slay the fear as he would a dragon.

It is not useful to be impatient with a fearful preschooler, or tease him, or say things like "Big boys are not afraid of monsters." This may only make him more anxious or make him try to hide his fears, even though they still bother him. As his experience of life grows, he will be able to deal with his fears better. In time, he will realize that monsters do not jump out of the television set and that nightmares are not a part of reality.

Children begin to welcome other children as friends throughout their fourth year.

Making Friends

Making a friend is an exciting, momentous step for a child, and she's usually ready for it sometime after her third birthday. Between thirty and thirty-six months of age, children enjoy time with other kids, but their play is parallel. They play side by side; they might copy each other's actions and run around together, but they don't interact very much. This interaction develops slowly throughout the fourth year. Your child needs to be with other children a few times a week to develop and practise her social skills.

By the time your child is four, he will likely have several friends. But he may come home from daycare and say things like, "Me and Coburn are best buds. But Mirko is not my friend anymore. He kicked me this morning." Knowing how to deal with friends has become important, and having a best friend is one of the major developments in his relationships with other kids.

Preschool boys tend to play more active games with their friends than girls do (as many parents will attest), although it's not clear whether this is because of parental expectations or because there is a gender difference. As your child becomes more social, give him pointers on the etiquette of friendship. Tell him, "Come to the door so we can say goodbye to Isaiah" or "There's Peter in the park. Do you want to go over and say hello?" Model the kind of behaviour and language that will help him both develop and maintain friendships. If your child is shy, you may want to give him opportunities to play with the same child often, rather than several different children consecutively. Repeated contact with a known person helps dispel shyness. Try not to make your child self-conscious about his shyness.

Kids, like most adults, don't like aggression. They avoid a child who hits, bites, or takes their toys away. If your child behaves in a way that makes him unpopular, work hard to help him figure out how to get along better. Reward him when he spends a peaceful time with a friend. Catch him being nice and tell him you noticed. If he acts rough with his friend, be very sympathetic to the injured party and talk with your child. End the playtime if your child continues to act out.

The Benefit of Preschool

At preschool, your child will have the opportunity on a regular basis to spend time with her friends. In fact, the most important reason to send your child to a preschool is to give her opportunities to socialize with other children her age. She'll learn to take turns, to be quiet and listen when others speak (other children as well as the caregivers), to follow a new routine with the group. And she'll probably make a truckload of neat items to decorate your fridge.

Most activities are designed to help children develop language skills and both fine and gross motor skills. Your child will work on learning colours; she'll learn to count and sort and match. And she'll do all of this as part of a group, learning not just from the teachers but from the other children.

As in any school setting, class size is important. Look for a school with one teacher and one assistant for every ten or eleven children. You may need to visit two or three schools in your area to get a good idea what's available. A good preschool usually invites the parents of prospective pupils to come in and spend a morning observing and asking questions.

Preschool may also help prepare a child for starting the regular curriculum in a regular school, since he has already made the transition to a more structured setting and to learning as a member of a group. When it's time for your child to start school officially, give him lots of opportunities to get used to the idea. Take him to visit the school and let him play in the school playground. Help your child get to know other children in the neighbourhood who will attend the school with him so that he sees some familiar faces when he does go.

Thriving As a Family

From the time your child was born, you've been developing routines to make family life go more smoothly. You may discover that some routines feel more like rituals that you and your partner and your children have come to expect. They are activities that make your family unique.

It might be that you always have a big pancake breakfast on Sunday morning, or that grandpa comes over to play cards every Friday night. Then there are the special occasions and holidays that bring their own special rituals—religious holidays, birthdays, Mother's Day, Father's Day. Rituals are the bricks and mortar of a well-rounded family life. They're the foundations of family traditions, and each member of the family retains individual memories of these traditions and rituals.

When your child becomes part of other worlds beyond his home, he starts to understand that everyone belongs to a family and that all families are different. His family's rituals help give him a sense of identity. They're important for the predictability they lend to his life. And they're also terrific fun for all of you.

One of the most pleasurable aspects of being parents is having the chance to create important moments in your child's life. Together you can decide how to celebrate special holidays, birthdays, the first day of school, graduations, as well as public holidays. Take into account each of your experiences as children but also strive to create rituals and traditions that are special to your family.

Celebrate your rituals—from the nightly after-bath mirror games to the grandest fête—with a passion. Your own particular rituals are what makes your family different from the one down the street. Your child will come to count on them. You may not even realize your peculiarities, but spend a Christmas or Hanukkah or Diwali with someone else's family and you'll see how family celebrations differ. The opportunity of establishing your own way of doing things is one of the greatest joys of becoming a family.

How you celebrate special days together will soon become family rituals—the backbone of family life.

But don't limit yourself to the celebrations the calendar recognizes. Some families institute a regular Friday games night. Or "pick-your-favourite-dinner" Tuesdays. Or Labour Day fireworks. Or even ritualistic gatherings in front of the television every Thursday at eight. Mostly, rituals develop without any help at all. One day, you'll think back and realize that a pattern has developed. Honour their regularity without being inflexible about it. Rituals are the backbone of family life.

Keeping Your Child Safe

When your child is walking and talking, he can become a more active part-ner with you in the big job of keeping him safe. You will be responsible for his safety for many years to come but, gradually over the years, you will teach him how to keep himself safe. Reward your child for spotting danger and telling you about it. Instead of saying, "Don't play with matches," when every kid knows that playing is fun, say, "Safety Kids always give matches to their moms or dads. Are you a Safety Kid?" You get the matches and your child gets the reward of being dubbed a Safety Kid.

Outside at Home

When your child begins to play outside more often, investigate your back-yard and the play area in the same way that you investigated the inside of your home when your child was first mobile. You still need to provide supervision, but eliminating hazards makes supervision easier. Look at everything from your child's point of view, and take the necessary precau-tions.

Plan an outdoor cleanup. Are there a couple of broken windows tucked out of sight behind the garage? Is there an unlocked shed that a four-year-old would find fascinating because it's full of broken tools and half-used garden pesticides? Don't overlook the items you've set aside for recycling or for garbage pick-up—they might be dangerous to a curious child.

Some float aids help children learn not to fear the water, which prepares them for swimming classes.

Take a look at your garage and driveway, and consider how to minimize any dangers to your child. Check what you can see in your rear-view mirror when you back up any vehicle. Could you see a small child on a tricycle? All vehicles can cause injury or death, but the family van is especially dangerous because the sight-line for drivers of vans is different from the sight-line for drivers of the average car. If your child plays on the driveway, he might impulsively run out into the street after an escaping toy, even with you watching. Identify a barrier at the bottom of the drive to remind him that he must stop and look for traffic.

The backyard pool
Half of all the drownings that occur in Canada take place in home pools. If you have a backyard pool, it's your responsibility to supervise not only your own children but also any other children invited and keep them safe.

> The pool's fence must meet your municipality by-laws; usually the fence must be at least 1.5 m (5 ft.) high and go around all four sides, including the side that leads to the deck and patio doors.
> Keep furniture away from the fence. Don't make it easy for children to hoist themselves over the fence to get in or out.
> Put two locks on the gate, a day lock and a heavy-duty night lock.
> Night lighting is essential.
> There should be a phone jack by the pool or, if there isn't, you should have a portable one to take out to the pool with you.
> Be very careful about the toys you let children bring to the pool. If a toy rolls into the water, children might reach into the water for it.
> Ride-on toys are particularly dangerous. Ban them from the area.
> Handle all the pool's chemicals yourself, and store them under lock and key.

> Write out Pool Rules to reduce the risks of injury or drowning. Post them and teach your child and visiting friends to read them. State the consequence for not following the rules: banishment!

Pool Rules:

-➤ No running.
-➤ No pushing.
-➤ No jumping in at the deep end.
-➤ No jumping on another swimmer.
-➤ No swimming without an adult.

Swimming classes for children three years and older should be a priority. If you're planning a children's pool party, hire a qualified lifeguard—the cost is not prohibitive. There may also be a teenager in your neighbourhood who has her lifeguard certification. But, when you are away from home, it may not be wise to let a teenage baby sitter supervise the kids in the pool. It's a huge responsibility.

Streetproofing

Streetproofing, instructing children about the risks and dangers of daily life, has taken on the meaning of protecting children from abduction by a stranger. Parents should, however, consider other more common risks and dangers to their children and streetproof them about traffic injuries, abuse by someone they know, getting lost, and dealing with other people's pets. There is no way to totally protect anyone. Streetproofing is as much about instilling in our children enough self-confidence that they will listen to their instincts as it is about giving them enough knowledge to be aware, but not fearful, of everything and everyone.

"I think our first mistake was giving our son a bike on his birthday. We treated it like it was a toy and so did he! It took us a while to turn it around and really teach him about road safety."

DAVID, FATHER OF TWO, KILBRIDE, ONT.

Traffic safety

Traffic injuries are the Number One cause of death and injury in children. One in two hundred children under the age of fifteen dies or is seriously injured in a traffic-related incident. One reason might be that children don't get the street-safety education that kids received a generation ago, although there are more cars on the roads. Parents and professionals are more likely to talk to children about stranger abduction.

It's up to parents to teach street safety. Children under the age of six should not go near the street or road without supervision, for several reasons: A child under six has poor depth perception and her peripheral vision is undeveloped; she is easily distracted; she's small and can't see over or around obstacles; she can't read signs or warnings; and a child this age probably thinks that, if she can see a car, the car's driver must be able to see her.

> ### Making Your Child More Aware
> ➤ Teach your child to look in both directions before crossing a street.
> ➤ Practise listening for traffic as well as watching for traffic.
> ➤ While driving with your child in the car, play road games such as Spot the Road Signs, Spot the Dangers, Spot the Bikes to increase your child's concentration and awareness of the road and of vehicles.

Praise or Punish for Safety Behaviour?

Even parents who disagree with the concept of spanking a child will use spanking as a last resort in traffic safety situations. But research done in New Zealand and Britain indicates that severe discipline might not work. One study showed that one out of three children who were killed by oncoming vehicles had previously been disciplined for playing on the road. One of the conclusions drawn was that children don't understand what being hit by a car means. "Mommy hit me and that didn't really hurt" may be a child's perception. Whenever possible, praise good road-safety behaviour.

Bikes & trikes and battery-driven vehicles

Don't allow children under six to ride their trikes or bikes near a street for the same reasons that you don't leave them unsupervised. When your preschooler is ready for a bike, she's also ready for an approved bike helmet. Make the rule "No helmet, No riding" even when she's going biking on a bike path. Most bike injuries don't involve cars.

Some tips

- ➤ Involve your child in a community bike-check and safety rally.
- ➤ Check your child's bike regularly; involve her in bike maintenance.
- ➤ Ride with your child in a safe place and teach road safety as you go.

Car safety

Until a child is 18 kg (40 lb.) or about 100 cm (40 in.) tall, he should be buckled into an appropriate car seat in the back seat. Maintain the back-seat rule until your child is at least twelve years of age to protect him from the dangers of an inflating air bag. Transport Canada recommends that children under twelve not ride in the front seat of vehicles equipped with air bags. But neither you nor your child will always know whether the car you're riding in has air bags.

Some car-riding tips

- ➤ Avoid giving a child hard candies, peanuts, grapes, or any food that may cause her to choke while she is in the car.
- ➤ Never leave a child alone in a car.
- ➤ Do not show a child how to start the car or work the controls, with the exception of the horn.
- ➤ Keep all the doors locked at all times while you're in the car.
- ➤ Teach your child to get out of a car on the non-traffic side.
- ➤ Teach your child to hold her caretaker's hand in a parking lot.

Sexual Abuse

It happens to more children than we care to think about, especially since statistics show that the person most likely to abuse a child is a family member, a close family friend, or someone with authority over the child.

How can you protect your child? Parents may give their children rules like "Don't let anyone touch your private parts" and "If anyone touches you, tell them *No!*" But rules like these make children feel totally responsible for their own safety when it's their parents who are responsible for their safety. A child, faced with an abuser, is not in a position to say *No!* He is frightened, alone, confused, and feels that he has no place and no person to turn to. Here are some ideas that may work.

- ➤ Tell your child, in words, that you love him, and add "There is nothing, you could do that would make me stop loving you."
  Why? A molester may say, "If your mom knew what you just did, she wouldn't love you anymore."
- ➤ Hug, cuddle, and touch your child.
  Why? You want to show her what appropriate touching is.
- ➤ Teach your child the correct names of his body parts.
  Why? There are no secret or dirty parts of the body. There are private parts, but all of the body is wonderful and every part has a name. If abuse occurs, it's helpful if a child can use the correct language.
- ➤ Talk openly about sexual matters. Answer questions like, "How come mommy can feed a baby, but daddy can't?" Let your child know that she'll never be admonished for asking questions.
  Why? A child who has been reprimanded or ignored for asking a question that some adults define as inappropriate will soon learn that she cannot confide in mommy and daddy.

Signs of abuse
Of the many causes for change in a child's behaviour, abuse is only one. Try to interpret sudden behavioural changes that have no immediate explanation. Some of these behaviours are:
- ➤ bedwetting.
- ➤ changing sleep patterns.
- ➤ including sexual references in her talk.
- ➤ unwilling to take off his clothes.
- ➤ acting clingy, distracted, or destructive.
- ➤ reacting in fear to someone your child knows.

It may seem natural for your child to want you to stay and the baby sitter to leave, but if your child reacts fearfully to a known caretaker, a baby sitter, or a visitor, be alert to possible abuse.

Child Abduction

The Royal Canadian Mounted Police (RCMP) and other law enforcement agencies classify abductions in several ways, including parental abduction and stranger abduction. Parental abductions represented 84 per cent of the total reported child abductions in 1995 in Canada.

Parental abduction

In Canada, the majority of children abducted by a parent are between three and seven years of age. Mothers and fathers are equally likely to abduct, although mothers tend to abduct *after* there's been a custody order while fathers tend to abduct *before* a custody order. Children are most likely to be abducted from the custodial parent's home; most of these abductions are short-term and are resolved within seven days. According to the RCMP's Missing Children's Registry, most parental abductions occur at the end of summer and Christmas vacations.

At one time, it was assumed that, if a child was with a parent, even one who abducted him, the child was safe. But such thinking has changed. With very rare exceptions, a parent abducts a child out of revenge. Seldom are the needs of the child taken into consideration. The abducting parent teaches the children to lie and to hide. They can't let them make friends or lead a normal life. They may not take them to a doctor or dentist for fear of being tracked down. This kind of parental behaviour is abusive but, in addition, the parent may abuse the child physically, verbally, and sexually.

> **With very rare exceptions, a parent abducts a child out of revenge.**

The policy of the RCMP's Missing Children's Registry is: "A child (who has been abducted) is never safe and (must) always (be) considered to be in a dangerous situation." If you believe that your child is in danger of being abducted by her other parent, seek legal help. While you're at it, take simple and unobtrusive precautions on your own.

➤ Record the licence plate number, model and make, and details of the other parent's car.

➤ Note what credit cards he or she carries.

➤ Keep track of addresses and telephone numbers of your ex-spouse's relatives and friends. Half of parental abductors rely on help from family, friends, or new spouses.

➤ Take snapshots of your ex-spouse with your child.

You may never need this file, but it helps you gain a sense of control. If the abduction does happen, you have a file to hand over to the police.

Stranger abduction

Most parents of young children fear stranger abduction. However, in 1995 the number of stranger abductions reported to police in Canada was 1.6 per cent of the total abductions and less than 1 per cent of the total number of missing kids. It's an unlikely and rare crime, yet it's a crime that gets a great deal of press because it cuts to the heart of who we are as civilized beings. There's not a parent alive who hasn't been stricken with terror at the thought of his or her child being stolen.

What to Say to Your Child

Begin with a realistic rule that will work, as this one does for many families.

"Don't go anywhere with anyone unless I (or name of caretaker, baby sitter) know about it. No, you can't even go with Aunt Heidi if I don't know about it, and it's not that Aunt Heidi would ever hurt you. I just have to know where you are at all times."

Notice that this instruction doesn't include the word *stranger*. Children have definite, but peculiar, ideas of just who is a stranger—a man in a black cape, a guy with a moustache, a woman like the witch in *Snow White*. Since abduction by strangers is rare, you want the rule your children remember to be realistic and inclusive.

Tell your child, if he's ever separated from you, to look for a mom with small children and ask for help.

If Your Child Is Lost

When separated from a parent in a public place, a child may run, hide, cry, or wander, or the very rare child may take the opportunity to revisit the toy department. It's hard to tell just what your child will do, but give it some thought. You may want to adjust your rules to suit your child's personality. If your child is very shy, for example, and you know he won't ask for help, caution him to "Stay still. Mommy will not be far away."

You may also call out for your child in a store. It's a good way to find her, and you are modelling for your child that, if she is lost or in danger, a loud voice is often the best defence.

It's not a good idea to tell preschoolers to look for a police officer. It's not likely they'll meet a police officer on patrol in a shopping mall just when they need her. You could tell your child to ask for help from a store clerk, but few clerks wear identifiable smocks or clothes, and even adults have a difficult time finding them. The best suggestion is to tell your child to look for a mom with small children and ask her for help.

Practise with your child until he knows:

→ his name, address, and phone number (including the area code).

→ his parents' full names and places of work.

→ how to use the home phone to get help (Dial 0 or 911).

→ how to use a pay phone (Dial 0 or 911).

→ who to ask for help.

Safety Tip

Keep a supply of your business cards or cards with your name, address, and telephone number to slip in your child's pocket.

Playground Safety

Because playgrounds are built for kids and are often on school board or municipal property, parents expect them to be safe. But not all playgrounds are safe and not all children play safely in playgrounds. Although municipal pools are obliged to have lifeguards on duty, usually there is no official supervision in a playground. However, there is an agency responsible for park management and for equipment.

For the most part, it's how children use the playground equipment that causes most injuries. If a child starts misusing a piece of equipment, there's a good chance that she has mastered it and is just plain bored. It may be time to move on to another activity. Teach your kids these rules:

➤ Always slide, hang, or jump feet first.

➤ Use equipment one at a time, and move away when you're done.

➤ Don't climb onto the roof of a covered slide.

➤ Only use equipment that you can reach.

➤ On swings, don't stand, don't climb on supports, don't ride double, and don't jump off mid-swing.

➤ Don't walk in front or behind when someone is swinging.

➤ Remove your bike helmet when playing on the equipment.

➤ Remove jackets with drawstrings or other clothing with features that could get caught in the mechanisms.

Before you allow your child to use a playground or a particular piece of equipment, give it a quick once-over and even a shake. In general, the metal equipment should be rust-free and any wood surfaces should be treated to prevent rotting. The best climbing bars have hand grips. Make sure the equipment is in good repair. Look for sharp points and edges or any loose pieces or protrusions that can catch clothes and pinch or break fingers. If you see the need for repairs, call the park management.

A Child's Point of View

My world is expanding to include friends, nursery school, new activities. Help me to make sense of all my new choices by establishing routines and setting limits for me.

Age Two-and-a-Half to Three

My Body

- I'm getting taller, but I still have that soft, round, baby look.

- Even though I get tired easily, I may be outgrowing my nap. I'll still need a quiet time in the afternoon.

- I have trouble sleeping. I might get out of my bed in the middle of the night and come into your bedroom.

- I'm more or less able to use the toilet during the day, although I need help with wiping. I'll need a nighttime diaper for a few more months or even a few more years.

- I'm more sure on my feet, and my balance is better.

- I try to dress myself, but I get my shirt on backward and my shoes on the wrong feet.

- I can play catch with a fairly big, soft ball.

- My fingers are working better for me. I can string macaroni necklaces and play with toys that have small parts.

- I can use a fork to feed myself.

- I can stack six or eight blocks. If they don't fall, I'll probably knock them down myself.

My Feelings

- My emotions go from one extreme to the other. I'm aggressive, then I'm painfully shy. I'm excited, then I explode into a tantrum.

- I'm bossy. I may seem as though I'm trying to control you, but it's because I feel so out of control myself.

- I need my special dolly or teddy or security blanket more than ever.

- I'm afraid of lots of things, including hurting myself. I worry that I might fall into the toilet or get sucked up by the vacuum cleaner.

- I get so tired that I whine. The more reaction I get from you, the more I whine.

- I need lengthy and elaborate routines to help me relax, especially at bedtime. If you leave out a line from my bedtime story, I might make you go back to the beginning.

My Feelings, continued

- I want things to be the same. Don't get a new hairstyle or rearrange the living room furniture.

- I might want to be a baby again. Let me use baby talk or suck my thumb. It'll soon pass.

My Mind

- I know hundreds of words and can understand thousands more. But I might use the same word for a whole category of things, such as *chicken* for all meat.

- I can't make choices. I want to experience the red socks and the blue socks at the same time. Please help me choose.

- I like things in a special order. I might line up my stuffed animals.

- I can get through the day better if you tell me in the morning what's going to happen. I understand time words like *this morning, after lunch*.

- I can say my whole name. I can name the objects in a simple picture book.

- I can copy simple strokes with a crayon or paint brush.

- I'm more interested in imaginative play, like dress-up or pretending a wagon is a boat.

- My sense of humour is growing. I like silly words, goofy faces, and clowning around with you.

My World

- I'm a homebody. I won't enjoy a full-day excursion as much as a walk around the neighbourhood.

- I want to orient myself in our community. It helps me if we always take the same route to familiar destinations.

- I want you to tell me about my birth and what I was like when I was a baby, so I can see how far I've come.

- I talk to other children, especially so they know which toys are mine.

- I might hit another child just to see what happens.

- If I keep having tantrums in the same place, like the supermarket, please stop taking me there.

- I save my worst behaviour for my most important people—my parents.

Age Three to Age Four

My Body

- I'm losing my babyish look—my round belly, the fine texture of my hair.

- If I haven't had my first visits to a dentist and optometrist, I should go now.

- I'm becoming more interested in my gender and its differences from the opposite sex.

- I use the toilet during the day, although I may need a nighttime diaper for a few more months or even another year or two.

- I can spend hours riding my tricycle.

- I still can't sit at the table for the duration of the meal. I need to get down and run, gallop, and play.

- I can unbutton, but I have trouble buttoning.

- Toward three-and-a-half, I lose some of my coordination for a few months. My hand is less sure when I'm stacking blocks, and I stumble and fall more. I may have continually bandaged knees.

My Feelings

- I start off the year calm and content.

- I begin to be interested in other people's feelings. I start becoming very sensitive to their reactions.

- As the year goes on, I become more insecure. I might bite my nails, chew my hair, or rub my genitals.

- I get more and more anxious. I whine more than ever before. I might be afraid of loud noises like an ambulance siren.

- Most of all, I'm increasingly terrified of being separated from you. Even if I've been fine at nursery school, preschool, daycare, or a friend's house, I may suddenly become hysterical when you leave.

- I sometimes get so stressed-out that I wet my pants.

- I protest loudly against things that didn't bother me before, like having a sweatshirt pulled over my head.

- I might threaten you with *I don't love you* or *You can't come to my party*. I don't mean it. In fact, I need constant reassurance of your love.

My Mind

- If I'm taught, I can recognize the first letter of my name when it's printed, or maybe my whole name. I can say my street and town, and I may even know what that means.

- I'm starting to realize that counting is not just a rhyme to be repeated, but that each number represents an additional object.

- I may start to have bad dreams.

- I like the idea of the new and exciting. I'm thrilled if you have a "surprise" or "secret" for me or if you say, "Guess what?"

- I play with words—*cookie, bookie, shookie*. I love rhymes and simple riddles. I like the sound of the words more than the meaning.

- If I haven't talked much up to now, I'll improve by leaps and bounds. I may stutter off and on for a few months.

- If you ask me how old I am, I'll hold up three fingers.

- My imagination is so vivid that I might create an imaginary friend.

- I draw stick people, but I usually leave out the body.

- I enjoy books. I turn the pages and mime reading them by myself.

My World

- I need to be around other children at least a couple of times a week. I'm starting to play with them instead of just beside them. I laugh more with them than with adults.

- Friends are very important to me. I have a few playmates or one special friend. Even if I have real friends, I might invent an imaginary person or animal as a companion.

- I'm beginning to understand that Grandma is your mother and Grandpa is your father.

- I "play doctor" with my friends to understand my body and its differences from theirs. I'll need you to set limits around this behaviour.

- I realize that I'll grow up to be a woman or a man. I might talk about wanting to marry my father or my mother.

- I'm interested in babies. I might ask if we can have one.

- Around age three-and-a-half, I often prefer staying home and doing crafts or baking cookies than going on an outing.

- To make sense of the world and to keep up a conversation with you, I ask a million *Why?* questions.

Ages Four and Five

My Body

- At four, I'm fast, noisy, and adventurous. I run around, swing high, shout, and yell. I can ride my tricycle or my bicycle with training wheels, but I don't have the peripheral vision to see cars very well.

- I play with toys that have lots of tiny parts that I can manipulate.

- I'm fascinated by my belly button.

- As the sensations in my genitals increase, I may start to fondle them more.

- I may show my genitals to friends. Or I may be so modest that I close the door when I go to the bathroom.

- I get better and better at climbing, skipping, and elementary acrobatics like somersaults.

- By age five, I may be eating more and running around a little less.

- I use the toilet during the day but, if I can't stay dry at night, I'll still need a diaper.

- My baby teeth may start to loosen. Or I may not lose any teeth for another year.

My Feelings

- I laugh a lot and cry a lot, sometimes in rapid succession.

- I worry. I may be fearful of large animals, loud noises, or people who look different from us.

- I may still be afraid of separating from you. I may develop the new fear that you will die.

- I have the occasional tantrum. I want my own way and I can be argumentative about getting it.

- Don't tell me too far ahead of time about an exciting event. I can easily become overexcited, then fall apart in tears and exhaustion.

- Having lots of room, indoors and out, to run around in helps me diffuse my overblown emotions.

- I enjoy testing limits to see how far you'll let me go.

- When I start school, I experience having conflicting feelings simultaneously. I know what it's like to feel excited and scared at the same time.

- Around five-and-a-half, I'm tense and anxious a lot of the time. I may need extra reassurance till closer to my sixth birthday.

My Mind

- I can learn to print some letters and numbers, although some may be backward. I can print my own name. I might ask, "What does *S-T-O-P* spell?"

- I'm beginning to show an interest in clocks and calendars and money.

- I love word play, especially when it involves bathroom humour. I say *You pee-pee head* or *I'm making poo-poo pie* and giggle hilariously.

- I can handle big words. I might know the names of all the different kinds of dinosaurs.

- On a walk, I want to study things like dog poop at close range.

- I draw things that are familiar to me in nature or in books, such as the sun, clouds, rainbows, my family and me. I add more detail, like fingers, to my stick people.

- I brag, tell tall tales, and exaggerate out of all proportion. I tell friends that my grandpa is 120 years old or that I have a million dollars in my piggy bank. I can watch a half-hour TV show and spend an hour telling you about it, adding myown invented details.

- My imagination is well-developed and quite flexible. I can take a big cardboard appliance box and change it from a house to a library to a pet shop within minutes.

My World

- I love playing with other children. I know how to share.

- I notice differences like skin colour and physical disabilities, and I may ask questions that embarrass you. Please try to give me simple, honest answers rather than tell me not to notice or ignore my questions.

- I'm very concerned with fair play. If someone got a bigger piece than I , I'll let you know.

- Boasting and other expansive behaviour reflect my growing sense of myself.

- At four, I love new and exciting outings. By five, I'm happier to stay around the house with you.

- Although I'm more and more interested in the anatomical differences between girls and boys, I don't care much about the gender of my playmates.

- I experiment with swearing, to try out the feel of the words and your reaction to them. I won't understand if you scold me. I don't know what the words mean.

- Once I start school, I have to have lots of free, unstructured time to daydream, try out ideas, deal with boredom, and spend time alone. I need to learn how I fit into the world.

Age Two-and-a-Half to Five

Family Resources

7

Cost of Raising a Child to Age 18*

Age	Food	Clothing	Health Care	Personal Care	Recreation Gifts School Needs	Transportation	Child Care	Shelter Furnishings Household Operation	Annual Total
Infants	1,354	1,678	192	0	0	0	4,383	1,973	**9,580**
1	908	464	192	86	374	0	5,963	2,063	**10,050**
2	982	472	192	86	374	0	4,988	2,031	**9,125**
3	982	472	258	86	374	0	4,988	1,999	**9,159**
4	1,352	482	258	86	374	0	4,988	1,999	**9,539**
5	1,352	482	258	86	474	44	4,988	1,999	**9,683**
6	1352	600	258	86	583	44	3626	1,999	**8,548**
7	1,462	600	258	83	843	44	3,626	1,999	**8,915**
8	1,462	600	258	83	843	44	3,626	1,999	**8,915**
9	1,462	637	258	83	843	44	3,626	1,999	**8,952**
10	1,649	637	258	83	843	44	3,626	1,999	**9,139**
11	1,649	637	258	83	843	44	3,626	1,999	**9,139**
12	1,649	1,100	271	151	840	370	0	1,999	**6,380**
13	1,799	1,100	271	151	840	370	0	1,999	**6,530**
14	1,799	1,100	271	151	935	370	0	1,999	**6,625**
15	1,799	1,041	271	222	1,133	370	0	1,999	**6,835**
16	2,093	1,041	271	222	1,133	370	0	1,999	**7,129**
17	2,093	1,041	271	222	1,133	370	0	1,999	**7,129**
18	2,093	1,041	271	222	935	370	0	1,999	**6,931**
Total	**$29,291**	**$15,225**	**$4,795**	**$2,272**	**$13,717**	**$2,898**	**$52,054**	**$38,051**	**$158,303**

*These projections are based on 1997 Budget Guides data and do not include inflation. Manitoba Agriculture.

Financing a Family

The old saying "If you wait until you can afford children, you'll never have any" tends to make prospective parents blanche. Parents in the midst of child-rearing are more likely to laugh—they recognize the irony of the quip.

Children do cost a lot of money and new parents worry about how they're going to manage. In fact, after the health of their soon-to-be-baby, family finances are the major concern. You probably began to make some adjustments in your spending even during your pregnancy. The nesting instinct that strikes many couples usually translates into more time spent at home. As your priorities shift, money that you once spent on other activities becomes available for your new focus.

The table opposite, produced by Manitoba Agriculture as guidelines for 1997, shows that it costs parents more than $150,000 to raise a child from birth to age 18. You could probably spend more without any problem, but you could also spend a lot less. The items of clothing and furnishings were priced as new one-time purchases, not taking into account sale prices, buying second-hand, or exchanging hand-me-downs. For many of your child-rearing costs, whether it's a service or a product, there's usually an alternative that costs less.

Childcare is usually the major cost, if one parent returns to work. Fees in Canada vary depending on where you live, whether you're in a rural or an urban community, how old your child is, and what kind of care you want. Generally, care of infants is the most labour-intensive and therefore the most costly. Fees tend to be less as your child grows older and more independent.

The Toronto-based accounting firm Woods Cowperthwaite Mehta, which specializes in accounting for not-for-profit organizations, estimates that the cost of childcare for infants up to 18 months of age ranges from $950 to $1,200 per month in either a commercial or a public centre. For toddlers up to age two and a half, the

monthly cost ranges from $800 to $1,000. For preschoolers, the rate drops further to between $650 and $850. Over the period that you may need full-time licensed daycare, the total cost could range from $34,000 to $45,000 for four years.

If you hire a live-in nanny, your costs might be $62,691.20 minimum in Ontario for four years, although you can deduct board. You won't pay more for a second child, but real savings over daycare begin with three children. A third option, the one chosen by most families, is family daycare, either licensed or unlicensed, in a daycare provider's home. The cost may vary from $300 to $800 with an average of $500 per month per child. Age is not a factor in this kind of childcare. No matter what kind of daycare you choose for your child, it pays to shop around for both quality and price.

When you're shopping for baby furniture, clothing, and equipment, there are many more opportunities for making cost-effective choices. In the figure for furnishings and household needs, the chart includes $1,678 for infant clothing, including cloth diapers, and $1,973 for bedding, furniture, and other baby items. If you replaced cloth diapers with disposables, the total would almost double, even taking into account the reduced costs of laundering. We all know that department stores run Baby Sales several times a year. Taking advantage of sale prices may lower your total costs from 10 to 50 per cent.

New vs. Used—It's a Big Deal

You could equip your baby with a brand-new layette or you could shop the second-hand route and save even more than by shopping sales. Used furniture and clothing stores are common in most communities. Some second-hand stores will resell your child's clothing, offering either a trade-in or cash. Usually the trade-in is the better value. In their younger years, kids usually grow out of clothes before they wear them out.

Buying second-hand is the niftiest recycling: you can clean out your child's closet and replenish his wardrobe at the same time for very little cost. (Remember not to remove the fabric care tags from items you expect to recycle.)

But this kind of shopping differs from ordinary retail shopping. You may need to make more than one trip to find what you're looking for. Regular frequent visits will net you the best bargains and allow you to scoop up the choicest merchandise. Or leave special requests with sales staff to notify you when something arrives that you particularly need. Remember that some products, such as bike helmets, should not be purchased second-hand.

Become a Yard Sale Pro

Yard sales may provide a gold mine of inexpensive goods, particularly for young families. Some of the best buys are items for babies and children—clothing, toys, furniture, and equipment. Yard sales offer a different experience from shopping at the mall. But some people find the exercise so productive that they seldom pay full retail price for products again.

Friends, relatives, and co-workers beat even yard sales for building up your supplies of baby stuff. Everyone delights in the arrival of a baby, so if people ask what you need, don't hesitate to let them know—especially if you suspect they are planning a shower. Mention the practical things you need. Hand-me-downs may be just as abundant; family and friends often help one another out by exchanging baby clothes and equipment, back and forth, as their offspring grow into and out of each age and stage. The second and third children, if not cheaper by the dozen, don't cost as much as the first. You've already got the equipment and supplies you need—and you've already got the pass-it-along network in place.

1997 Price Comparison, Ottawa

New		Used	
Crib, change table and matching dresser	$ 700	Crib and mattress*	$ 100
		Change table	$ 40
Mattress	$ 50	Dresser	$ 40
5-piece linen set	$ 140	5-piece linen set	$ 15
Infant car seat	$ 60	Infant car seat*	$ 25
Undershirt	$ 9	Undershirt	$ 2
Stretchy sleeper	$ 15	Stretchy sleeper	$ 2
Two-piece outfit	$ 20	Two-piece outfit	$ 5
Knit sweater, cap and booties	$ 20	Knit sweater, cap and booties	$ 5
Total	$ 1,014	Total	$ 234
		*meets safety standards	

➤ Start planning by checking your community newspaper. Yard sales are usually clustered on weekend mornings. List the ones you want to go to in order of preference and location—a map is really helpful for plotting your route.

➤ Get an early start. If the sale begins at 8 a.m., plan to be there at 7:45. Sellers have usually set up the night before and may not mind early arrivals.

➤ Carry a list of the items you're looking for and the price you're willing to pay. If you spot something that's not on your list, but screams "Great deal!" ask yourself if you really need it. Your objective is to save money, and a list with prices may save you from yourself.

➤ Check carefully each item that interests you. If it's badly stained or in poor repair, it's no bargain.

➤ Offer a lower price than the one marked if you think you could get it for less—dickering is usually acceptable.

➤ Carry lots of change and small bills. Sellers can't always make change, and it helps your bargaining position if you're negotiating for a $4 item with toonies in hand rather than a $5 bill.

Dollar Decisions in the Early Years

Some of the decisions you make on behalf of your children and family will be based solely on the bottom line. Others will be made on a less tangible foundation. Either way, there is usually opportunity to save money depending on your options and your inventiveness.

Maternity Clothes. If you and your friends or family members are going through the baby years around the same time, pool your maternity clothes and pass them around as needed.

Diapers. You've got three basic choices and the differences can add up to $1,700 over the two-and-a-half-year period you'll be dealing with

them. The cheapest route is to buy cloth diapers and launder them yourself. That will cost between $600 and $1,000, depending on whether you buy plain diapers or the fitted kind with Velcro tabs. A diaper service—which provides an unlimited supply of diapers, picks up the dirty ones and delivers the clean—could cost between $1400 and $1900 for two and a half years. Disposable diapers for the same period of time could cost up to $2,300.

Infant Feeding. On top of all its other qualities, breast-feeding beats formula hands down. One year's worth of formula costs anywhere from $1200 to $3,600. Compare that to what you pay to breast-feed!

Baby Equipment. New parents face a long list of supplies to buy, but ask yourselves if everything is absolutely necessary. A dresser top, if it's the right height, can double as a change table. A playpen is an expensive toy box if your baby doesn't tolerate being confined. Check with friends and family for their experiences.

Toddler Bed. Instead of buying a $200 bed with built-in side rails to cushion the transition from crib to bed, put a mattress on the floor.

Birthday Parties. Start a family tradition of celebrating just certain birthdays—every third or fourth one—with a bang, and keep the ones in-between as simple family celebrations. Dollar stores have great buys for decorations. Use plain paper bags for loot bags, and have the guests decorate them as part of the party fun. Prizes for games played during the party can be the loot for the bags. Or if you are planning a special activity for a birthday party, like a trip to the movies or the playground, tell your youngster in advance that the activity replaces loot bags. Invitations to birthday parties often arrive like little cluster bombs, ripping big holes in your budget. Stock up on birthday presents when you spot great buys and keep a special storage spot for them.

Back to Work or Not?

You won't find any clear answers on the financial implications of staying home versus going back to work after your baby is born. But consider both the short-term costs of staying home and the long-term implications for lost income.

If you decide to stay home with your child, there will be savings that partially offset your loss of income: You won't pay childcare expenses of up to $1,200 a month for infants; your wardrobe will probably be more relaxed and less costly; restaurant lunches will disappear from your budget; transportation expenses, including insurance premiums, will shrink.

But you and your spouse need to consider the long-term implications of time away from the job. If you work in the service sector, they are not so drastic. But for many people, a chunk of time spent away from their career means a loss of career opportunities and future earning power. Unless you actively stay abreast of new developments in your field, you will find your knowledge and skills become outdated in no time. Also, the longer you are out of the employment loop, the more difficult, psychologically, it can be for you to get back in.

The Canadian Council on Social Development (CCSD) depicts a chilling scenario for new mothers. In a 1996 study, the council advised that "the costs of leaving the full-time labour force to have children may be rising for women." The CCSD found that a large part of new employment opportunities since the 1991-1992 recession are made up of part-time jobs. These jobs are mostly in the lower-paying service sector with few, if any, benefits. A woman who wants to return to her career after a few years raising a child may be unable to break back in.

In her 1997 book *Career Intelligence: Mastering the New Work and Personal Realities,* Toronto author Barbara Moses agrees that there might be no job to return to after a leave, but she argues that, in many sectors, the job might be lost whether you take time off or not. The upside, she claims, is that careers are less likely to stall because of a parental leave—more companies accept the practice. There is also less of a threat that you will miss out on a mid-level promotion as middle management is re-engineered out of the workplace. Although fifteen years ago a gap of employment time on your résumé would have caused potential employers concern, it's no longer rare and may even be viewed as a positive.

Moses cautions people on leave to keep up contacts throughout their time away, not just when they're anxious to get back to work. Maintain some links to your job with part-time work to keep your skills fresh, if that's possible. There is lots to think about if you want to maintain your career because you love your work. But there are other good reasons for minimizing the distance between yourself and your own income. If you are at all concerned for the viability of your marriage, you don't want to jeopardize your ability to support yourself and your child.

Saving for Your Child's Education

When planning for your child's university education, allow between $10,000 and $15,000 per year for tuition, books, room and board, and other expenses. It's a problem to start putting money aside now for something that seems so far away—there is always a more immediate expense to deal with. But the earlier you start saving, the easier you'll have it. Tuck away $26.50 a week starting now and in 18 years, assuming an 8 per cent compound interest rate, you'll have $50,000. No ordinary savings account today will give you that kind of return, but there are different methods that help you reach your goal.

The most advantageous way is to set up a flexible trust, which can be done through a bank or a financial house. You contribute money regularly to buy mutual funds which are held in trust for your child—but you retain control of the funds. Buying mutual funds in your child's name over a ten-year period or longer tends to bring the highest rewards, and the child pays tax only on the capital gains when cashed out. There are no limits on how much you can contribute to such a savings plan, and you control how and when the money is spent. If your child decides against going to university, you can use the money for something else. Also, the fees involved are usually lower than those for some registered plans. With a flexible trust fund, you have easy access to your savings—which can be good or not so good if you are faced with a large, unexpected expense down the road. The money is accessible, but spend it and you've spent your child's university fund.

Another way to save is by paying down your mortgage on your house so that you are debt-free by the time your child is ready for university. You can then use that monthly amount to pay for tuition. This is another flexible option where you remain in control and there are no extra fees, but it requires a whack of self-discipline to see it through.

With a Registered Education Savings Plan (RESP), you contribute a monthly amount to a plan, usually a mutual fund or guaranteed investment certificate (GIC), beginning when your child is very young. There are annual limits to how much you can contribute. There are up-front fees, but your capital and all income is tax-deferred until it is paid out. The major catch is that, if your child doesn't go on to post-secondary studies, you lose the interest, unless there are opportunities to slide the capital into your Registered Retirement Savings Plan or accept being taxed at an elevated rate.

A Scholarship Trust works much like an RESP, but your contributions are invested in a more conservative vehicle such as a GIC, which means less growth potential. You won't pay any tax on the earnings, but you will pay sales commissions. There are annual and lifetime limits on the amount you can invest. If junior doesn't scamper off to university in the prescribed time, there are different outcomes, depending on what you signed up for. So make very careful comparison of what plans will work best for you and your child.

Balancing Act

If you were a new mother in Canada in 1997, chances are that within the first six months of your baby's life you were back at work outside the home. Your family needed your income to pay the bills, or your employer wanted you back on the job because she couldn't afford to hold your position open any longer. Whatever the reason for your return, know this: You are not alone.

Working mothers with preschool-age children now make up a significant part of the Canadian labour market. Statistics Canada reports that, in 1991, 66 per cent of mothers with at least one child under the age of six were in the labour force. In addition, today's mother is more likely to be working full-time than part-time.

Longer maternity leave, sometimes topped up by an employer, has made it easier for new mothers to stay home with a newborn, and the federally legislated parental leave can be taken by either parent. Although the paid time away from work can be as much as 25 weeks and some employers offer longer unpaid time as "care and nurturing" leave, most new parents return to their jobs within one to six months.

For many families, parenting a child and managing two full-time jobs can be very stressful. One survey by The Conference Board of Canada revealed that 80 per cent of Canadian employees experience some degree of anxiety or stress related to competing demands of family and work. A 1994 Angus Reid poll reports that half of Canadians say they haven't achieved a good balance between work and family.

Employment Statistics
- In 1991 it took 65 to 80 hours of work per week to support a Canadian family.
- In 1970 it took 45 hours per week.
- The number of families living below the poverty line would increase by 78 per cent if one parent in a two-parent family withdrew from the work force.

But in spite of the pressures, most families don't have a lot of choice. Three-quarters of Canadian families currently require two incomes to stay above the poverty line. Now more than ever, it's important to find a balance because the conflicts between work and family lead to increased stress, poorer health, and lost income.

Is your company "family-friendly" ?

Some employees are fortunate to work for a company that offers options, even one of which could make your family life much more manageable. Among the options are flextime, job-sharing, part-time work, and telecommuting. Parents in skilled occupations, like banking, tend to have greater access to part-time work and job-sharing, according to the National Child Care Survey conducted by Statistics Canada.

With the exception of family-friendly companies, most companies and industries have made available only to middle and senior managers the perks of flexible work schedules and paid leave to handle family responsibilities. What can the rest of the work force do?

To single-handedly take on an employer or a union in a fight to win family-friendly policies is time-consuming. Although it's worthwhile becoming involved in efforts to improve working conditions, it's important to understand that change takes time. And time, for parents of young children, is in short supply. But there are two things you can do immediately to get the ball rolling: Raise the issue with union leaders or your managers; develop a business case to demonstrate why your proposal for a flexible work schedule (or other arrangement) will benefit the company.

Find out who in the company or union is responsible for employee benefits and approach him or her about improving existing policies. Volunteer to become the company's pilot project. But before you make the pitch, do your homework. Research other companies to find out what has worked and what hasn't. Companies that win applause for their workplaces will be happy to share information with you. Don't be shy about calling or writing the Human Resources department for copies of their family-friendly policies. Labour organizations and unions can also be good sources of information. Even if your workplace isn't unionized, the research collected by labour groups can be applied in many different organizations.

With research in hand, decide what would work best for you and make your proposal worth adopting. Avoid the pitfall of casting doubt on your own ability to do your current job within the current structure. Don't tell your employees how tough you find it to manage at home and at work, even if it's true. Instead develop your proposals in terms of benefits to the company. One woman who needed an extra hour in the morning so she could take her four-year-old to junior kindergarten was careful not to mention that fact; instead, she requested a change in hours so she could be at her desk later in the day when a number of clients were making last-minute requests for assistance. By framing her proposal as a benefit to the company, she made it possible for her manager to sell the idea to his boss and to other staff who might question why she was coming in late every day.

Make-It-Work Strategies

- ➤ Identify your needs.
- ➤ Identify your employer's needs.
- ➤ Try to anticipate employer's reaction.
- ➤ Tell your employer why your request benefits the company.

- ➤ Learn to be more efficient at work. Don't fritter away the day.
- ➤ Don't feel guilty when you leave work "early" after eating lunch at your desk. It's not how much time you spend, it's what you accomplish that counts.

Workday Options

Flexible hours

Flexibility in a work schedule helps parents balance the demands of a full-time job with family responsibilities. It allows you to pick up a child before the daycare centre closes, take a child to the doctor's for a regular check-up, or come in late when a caregiver is ill and has left you scrambling to make other arrangements. Employers can benefit too. The option of flexible hours reduces absenteeism and stress, and increases employee and corporate productivity. The flextime programs that companies have developed include:

➤ a work day of the usual 7 or 8 hours, but starting earlier (7 a.m. to 10 a.m.) or ending later (3 p.m. to 6 p.m.)

➤ a compressed workweek in which you work fewer hours or not at all on some days and longer hours on other days

The Co-operators Group, a national insurance company, offers employees several options in a compressed 36-hour workweek schedule, in which employees choose one of the following:

➤ standard 7.2-hour days, 5 days a week.

➤ 8-hour days for 4 days with a half day on the 5th.

Whole or part days off give parents time to schedule medical or dental appointments or meet other family obligations.

One problem caused by offering flextime on an individual basis is the resentment created among other workers who see someone leaving early or coming in late, according to the company's stated policy. If flextime isn't made available to all employees in your workplace, ask that the company conduct education sessions with staff about work and family issues. If that's not possible, be straightforward with your co-workers and tell them how your working arrangements have been changed. Many colleagues will be supportive of your efforts and, who knows, you could blaze a new trail for others to follow.

Will flextime work for you?

➤ How would I manage my time effectively to get the work done?

➤ Can I take the initiative in my work?

➤ Can I make decisions when my manager isn't there?

➤ How would I meet deadlines on cooperative projects, if I work flexible hours?

➤ How would I supervise and support people who report directly to me if I work different hours or days than they do?

➤ Would I find it physically tiring to work an extended day?

Job sharing

When two people share the responsibilities for one job, it's called job sharing. Working part-time at a full-time job is appealing because it offers employees the opportunity to stay connected with a career, maintain a steady income, and still allow time for child-care responsibilities.

The drawback to job sharing is, of course, financial. Because it means a pay cut, job sharing is only possible for couples who can live on one-and-a-half salaries. Benefits such as life insurance or dental and medical plans may also be reduced or prorated. Most importantly, unless job sharers are protected by a collective agreement, they may not be able to return to a full-time job. To protect yourself, negotiate the agreement so that the employer agrees to find you full-time work when the job sharing ends.

Even job sharing will not solve the issues involved in juggling family and work responsibilities. In many cases, job-sharers end up taking home unfinished work when unsupportive managers assign tasks at the last minute. If you job share and find yourself working for free on your unpaid days, it's important to tell a supervisor that the company has too high an expectation about the amount you can accomplish in a half day and that the tasks should be re-evaluated.

Are you ready to job share?

➤ How would work get done when I'm not in the office?

➤ Does my job require teamwork and meetings? If so, how do I participate on days off?

➤ What plans should I develop to communicate with my job-sharing partner?

➤ How do I really feel about sharing my work with someone else?

Telecommuting

Remember when the telecommunications revolution was supposed to make it easy for everyone to work from home? You would need only a computer and a place to plug it in. For many jobs, telecommuting is still science fiction, but some people may convince their managers that work can get done even when an employee doesn't show up at the office.

Working in sweat suits and slippers is one of the advantages of telecommuting. When you work from home, you eliminate commuting time and costs, you save money on clothes, coffee, and lunches, and you have more time to spend with your family at the beginning and end of a day.

Depending on your work habits, it may also increase your productivity. Many employers are unaware of how much office time gets eaten up by unforeseen interruptions: non-business telephone calls, polite conversations with fellow workers, and endless meetings.

But telecommuting can pay off for employers also in several ways. Some may save money on office space rentals. At the Canadian Imperial Bank of Commerce (CIBC), one department saved $70,000 in office rent when 30 of the 40 people employed in the Securities Department became telecommuters, including the vice-president of sales and service, Roger Brandvold, who works out his home in Regina, Saskatchewan. He says that the sales and service team's communication skills made them naturals for telecommuting. In discussions with staff, however, Brandvold discovered that some telecommuters were working

longer hours because they were based at home. "We don't need to be afraid that people are at home watching *Oprah* in the afternoon. We need to be concerned about people spending more time at work because it is conveniently located."

Working from home won't solve your childcare problems. Childcare will be crucial if you have infants or toddlers at home. Few people are capable of watching an energetic toddler or caring for a baby while they do a full-time job. The big advantage of telecommuting is that, should you finish the work early, you can spend the time with your family.

Will telecommuting work for you?

➤ Can I work at home without distractions?

➤ Will I be tempted to do homemaker tasks instead of the work I'm being paid to do?

➤ Will I miss the social interaction?

➤ What will I need to work at home, and will my employer supply them, or will I have to purchase them? (a computer, an extra telephone line, modem, Internet Service Provider for E-mail, and a private workspace)

➤ Does my job require teamwork?

➤ Do I need access to files or information available only at the office?

Self-Employment

When some people can't fit their life into the mould of a typical job, they look to themselves to provide employment. A great idea and a flair for organization can spell success for the entrepreneur, but not everyone has the temperament to be entrepreneurial. Self-employment offers flexibility in work arrangements, but the financial payback isn't always satisfactory. Self-employed people who work primarily on their own have lower average incomes than other workers. They also have no company-sponsored health benefits or paid vacations, and they must find their own employment and disability insurance and pay both employer and employee Canada Pension Plan (CCP) contributions.

Becoming your own boss isn't something you should do lightly. Before you leave a full-time or part-time job, make certain that self-employment is what you really want. Seek advice from other professionals such as accountants, marketing experts, and successful business people. Contact your local college or university to see if the Business faculty has graduate students who might help you research your potential market and draw up a business plan.

The self-employed, like telecommuters, still require caregivers for their children. When you're in a business that requires you to meet deadlines, make telephone calls, or meet with clients, someone else has to care for your child or children. It's revealing that self-employed people tend to work longer—40 hours per week compared to the average worker's 37 hours per week—according to a 1991 study from Statistics Canada.

Are you ready to be an entrepreneur?

> Is there a demand for my product or service?

> Am I a self-promoter?

> Can I do without company-paid benefits, that is, pay for my own benefits?

Home business opportunities

Communications. Freelance writer or editor, translator, publicist, desktop publisher, scriptwriter, media trainer.

Office support. Word processor, proofreader, mailing list organizer, clipping service, bookkeeping.

Professions. Lawyer, doctor, dentist, chiropractor, hairdresser, management consultant, speech and language pathologists, caterer, travel agent.

Computers. Trainer, repair person, software designer, programmer.

Education. Tutoring, childcare.

Sales/Marketing. Real estate agent.

Home repairs and renovations. Architect, interior designer, landscaper, upholsterer, refinisher, painter, handyperson.

Personal services. House cleaner, dog walker, house sitter, dressmaker.

Part-Time work

For many people, the balance between work and family can only be achieved through part-time work. In a 1992 federal government survey, 19 per cent of full-time workers said they were highly stressed for time compared with 11 per cent of part-time workers. Working part-time can be a successful strategy for balancing work and family. However, most part-time workers pay for the convenience in wage and benefit concessions.

Part-time work is generally lower paying, often at minimum wage. And many workplaces do not offer benefits such as medical, dental, or pension plans to part-time workers. Statistics Canada reports that only 27 per cent of part-time workers have employer-sponsored pension plans compared with 54 per cent of full-time workers.

Sharing the Load

Survival as a working parent often depends on your support network. Family and friends may be called on in an emergency, such as a sick child who needs nursing, but the person you will really count on is your spouse. Now that you're parents, it's time to discuss what will happen if the baby gets sick or child-care arrangements fall through. Which of you will stay home from work?

And what about the household duties—cooking, cleaning, and shopping? Sharing the load places less stress on the marriage, but the reality is that, when work and family responsibilities collide, it's women who step in to clean up the mess. Even in dual-income families, women with children under the age of six spent, on average, just over 14 hours per day on paid and unpaid work, and fathers 12 hours a day. Being aware of who does what in the family, even to the point of posting a list of chores and who is responsible for each chore, helps ease parental tensions when juggling work and family becomes too much.

A Working Parent's Survival Tips

➤ Learn to say *No!* without guilt.

➤ Set priorities. Focus on the first priority, then move on.

➤ Put some space between work and family. If you commute, use the time to relax and unwind. If you drive to work, park far away from the office; the walk is good exercise and it will buy you some quiet time.

➤ Schedule time for your family the way you schedule time for a meeting.

➤ Don't answer the phone during dinner.

➤ Take time for yourself. When you're over-stressed, it's easy to take your frustrations out on your family.

Troubleshooting

Even in the perfect job with the perfect boss, things can go wrong. When it happens to you, and it will, keep your cool by being prepared.

A Sick Child

It's Monday morning. The plant where you work is expecting a big shipment of parts and you're supervising the job. Dressed and ready to go, you head to your child's room to wake him and get him prepared for daycare. One look at his feverish brow and you know he's not feeling well enough to leave his bed, let alone spend the day at a caregiver's.

With less than an hour before you have to be on the road, you execute your plan of action. If all goes well, grandma will be on her way and at your door just in the nick of time. But the telephone call goes unanswered—grandma has an appointment of her own and is already out the door. Now what? You need a second back-up plan.

Try contacting the local office of the YMCA or your local public health unit. Also many community organizations have a list of emergency caregivers, some of them trained nurses. You should have already checked out the availability of this kind of service and even tested them. If not, do so now, so that you'll be prepared the next time.

Recognizing that one working parent of a sick child has to miss work, some Canadian companies have begun to provide on-call services for such emergencies. Several employers in eastern Ontario are working with the Victorian Order of Nurses (VON) to offer short-term care for a child who is mildly ill. Employees call a central number and, within an hour, a certified health-care worker arrives at their home. In some cases, the cost of the VON was paid for by the employer; in other instances, employees split the cost.

The Business Trip

An out-of-town business trip can be a working parent's nightmare. Even with a supportive spouse, it often takes two adults to work around the child-care schedules. If business trips are in your future, consider hiring a live-in nanny or signing up a supportive relative who is happy to pack an overnight bag and be your stand-in.

Prepare for the trip well in advance. Think about what needs doing and get it done before you leave. If your child is old enough to know that mommy or daddy is away for a period of time, discuss the trip. Get a map and show her where you'll be. Arrange for a time to call and talk to her.

When a trip happens unexpectedly and you can't find a sitter to fill in, consider staying at a hotel that offers childcare on the site. Many hotel chains offer childcare as an incentive to attract convention business and, with it, the parents who must travel on business.

If your best efforts to make child-care arrangements fail and you have to cancel the trip, make the best of it. Call the client to see if you can arrange another meeting. Then explain to your boss all the efforts you've made to accommodate work, apologize, and just move on.

Childhood Illnesses

Adapted from Chapter 3, "Managing Illness," *Well Beings*, 2nd ed., 1996, Canadian Paediatric Society

Basic information for parents and caregivers about common childhood infections and illnesses is presented in the four charts on pages 286 to 291: Respiratory Infections, Skin and Scalp Infections, Gastrointestinal Infections, and Other Common Infections. In the columns, key points are presented about how each infection is transmitted, what its signs and symptoms are, how long a child might remain infectious to others, and what a parent should do or expect after contacting a doctor. Most family doctors can provide helpful guidance in telephone discussions, but they will want to see the child to diagnose any illness and prescribe or recommend treatment. They are also best able to discuss any precautions that parents might take for other family members or the child's wider circle. In remote areas, the public health nurse or outpost nurse may be the only qualified person available to diagnose an illness.

Find out and post near your telephones the contact numbers for your family physician, your child's doctor, the local hospitals and hospital emergency rooms, the local public health agency, and any other known sources of medical help in urgent situations.

Signs and Symptoms of Infection

The middle column of each chart, "Signs and Symptoms," uses one or more of the following terms; the paragraphs below offer a fuller explanation of the terms. No matter what the cause of a child's symptoms, the behaviour always provides an important key to help judge how serious the illness is. Children who exhibit lethargy or unusual sleepiness, irritability, persistent crying, or other signs of possible severe illness should be seen by their physician as soon as possible.

Runny Nose. In a viral infection, the nasal discharge usually starts as clear, colourless mucus. In a day or two, it often becomes thick yellow or green. The colour change in itself is not a sign of more serious infection; however, if nasal discharge persists for more than ten days, the child should be checked for the possibility of a sinus infection. The most common cause of a runny nose in young children is a viral infection such as the common cold; other causes include allergies (environmental or food) and chemical irritations.

Coughing can be triggered by irritation anywhere in the respiratory tract, from the nose to the lungs. The causes of coughing include allergies, asthma, chemical irritations (such as cigarette smoke), cystic fibrosis and other chronic lung diseases, an inhaled object, a habitual response, and the child's psychological state. Many children with a common cold will cough. There are many symptoms of a viral infection in the respiratory tract—such as a runny nose, sore throat, cough, loss of appetite, fatigue, aches and pains—but the cough lasts the longest.

Croup describes both a symptom and an illness. Due to an inflammation of the windpipe below the vocal chords (larynx, voice-box), the child's voice gets hoarse and a barking-like cough develops. The child's breathing may get very noisy or "croupy." In severe cases, the airway (or windpipe) may become obstructed. The louder the noise and the harder the child works to breathe or inhale when resting, the more serious the airway obstruction.

Wheezing refers to noises made during breathing, mainly breathing out. The sounds are often musical. Wheezing is caused by a combination of narrowing and excess mucus in the major airways (or bronchi) of the lungs. The most common cause of wheezing in young children is a viral infection. The child's rate of breathing and the amount of effort required to breathe indicate how serious the problem is. You can see the child's effort as a sucking-in of the chest muscles between, above, or below the ribs.

Vomiting. Children vomit much more readily and easily than adults and often with much less discomfort. Vomiting may be due to the general effects of an infection rather than specific irritation to the stomach. Vomiting itself is not usually dangerous unless the child chokes and inhales the vomitus, or the child vomits frequently enough to cause dehydration.

Diarrhea means a change in the normal pattern of bowel movement, resulting in a substantial increase in the number of stools and/or a change in the consistency of the stool to watery or unformed. Diarrhea occurs when the bowel is stimulated or irritated by infection or other causes. It can be dangerous. If the amount of water lost through the bowel movement is greater than the amount the child drinks, dehydration may occur. Abdominal cramps or stomach-ache often occur with vomiting or diarrhea.

Dehydration means a loss of water from the body, impairing the circulation of the blood. Dehydration occurs much more rapidly in infants with diarrhea than in older children or adults. The risk of dehydration is greater if the child is also vomiting.

Any Change in Skin Colour A sudden onset of paleness or yellowing of the whites of the eyes or skin is a symptom of illness.

Rashes have many causes and require a physician's examination and further information before the cause can be determined. Children who have a rash but no fever or change in behaviour may, nevertheless, need to be seen by a physician.

Fever

Fever is often the most significant sign of an illness. Fever is a temperature higher than normal. Its presence often means infection, although other conditions without infection may also cause fever. A fever may occur following a child's vaccination (or immunization). Overdressing your child or strenuous exercise, especially during hot weather, may increase his body temperature. Fever is not caused by teething. Infants with serious infections may have below-normal temperatures rather than a fever.

Normal body temperature is 37°C (98°F). Body temperature varies throughout the day, following a regular cycle. The lowest body temperature occurs in the early morning hours (2:00 a.m. to 4:00 a.m.), and the highest temperature occurs in late afternoon. The difference between the lowest and highest temperature may be as much as 0.5°C (1°F). A fever is indicated by one of the following:

➤ a <u>rectal</u> temperature equal to or higher than 38.5°C (101.3°F).

➤ an <u>oral/tympanic</u> temperature equal to or higher than 38°C (100.4°F).

➤ an <u>axillary</u> (in the armpit) temperature equal to or higher than 38°C (100.4°F).

How high is "high"?

Although some serious infections may cause high fever, it is not safe to assume that the higher the fever, the more serious the illness. A mild viral infection can cause a fever as high as 40°C (104°F), while a severely ill child with meningitis may have a fever of only 38.5°C (101.3°F), or even lower. If a child feels warm or feverish, it is much more important to observe her behaviour than to take her temperature.

Is fever dangerous?

No, but it can serve as a valuable warning sign. A fever almost always means infection in young children—fever is an important defence mechanism that helps the body fight or react to an infection. However, some children may be susceptible to febrile seizures (convulsions) when their body temperature goes up suddenly.

Are febrile seizures (convulsions) unusual?
These seizures are fairly common—approximately 3 per cent of normal children have at least one febrile seizure between the ages of six months and six years. The tendency runs in families—febrile seizures last less than fifteen minutes and do not cause brain damage or epilepsy. Children who are prone to febrile seizures may have a seizure whenever they develop a fever, especially if the body temperature rises rapidly. Often, the seizure is the first sign of a fever. Seizures may also occur as part of a more serious infection, such as meningitis (an infection of the membrane and the fluid that covers the brain). Therefore, take any child with fever and a seizure promptly to a physician for evaluation.

When does a fever indicate serious illness?
In a child with fever, certain types of behaviour or symptoms suggest a serious illness. These are:

➤ excessive listlessness, drowsiness, sleepiness, or lack of interest in surroundings
➤ irritability, fussiness, crankiness, inconsolable crying, high-pitched crying or screaming, or a weak cry
➤ poor skin colour or pallor
➤ rapid breathing (faster than 40 breaths per minute)
➤ difficulty breathing
➤ a fever with a rash
➤ excessive drooling

In particular, infants who appear feverish and who are less than six months of age should be evaluated by a physician as soon as possible.

Things to do when a child has a fever
1. Fever can be lowered by allowing the heat to leave the child's body in one of two ways:

Undress the child to his diaper or underwear, or allow the child to sweat—the body cools as the sweat evaporates. If the skin is cooled too much, it may cause shivering. The muscular activity of shivering will raise body temperature. Any child who is shivering should be wrapped up and kept warm until the shivering stops and the skin feels warm to touch, then remove most of the blankets or clothes so the child's body heat can be lost to the air.

Sponging and tepid (or warm) water baths will lower fever, but children rarely enjoy this bath and usually struggle.

2. Children with infections causing fever often have headaches and other aches and pains. Medication with acetaminophen (Tylenol, Tempra, Panadol, and others), which lowers fever, also relieves pain. The main reason to use such medicine is to make the child feel better. The correct dose is listed on the bottle or package. It should be given at the dose recommended, and not more often than every four hours, until the child's temperature comes down. The temperature usually drops in 1 to 2 hours; sometimes it may rise again, so that the medication may have to be repeated.

Note: Don't use Aspirin [acetylsalicylic acid (ASA)] to treat fever in children or teenagers. When aspirin is given to a child with chickenpox, influenza, or some other viral infection, there is an increased chance that the child may develop Reye's syndrome, a very serious condition that can damage the liver and brain.

Immunization

The Canadian Paediatric Society has published a book, *Your Child's Best Shot: A Parent's Guide to Vaccination* (1997, 154 pages, $25), which provides parents with more information on some of the illnesses and infections listed in the following charts. In the book, parents will also find a full description of each illness or infection with the recommended vaccination listed in the immunization chart. (See page 292.) The descriptions include the topics: History, The Germ, The Illness, The Vaccine, The Results of the Vaccination, and Summary. In Chapter 12, readers will find answers to twenty-six questions that parents most often ask their doctors about vaccinations.

Respiratory Infections

Infection	Transmission	Signs and Symptoms	Infectious Period	Things Parents Can Do
Common Cold	Spread person to person via droplets; indirect spread via contaminated hands, objects, surfaces. Almost always viral.	Runny nose, sore throat, cough, decreased appetite.	1 day before to 7 days after onset.	Contact doctor if child shows any of the following signs: earache; fever higher than 39°C (102.2°); excessive sleepiness, crankiness, or fussiness; skin rash; rapid breathing or difficulty breathing, or persistent coughing.
Colds with Fever	Same as above.	Same as above, plus: fever, headache, muscle aches.	Same as above.	
Ear Infections (Otitis Media)	Usually follows a cold, but is caused by virus and bacteria.	Earache, fever and cold symptoms. Infant may simply show unusual behaviour by becoming irritable and fussy.	Not infectious.	Contact your doctor, if you suspect your child has an ear infection. These are usually treated with an antibiotic—it's important to take all of any medication prescribed.
Pinkeye (Conjunctivitis)	Spread person to person by contact with secretions from eye. Caused by rubbing eye excessively, by allergy, by a virus, or by bacteria.	Redness, itching, pain, discharge from eye.	For duration of illness or until 24 hours after treatment is started.	Contact your doctor. If discharge is pus (yellow, thick), exclude from other activities until the antibiotic has been taken for 1 full day.
Pneumonia	Spread person to person via droplets; indirect spread via contaminated hands, objects, surfaces. May be caused by virus and bacteria.	Cough, rapid or noisy breathing, pale or blue colour; fever may also be present.	Varies with cause.	Contact your doctor immediately, or seek emergency help if your child has difficulty breathing.
Strep Throat	Spread person to person by droplets (bacteria in the saliva). Scarlet fever is a form of strep throat infection; rheumatic fever may be one serious complication.	Fever; sore throat; swollen, tender glands in the neck.	Until 24 hours after treatment is started.	Contact your doctor. Cultures positive for strep throat will be treated with antibiotics. It's important to take all of any medication prescribed.

Skin and Scalp Infections

Infection	Transmission	Signs and Symptoms	Infectious Period	Things Parents Can Do
Head Lice	Spread person to person. Requires close, direct contact. Infested hats, clothes may also be involved in the spread.	Most children have no symptoms. Some will have itching of scalp. Nits (eggs) are seen attached to hairs near scalp.	Until treated.	Use over-the-counter medication with care and as directed. Exclude from activities with other children until treated. Removal of all nits may be necessary to cure some cases.
Herpes Simplex	Spread person to person. Virus is in saliva and infected sores.	Many infections occur without symptoms. May cause high fever; many painful ulcers in mouth. May recur as cold sores.	For one week during first infection; 5 days during recurrent cold sores.	Contact your doctor: Exclude from activities with other children for severe illness, not for recurrent cold sores.
Impetigo (caused by strep and staph bacteria)	Spread person to person by direct contact.	Pustules or crusted rash on nose, mouth, or exposed parts of body (arms or legs).	From onset of rash until 1 day after start of treatment with antibiotics.	Contact your doctor: Exclude from general activities until antibiotic treatment has been taken for 1 full day.
Scabies (an infestation)	Spread person to person by mites that burrow into the skin. Requires close, direct contact.	Very itchy rash; looks like curvy white threads, tiny red bumps, or scratches appearing anywhere on the body in infants under 2 years; in older children, rash usually appears on fingers, elbows, armpits, or abdomen.	Until treated. The mites can live on clothing, other objects, and skin for four days.	Contact your doctor; if she confirms scabies, every member of the family may have to be treated. Children may be excluded from other activities to control outbreak. Wash bed linens, towels, and clothes in hot water and dry at the hottest setting.

Gastrointestinal Infections

Infection	Transmission	Signs and Symptoms	Infectious Period	Things Parents Can Do
Vomiting	Germ likely to be excreted in vomitus and stool. Spread directly from person to person and indirectly from hands to objects, surfaces, food, or water contaminated with germs (young children frequently put fingers and objects in mouth).	Vomiting may be dangerous in infants and young children because the loss of fluid may cause dehydration.	For duration of vomiting.	Contact your doctor if there are 2 or more episodes in a day, or if vomiting does not stop after 4 to 6 hours, and if your child shows signs of dehydration.
Diarrhea	Germ excreted in stool. Spread directly from person to person; indirectly by hands; stays on objects, surfaces, food, water contaminated with germs (young children frequently put fingers and objects in mouth).	Increase in frequency of stools and/or change to unformed, loose, or watery stool. Fever, loss of appetite, nausea, vomiting, abdominal pain, mucus or blood in stool may also occur. Diarrhea may be dangerous in infants and young children since loss of fluid may cause dehydration.	For duration of diarrhea.	Contact your doctor if any of the following are present: diarrhea with a fever over 38.5°C (101.3°F); repeated vomiting; dehydration; blood or mucus in stool, or your child is less than six months of age. As soon as diarrhea starts, give your child an oral rehydration solution (ORS) because it contains the ideal balance of water, salts (electrolytes), and sugar. [Gastrolyte™, or Pedialyte™ are commercial sources.]
Campylobacter	Germ excreted in stool. Poultry, beef, unpasteurized milk or other food may be source of infection.	Fever, diarrhea, blood in stool, cramps.	For duration of diarrhea.	As above. (Your doctor may have to take stool samples to confirm the diagnosis.)
Escherichia coli (E. coli)	Germ excreted in stool. Poultry, beef, unpasteurized milk or other food may be source of infection.	Fever, diarrhea, blood in stool, cramps	For duration of diarrhea.	As above.
Giardia (a parasite in the stool that causes bowel infection)	Germ in stool. Spread from person to person. Common in child care.	Most children have no symptoms. May have loss of appetite, vomiting, cramps, diarrhea, mushy stool, excessive gas.	Infectious until cured.	As above.

Gastrointestinal Infections, continued.

Infection	Transmission	Signs and Symptoms	Infectious Period	Things Parents Can Do
Norwalk Virus	Spread from person to person via air.	Vomiting and prostration for 1 to 2 days.	For duration of illness.	As above.
Rotavirus	Virus in stool. Spread from person to person. Most common cause of diarrhea in child care.	Fever and vomiting precede watery diarrhea. Dehydration may occur rapidly in infants.	For duration of illness.	As above.
Shigella	Germ in stool. Spread person to person.	Diarrhea, fever, blood and/or mucus in stool, cramps.	For duration of diarrhea. Highly infectious.	As above.
Food poisoning	Acquired from contaminated food	Nausea, vomiting, cramps, diarrhea.	Not infectious, but all who ate the food may experience symptoms.	Contact your doctor if reactions are severe.
Salmonella	Acquired mainly from food, especially eggs and egg products, beef, poultry, and unpasteurized milk.	Diarrhea, fever, blood in stool.	While having diarrhea.	As above.
Hepatitis A (a liver infection caused by a virus)	Virus in stool. Spread from person to person; may also be spread in food or water.	Most children have no signs of illness. May have fever, loss of appetite, nausea, vomiting, jaundice (yellow colour in skin and eyes).	2 weeks before to 1 week after onset of jaundice.	Contact your doctor. Immune globulin vaccine may be indicated for child and family members.

Other Common Infections

Infection	Transmission	Signs and Symptoms	Infectious Period	Things Parents Can Do
Chickenpox (Varicella-Zoster virus)	Spread person to person and via air. Infectious, but it's almost impossible to stop the spread of the virus.	Rash with small blisters on top which become crusted; along with fever; itching.	2 days before to 5 days after onset of rash; appears 2 to 3 weeks after the first family member is infected.	Do not give aspirin [acetylsalicylic acid (ASA)] or any products that contain aspirin. Infection may be severe for adults (especially pregnant women or someone with an immune system disorder) who have not had chickenpox or shingles.
Cytomegalovirus (CMV)	Spread person to person. Requires intimate contact. Virus in urine and saliva. Can infect the fetus of a pregnant woman.	Usually causes no illness.	Whenever virus is present in urine or saliva.	No need to exclude from activities.
Hepatitis B	Virus present only in blood and certain body fluids (semen, cervical secretions). Virus is not in stool. Spread by contact with blood or by sexual intercourse.	Illness uncommon in children. Illness in adults is more severe and more prolonged than hepatitis A. May cause severe liver disease or liver cancer.	From weeks before onset to months or years after recovery from illness. May be infectious for life.	No need to exclude from activities unless open sores are present. Hepatitis B vaccine and/or hepatitis B immune globulin may be indicated under special circumstances.
Measles (Most children receive the vaccine at 1 year of age)	Virus in respiratory secretions. Spread person to person. Very infectious.	Fever, cough, runny nose, inflamed eyes for 1 to 3 days before onset of rash. Rash is large red spots which often join together; starts on face and spreads rapidly over body. Illness lasts 5 to 10 days.	2 days before onset of fever and cough (3 to 5 days before onset of rash) until 4 days after onset of rash.	Measles, caused by a virus, can only be prevented by immunization—there is no antibiotic. Contact your doctor for suggestions as to how to make your child feel better. Exclude from contact with others until at least 4 days after onset of rash.

Other Common Infections, continued.

Infection	Transmission	Signs and Symptoms	Infectious Period	Things Parents Can Do
Meningitis (an infection of the lining of the brain)	Meningococci meningitis is spread person to person through continual close contact.	Fever; excessive fussiness or sleepiness, vomiting, rash (like blotchy or pinpoint red spots or bruises), stiff neck.	Very infectious until treated.	Contact your doctor immediately; child may need antibiotics; vaccine may be used in special circumstances.
Mumps (rare because most children receive the vaccine at 1 year of age)	Virus in respiratory secretions is spread person to person;	Enlargement of salivary glands causes swelling of cheeks and face. May have fever, headache, abdominal pain. Many children may not even have swollen glands, but mumps can be more severe in adults.	From 7 days before to 9 days after swelling. Most infectious 2 days before onset of swelling.	Mumps, caused by a virus, can only be prevented by immunization—there is no antibiotic. Contact your doctor for suggestions as to how to make your child feel better.
Rubella (German Measles) (most children receive the vaccine at 1 year of age)	Caused by a virus, can be spread person to person in respiratory secretions. There is risk of severe damage to the fetus if a pregnant woman gets rubella during the first trimester.	Many have no illness, although infected. May have mild fever, sore throat, swollen glands in neck but no rash. Rash consists of small red spots which start on scalp and face and spread rapidly over entire body.	From a few days before until 7 days after onset of rash.	Your doctor can diagnose rubella and immunity to it by doing a blood test, but there is no medication to cure it. Exclude your child from general activities for 7 days after onset of rash.
Shingles (zoster virus, same as the chickenpox virus)	Spread person to person in people who have already had chickenpox. Requires close direct contact.	Rash with small blisters on top which become crusted; itching.	Very infectious during rash; it's possible to infect someone who has not had chickenpox.	Contact your doctor. If lesions cannot be covered, exclude from other activities until all the blisters have crusted.
Whooping Cough (Pertussis)	Bacteria in respiratory secretions. Spread person to person. Very infectious.	Begins as cold with profuse runny nose and cough. Cough gets progressively worse and occurs in paroxysms, or spasms. Face red or purple during coughing spells and child may vomit. Fever uncommon.	From onset of runny nose until 3 weeks after onset of paroxysms or whooping.	Contact your doctor immediately. Exclude from regular activities until 5 days after start of antibiotics or 2 weeks if no treatment given. Other people who have been in contact may need antibiotics or vaccine.

Recommended Immunization Schedule for Infants and Children

NATIONAL ADVISORY COMMITTEE ON IMMUNIZATION (NACI), HEALTH PROTECTION BRANCH, HEALTH CANADA

Vaccine	Age in Months						Age in Years			
	2	4	6	12	18		4 to 6	9 to 13	14 to 16	
Hepatitis B*			3 doses							
Diphtheria, Pertussis, and Tetanus (DPT)	DPT	DPT	DPT		DPT		DPT		Td**	
Haemophilus influenzae type b*** (Hib)	Hib	Hib	Hib		Hib					
Polio (inactivated polio vaccine/oral polio vaccine)	Polio	Polio	Polio****		Polio		Polio		Polio****	
Measles, Mumps, and Rubella (MMR)*****				MMR	MMR*****					

NOTES:

*   Adolescents who have not received hepatitis B vaccine in infancy should receive it through school programs according to the provincial and territorial policies.

**   Td: Tetanus and diphtheria toxoids; adult formulation for 12 years and older.

***   Recommended schedule for both Hib-TITER® and Act-HIB®.

****   If oral polio vaccine is used exclusively, boosters at 6 months and 14 to 16 years of age may be omitted.

*****   The 2nd dose of MMR is routinely recommended at either 18 months or at 4 to 6 years of age. It should be given anytime before school entry provided that there is at least a 1-month interval between receipt of the first and second doses.

Selected Canadian Resources

Organizations, Help Lines, & Web Sites
Many of these resources offer information, fact sheets, and publications.

AboutFace
99 Crowns Lane, 4th Floor
Toronto, ON M5R 3P4
1-800-665-3223
Provides information and emotional support for individuals and families who are touched by facial differences.

Alberta Cord Blood Bank
Clinical Sciences, Building
University of Alberta
Edmonton, AB T6G 2G3
(403) 492-2673
Fax: (403) 492-8704

Allergy/Asthma Information Association (AAIA)
30 Eglinton Ave. W., Suite 750
Mississauga, ON L5R 3E7
(905) 712-2242
1-800-611-7011

(The) Alliance for Children and Television
60 St. Clair Ave. E., Suite 1002
Toronto, ON M4T 1N5
(416) 515-0466

Asthma Society of Canada
130 Bridgeland Ave., Suite 425
Toronto, ON M6A 1Z4
(416) 787-4050
1-800-787-3880

Autism Society Canada
129 Yorkville Ave., Suite 202
Toronto, ON M5R 1C4
(416) 922-0302
Fax: (416) 922-1032

Between Moms
<http://www.cadvision.com/moms>

Big Brothers & Sisters of Canada
5230 South Service Rd.
Burlington, ON L7L 5K2
(905) 639-0461
1-800-263-9133

Call Mom
1-900-451-MOMS, $2.95/min
E-mail: callmom@mts.net
National help line re parenting dilemmas and household conundrums.

Canada Safety Council
1020 Thomas Spratt Place
Ottawa, ON K1G 5L5
(613) 739-1535

Canadian AIDS Society (CAS)
100 Sparks St., Suite 400
Ottawa, ON K1P 5B7
(613) 230-3580
1-800-499-1986
Fax: (613) 563-4998
<http://www.cdnaids.ca>

Canadian Association of Family Resource Programs
101–30 Rosemount Ave.
Ottawa, ON K1Y 1P4
(613) 728-3307

Canadian Association of Speech-Language Pathologists and Audiologists (CASLPA)
#2006, 130 Albert St.
Ottawa, ON K1P 5G4
(613) 567-9968
1-800-259-8519
<http://www.caslpa.ca>

(The) Canadian Association of the Deaf
2435 Holly Lane, Suite 205
Ottawa, ON K1V 7P2
Voice/TTY (613) 526-4785
Fax: (613) 526-4718

Canadian Automobile Association
Child Restraint Information Program (CRIP)
A public service run by the CAA in cooperation with Transport Canada. Contact your local CAA office. <http://www.caa.ca>

Canadian Cancer Society
10 Alcorn Ave., Suite 200
Toronto, ON M4V 3B1
(416) 961-7223
Fax: (416) 961-4189
also **National Cancer Institute of Canada**
National Toll-Free: 1-888-939-3333
<http://www.cancer.ca>

Canadian Child Care Federation (CCCF)
30 Rosemount Ave., Suite 100
Ottawa, ON K1Y 1P4
(613) 729-5289
1-800-858-1412
Fax: (613) 729-3159
E-mail: ccf@sympatico.ca
Child & Family Canada, initiated by CCCF
<http://www.cfc-efc.ca>

Canadian Cystic Fibrosis Foundation (CCFF)
2221 Yonge St., Suite 601
Toronto, ON M4S 2B4
National Office: (416) 485-9149
1-800-378-2233
<http://www.ccff.ca/~cfwww/index.html>

Canadian Dental Association (CDA)
1815 Alta Vista Dr.
Ottawa, ON K1G 3Y6
(613) 523-1770
Fax: (613) 523-7736
<http://www.cda-adc.ca>

(The) Canadian Dermatology Association
774 Echo Dr., Suite 521
Ottawa, ON K1S 5N8
(613) 730-6262

Canadian Diabetes Association (CDA)
15 Toronto St.
Nat'l Office: Suite 1001
Ontario Division: Suite 800
Toronto, ON M5C 2E3
(416) 363-3373
Fax: (416) 363-3393
National Toll-Free: 1-800-226-8464
(ON) 1-800-361-1306
<http://www.diabetes.ca>

Canadian Down Syndrome Society
811-14th St. N.W.
Calgary, AB T2N 2A4
(403) 270-8500
Down Syndrome Association of Metro Toronto
<http://www.io.org/~dsamt/index.htm>

Canadian Hemophilia Society
#1210, 625 ave. Président Kennedy
Montreal, QC H3A 1K2
(514) 848-0503
Fax: (514) 848-9661

Canadian Institute of Child Health (CICH)
885 Meadowlands Dr. E., Suite 512
Ottawa, ON K2C 3N2
(613) 224-4144
Fax: (613) 224-4145
<http://www.cich.ca>

Canadian Juvenile Products Association
PO Box 294 or 10435 Islington Ave.
Kleinburg, ON L0J 1C0
(905) 893-1689

Canadian Liver Foundation (CLF)
National Office
#200, 365 Bloor St. E.
Toronto, ON M4W 3L4
(416) 964-1953
1-800-563-5483
Fax: (416) 964-0024
<http://www.liver.ca>

Canadian Living: Your Family Magazine
<http://www.canadianliving.com>
Christine Langlois is Canadian Living's *health and family editor and moderator of its Health and Family forum online.*

Canadian Lung Association
#508, 1900 City Park Dr.
Gloucester, ON K1J 1A3
(613) 747-6776

Canadian MedicAlert Foundation
#301, 250 Ferrand Dr.
Toronto, ON M3C 3G8
(416) 696-0267 or (416) 696-0142
National: 1-800-668-1507

Canadian Mental Health Association (CMHA)
2160 Yonge St., 3rd Floor
Toronto, ON M4S 2Z3
(416) 484-7750
Fax: (416) 484-4617
<http://www.icomm.ca/cmhacan>

Canadian Mothercraft Society
32 Heath St. W.
Toronto, ON M4V 1T3
(416) 920-3515
Promotes healthy infant & early childhood development through partnership with family & community; offers ECE training and certification. Affiliated with
  Breaking the Cycle
  63 Lombard St.
  Toronto, ON M5C 1M2
  (416) 364-7373

Canadian Motor Vehicle Safety Standards (CMVSS)
Transport Canada
Ottawa, ON K1A 0N5
(613) 998-1978
<http://www.engr.usask.ca/tc/crs/keep.html>
<http://www.tc.gc.ca>

Canadian National Institute for the Blind (CNIB)
1929 Bayview Ave.
North York, ON M4G 3E8
(416) 975-0010
<http://www.cnib.ca>

Canadian Paediatric Society (CPS)
2204 Walkley Rd., Suite 100
Ottawa, ON K1G 4G8
(613) 526-9397
Fax: (613) 526-3332
E-mail: info@cps.ca
<http://www.cps.ca>

Canadian Parents Online
<http://www.canadianparents.com>
Offers chat forums, product information, and Canadian experts to answer questions.

Canadian Red Cross
National Office
1800 Alta Vista Dr.
Ottawa, ON K1G 4J5
Western Zone: (413) 541-4400
Ontario: (905) 890-1000
Quebec: (514) 362-2929
Atlantic: (506) 648-5000
<http://www.redcross.ca>

Canadian Toy Testing Council
22 Hamilton Ave. N.
Ottawa, ON K1Y 1B6
(613) 729-7101
Fax: (613) 729-7185
<http://cfc-efc.ca.cymbiont.ca/ttc/>

Candlelighters
Childhood Cancer Foundation Canada
55 Eglinton Ave. E., Suite 401
Toronto, ON M4P 1G8
(416) 489-6440
1-800-363-1062

Child Care Advocacy Association of Canada
323 Chapel St.
Ottawa, ON K1N 7Z2
(613) 594-3196

Children's Oncology Care of Ontario (COCO)
Ronald McDonald House (#1 1981)
  356 Dundas St. W.
  Toronto, ON M5T 1G5
  (416) 977-3300
Ronald McDonald House (#2 1991)
  26 Gerrard St. E.
  Toronto, ON M5B 1G3
  (416) 977-0458

Children's Rehabilitation and Cerebral Palsy Association
The Neurological Centre, 2805 Kingsway
Vancouver, BC V5R 5H9
(604) 451-5511

(The) Children's Wish Foundation of Canada
#8C, 1735 Bayly St.
Pickering, ON L1W 3G7
(905) 420-4055
1-800-267-9474(WISH)
Fax: (905) 831-9733
<http://www.childrenswish.ca>

(The) College of Family Physicians of Canada
(CFPC)
2630 Skymark Avenue
Mississauga, ON L4W 5A4
(905) 629-0900
<http://www.cfpc.ca>

Crohn's and Colitis Foundation of Canada
#301, 21 St. Clair Ave. E.
Toronto, ON M4T 1L9
(416) 920-5035
1-800-387-1479

Dads Canada Initiative
105-396 Queens Avenue
London, ON N6B 1X8
(519) 858-8867
1-888-DADS CAN

Doulas of North America (DONA)
(206) 324-5440

Easter Seals Society Canada
511-90 Eglinton Ave. East
Toronto, ON M4P 2Y3
(416) 544-1715
Fax: (416) 932-9844

Epilepsy Canada
#745, 1470 rue Peel
Montreal, QC H3A 1T1
(514) 845-7855
1-800-860-5499
Fax: (514) 845-7866

Family Service Canada
383 Parkdale Avenue, Suite 404
Ottawa, ON K1Y 4R4
(613) 722-9006
1-800-668-7808
Fax: (613) 722-8610
E-mail: fsc@igs.net
A network of over 100 family-serving member agencies in communities across Canada; established to promote and strengthen family life in Canada.

Health Canada
<http://www.hc-sc.gc.ca>
Health Protection Branch HPB
   Product Safety Directorate
   Vancouver (604) 666-5003
   Toronto (416) 973-4705
   Montreal (514) 646-1353
Health Promotion & Programs Branch HPPB
   National Clearinghouse on Family Violence
   1-800-267-1291
Publications
   Health Canada, Ottawa, ON K1A 0K9
   (613) 954-5995

(The) Hospital for Sick Children
555 University Avenue
Toronto, ON M5G 1X8
(416) 813-1500
<http://www.sickkids.on.ca/>
Centre for Health Information & Promotion
   (416) 813-5819
Poison Information Centre
   1-800-268-9017

Infant Feeding Action Coalition INFACT Canada
10 Trinity Sq.
Toronto, ON M5G 1B1
(416) 595-9819
Fax: (416) 591-9355
E-mail: infact@ftn.net
<http://www.infactcanada.ca>

Infant & Toddler Safety Association (ITSA)
385 Fairway Rd. S.
Kitchener, ON N2C 2N9
(519) 570-0181

(The) Kidney Foundation of Canada
#300, 5165 Sherbrooke St. W.
Montreal, QC H4A 1T6
(514) 369-4806
1-800-361-7494
Fax: (514) 369-2472
<http://www.kidney.ca>

Kids Help Phone/Jeunesse J'écoute
439 University Ave., Suite 300
Toronto, ON M5G 1Y8
Regional Referrals: (416) 586-5437
1-800-350-5437
Counselling for kids in distress, 24-hour.
1-800-668-6868
*A national Toronto-based, bilingual telephone
service available free of charge to any child or
teenager in Canada.*
<http://kidshelp.sympatico.ca>

Labour Support Association & Registry (LSAR)
(905) 842-3385 or (905) 844-0503
For information about doulas in your area.

La Leche League Canada
18C Industrial Drive, P.O. Box 29
Chesterville, ON K0C 1H0
(613) 448-1842
Fax: (613) 448-1845
　Breastfeeding Referral Service:
　1-800-665-4324
*Check the Business section of your telephone
book for local groups. Request the LLLI
catalogue of publications, a directory of
contacts, and information on memberships
and subscriptions.*
<http://www.lalecheleague.org/>
<http://www.ncf.carleton.ca/ip/social.services/
leche>

Lamplighters Leukemia Association
PO Box 1285, Station H
Montreal, QC H3G 2N2
(514) 933-5384

Learning Disabilities Association of Canada
#200, 323 Chapel St.
Ottawa, ON K1N 7Z2
(613) 238-5721

Midwifery Collectives
*Check the Business Section of your telephone
book for local groups.*

MotheRisk
The Hospital for Sick Children, Toronto.
(416) 813-6780 (M-F: 9-5)
<http://www.motherisk.org>
*Provides authoritative information and guidance
to pregnant or lactating patients and their
health care providers regarding the fetal risks
associated with drug, chemical, infection, disease, and radiation exposures during pregnancy
and lactation.*

Multiple Sclerosis Society of Canada
#1000, 250 Bloor St. E.
Toronto, ON M4W 3P9
1-800-268-7582

**Muscular Dystrophy Association of Canada
(MDAC)**
#900, 2345 Yonge St.
Toronto, ON M4P 2E5
(416) 488-0030
1-800-567-2873
Fax: (416) 488-7523
<http://www.mdac.ca>
*Offers information on neuro-muscular disorders;
provides info on regional offices and chapters.*

National Cancer Institute of Canada
See Canadian Cancer Society

National Institute of Nutrition (NIN)
#302, 265 Carling Ave.
Ottawa, ON K1S 2E1
<http://www.nin.ca>

One Parent Families Association of Canada
National Office
6979 Yonge Street, Suite 203
Willowdale, ON M2M 3X9
(416) 226-0062

Ontario Coalition for Better Child Care
500A Bloor St. W.
Toronto, ON M5S 1Y8
(416) 538-0628
Fax: (416) 538-6737

Family Resources

Parenting Today
2762 Wall St.
Vancouver, BC V5K 1A9
(604) 258-9074
kathy_lynn@mindlink.bc.ca
A parent education company in Vancouver;
owner Kathy Lynn; audio books, newsletter.

Parents of Multiple Births Association of
Canada (POMBA)
240 Graff Avenue
Stratford, ON N5A 7V6
(519) 272-2203

Parent-to-Parent Link
Easter Seals Society Ontario
250 Ferrand Dr.
Toronto, ON M3C 3P2
(416) 421-8377
1-888-377-5437
Provides one-on-one support to parents of
children with disabilities.

Postpartum Adjustment Support Services
Canada (PASS-CAN)
c/o Christine Long,
P.O. Box 7282 Station Main,
Oakville, ON L6J 6L6
(905) 844-9009

Reye's Syndrome Foundation of Canada
Children's Hospital of Western Ontario
RR#2 Kerwood, ON N0M 2B0
(519) 685-8484

Ronald McDonald Children's
Charities of Canada
McDonald's Place
Toronto, ON M3C 3L4
(416) 443-1000
1-800-387-8808
Provides information on R.M. Houses across
Canada.

Royal Canadian Mounted Police
Missing Children's Registry
1200 Vanier Parkway, P.O. Box 8885
Ottawa, ON K1G 3M8
(613) 993-1525
Fax: (613) 993-5430
<http://www.childcybersearch.org/>

St. John Ambulance Canada
National Headquarters
312 Laurier Avenue E.
Ottawa, ON K1N 6P6
(613) 236-7461
Fax: (613) 236-2425
<http://www.sja.ca>
Check the Business section of your telephone
directory for local branches. SJA offers First
Aid products, training, and services.

SMARTRISK Foundation
658 Danforth Ave., Suite 301
Toronto, ON M4J 5B9
(416) 463-9878
1-888-537-7777
E-mail: choose@smartrisk.ca
<http://www.smartrisk.ca>
A national nonprofit injury-prevention
organization based in Toronto.

(The) Toronto Hospital
Umbilical Cord Blood Bank
(416) 340-3323

Victorian Order of Nurses
VON Canada
5 Blackburn Ave.
Ottawa, ON K1N 8A2
(613) 233-5694
Fax: (613) 230-4376
<http://www.von.ca>
Offers counselling for breast-feeding; for post-
partum depression; for second-time moms,
pre- and post- natal.

(A) World of Dreams Foundation Canada
#708, 465 rue St. Jean
Montreal, QC H2Y 2R6
(514) 843-7254
1-800-567-7254
Fulfills dreams for critically and chronically ill
children across Canada.

Specialized Sources

(The) Canadian Children's Book Centre (CCBC)
35 Spadina Rd.
Toronto, ON M5R 2S9
(416) 975-0010
Planned for end of 1997
<http://www3.sympatico.ca/ccbc/>

Parentbooks
201 Harbord St.
Toronto, ON M5S 1H6
(416) 537-8334
1-800-209-9182
Fax: (416) 537-9499

Selected Pamphlets, Books, & Videocassettes
alphabetized by title

All shapes and sizes: Promoting fitness and self-esteem in your overweight child, Teresa Pitman and Miriam Kaufman. 1994. A Today's Parent Book, HarperPerennial, Toronto.

Alternatives in diapering
Baby Love Products
5015-46th Street
Camrose, AB T4V 3G3
(403) 672-1763
A booklet published by the Peace River Childbirth Education Association. Contains information about the wide range of diaper products available, prevention and treatment of diaper rash , washing instructions for cloth diapers; comparisons of the relative cost and both health and environmental considerations of disposable and cloth diapers.

(The) Art of breastfeeding, videocassette: 60 min. La Leche League Canada

(The) Breastfeeding answer book, expanded to 608 pages, Nancy Mohrbacher and Julie Stock. 1997. La Leche League International. (Professional)

Breastfeeding twins, 2nd ed. 1996. Parents of Multiple Births Association of Canada (POMBA) (519) 272-2203

Camping with kids, Rosemary Rawnsley and Jacquie Stinson. 1989. Brighouse Press, Vancouver.

Canada's food guide to healthy eating. 1992.
Using the food guide. 1992.
Using food labels to choose foods for healthy eating
Food guide facts: Background for educators and communicators.
Canada's food guide to healthy eating: Focus on preschoolers, Background for educators and communicators. 1995.
Publications, Health Canada
Ottawa, ON K1A 0K9
(613) 954-5995

(The) Canadian babysitter's handbook: The essential guide for everyone entrusted with the care of babies & young children, St. John Ambulance. 1995. Random House of Canada, Toronto.

Canadian Injury Prevention Program (CIPP) Publications sponsored by SANDOZ and the Canadian Medical Association

Career intelligence: Mastering the new work and personal realities, Barbara Moses. 1997. General & Stoddart Publishing, Toronto.

Chalk around the block, Sharon E. McKay and David MacLeod. 1993. Somerville House Books Limited, Toronto.

Child care: A practical guide, 3rd ed., 1991. St. John Ambulance.

Childhood asthma: A handbook for parents, 4th ed. Gerard J. Canny and Henry Levison. 1993. Asthma Clinic, The Hospital for Sick Children.

Cinderella revisited: How to survive your stepfamily without a fairy godmother, Peter Marshall. 1993. Whitecap Books Ltd., North Vancouver.

(The) Complete Canadian health guide, June Engel and The University of Toronto Faculty of Medicine. 1993. Key Porter Books, Toronto.

(The) Enlightened eater, 4th ed., Rosie Schwartz. 1994. Macmillan Canada, Toronto.

Exploring the joy of music, David Welton Watts. 1991. Scholastic Canada Ltd., Toronto.

Family matters, Judith Timson. 1996. HarperCollins Canada Ltd., Toronto.

Familytips: An illustrated guide to discipline, Ellie Presner. Jerell Publishing, P.O. Box 365, Westmount, QC H3Z 2T5

Feeding your baby in the '90s: From conception to age two, 2nd ed. rev., Louise Lambert-Lagace. 1992. Stoddart Publishing Co., Limited, Don Mills.

Feeding your preschooler: Tasty nutrition for kids two to six, Louise Lambert-Lagace. 1993. Stoddart Publishing Co., Limited, Don Mills.

Hi! I am the new baby, Tina Powell. 1995. Moulin Publishing Limited, Toronto.

Raising kids without raising Cain, Gary Direnfeld. 1993. Dundas.

I don't want to go to school today: A guide for parents, Greg Anderson. 1993. Trilobyte Press, Oakville.

INFACT Canada Newsletter. Articles on health, social, environmental, scientific, political and ethical issues related to breast-feeding.
Infant Feeding Action Coalition INFACT Canada
10 Trinity Sq.
Toronto, ON M5G 1B1
(416) 595-9819
Fax: (416) 591-9355
E-mail: infact@ftn.net
<http://www.infactcanada.ca>

It takes two to talk, 3rd ed. rev., Ayala H. Manolson. 1992. A publication of The Hanen Centre (for speech pathology), Toronto. (416-921-1073)

Keep your child safe, Canadian Paediatric Society. 1990. Ross Laboratories Ltd., Montreal.

Keys to parenting your anxious child, Katharina Manassis, The Hospital for Sick Children. 1996. Barron's Educational Series, Inc., Hauppage, N.Y.

Kidtips, Ellie Presner. Jerell Publishing, P.O. Box 365, Westmount, QC H3Z 2T5

Learning language and loving it, Elaine Weitzman. 1992. A publication of The Hanen Centre (for speech pathology), Toronto. (416-921-1073)

Let me play, Elizabeth A. Munroe. 1991. Scholastic Canada Ltd., Toronto.

Little well beings: A handbook on health in family day care 1994. Canadian Paediatric Society, Ottawa, ON (613) 526-9397 ext. 245.

(The) Live-in caregiver program, a kit, from Citizenship & Immigration Canada, Ottawa.

Love, limits and consequences: A positive practical approach to kids and discipline, Teri Degler and Yvonne Kason. 1990. Summerhill Press, Toronto.

Management of children with developmental coordination disorder: At home and in the classroom. School of Occupational Therapy and Physiotherapy, McMaster University, 1280 Main St. W., Hamilton, ON L8S 4K1
For a copy send a cheque, payable to McMaster University, for $2 to Cheryl Missiuna at the above address; enclose a S.A.S.E., 9" x 6" with 90 cents postage.

Mom's the word, videocassette: Mothercraft Society. 1987. Berns Baby Productions, Toronto.

(The) mother zone: Love, sex, and laundry in the modern family, Marni Jackson. 1992. Macfarlane Walter & Ross, Toronto.

National breastfeeding guidelines for health care providers, revised. 1996. Canadian Institute of Child Health, Ottawa.

Of cradles and careers: A guide to reshaping your job to include a baby in your life, Kaye Lowman. La Leche League.

Our strength for tomorrow: Valuing our children, Report on Child Health. May 1997. Based on the work of the CFPC Task Force on Child Health, The College of Family Physicians of Canada, (905) 629-0900.

Pam's kitchen: Recipes for children, Pam Collacott. 1990. Macmillan of Canada, Toronto.

Parenting your newborn baby, Linda McHarg. videocassette: 66 min., col. 1993. Dr McHarg's series Growing up with your child, Dab Communications.

(A) Parent's guide to the Suzuki method, Alinta Thornton. 1989. Omnibus Press/Monarch Books of Canada, Downsview.

Paediatric child health, magazine produced by the Canadian Paediatric Society

(The) Picky eater: Recipes and survival tips for parents of fussy eaters, Sharon E. McKay. 1993. A Today's Parent book, HarperPerennial (HarperCollins Canada Ltd, Toronto).

Please make my world safe, 4th ed., 1986. The Hospital for Sick Children Foundation, Toronto.

Starting right, revised 1996. Published by H.J. Heinz Company of Canada Ltd in cooperation with the Canadian Paediatric Society.

Stepfamily. A newsletter by the Canadian Stepfamily Association, published every two months; subscribe at:
Canadian Stepfamily
R.R. 4, G.B. 96, Site 11
Colborne, ON K0K 1S0
1-800-268-5509

Ups and downs: A new mother's guide (re post-partum depression syndrome), Eileen Beltzner. 1997. PASS-CAN, Oakville.

Welcome to parenting A five-part videocassette (2.5 hours) on children ages 0 to 6, with key information on children's body, mind, safety, and behaviour. Health Canada.
Available from Family Service Canada, $17.99, 1-800-668-7808

Well Beings: A guide to promote the physical health, safety, and emotional well-being of children in child care centres and family day care homes, 2nd ed., A project of the Canadian Paediatric Society. 1996. CPS, Ottawa, ON (613) 526-9397 ext. 245. (Professional)

What every babysitter should know: Babysitting course, 2nd ed. 1993. St. John Ambulance.

(The) Womanly art of breastfeeding, 6th rev. ed., 40th anniversary ed. 1997. La Leche League International. Also an Audio Guide: 2 90-min tapes.

Women in the know: How to build a strategy to achieve financial success, Janice Book, Sandy Cimaroni, Susan Swayze. 1996. Key Porter Books Limited, Toronto.

You make the difference in helping your child learn, Ayala H. Manolson with Barbara Ward and Nancy Dodington. 1995. A publication of The Hanen Centre (for speech pathology) Toronto. (416-921-1073)

Your child's best shot: A parent's guide to vaccination, the Canadian Paediatric Society. 1997. Canadian Paediatric Society, Ottawa, ON (613) 526-9397 ext. 245.

Index